When it comes to your scores,
don't settle for less…

Settele for more!

SAT® Math Packets

Practice Materials and Study Guide for the SAT Math Sections

By Mike Settele

Los Angeles, CA

www.setteletutoring.com

2020 Edition

Settele
Tutoring

Published by Settele Tutoring
For permissions and other inquiries, contact by email at mike@setteletutoring.com

The SAT® is a trademark registered by the College Board, which is not affiliated with, and does not endorse, this product.

Note: All Khan Academy content is available for free at (www.khanacademy.org). Khan Academy is not affiliated with, and does not endorse, this product.

This publication is designed to help students improve on the SAT. However, nothing in this publication should be construed as a guarantee of score improvement.

ISBN-13: 978-1686243875

Thank you for purchasing!

I strongly believe that everyone should be able to achieve their best scores, and the cost of test prep should not limit any student's potential. I'm grateful that you've chosen Settele Tutoring to help you reach your goals.

If you received this copy of the SAT Math Packets from a friend or other source, please consider purchasing your own copy at:

www.setteletutoring.com

Purchasing this book supports a small business and helps me produce more practice materials. Creating these packets required a lot of effort, but my goal is to keep the price low so that more students can benefit from using them. At the same time, I have plenty of free test prep resources available on my website and social media. Subscribe and follow for more!

YouTube.com/SetteleTutoring

Instagram @SetteleTutoring

Twitter @SetteleTutoring

Facebook @SetteleTutoring

Email mike@setteletutoring.com

Author's Note

Dear Hardworking Student,

Thanks for buying my book! I hope it helps you improve your scores, not only by teaching you the topics tested on the SAT, but also by boosting your confidence in yourself.

I've been an SAT and ACT tutor since 2006, and I consistently find that students tend to be overwhelmed and intimidated by the standardized testing process. The scope of the exams is massive, and the pressure to succeed is intense. Maybe it's the stress, maybe it's the wording of the questions, but something about the SAT makes students doubt themselves. They feel like there's just too much that they don't know. But let me be clear — **you're smarter than you think you are**.

In fact, this book wasn't designed to teach you anything new. Instead, it's meant to remind you of what you already know. Still, I've included several test-taking strategies to help you apply your knowledge to the weird world of the SAT. This test is absolutely trying to trick you. But once you learn to see through their traps and disguises, you'll be able to solve and answer with confidence.

I also recommend purchasing *The Official SAT Study Guide* and registering for free SAT prep on the Khan Academy website. Both are great resources, but they can be just as overwhelming and intimidating as the SAT itself if you don't know where to start. This book will help you sort through it all, and you can get even more practice and advice by connecting with me on social media. I post an SAT or ACT question on Instagram every day, and my YouTube channel has free, comprehensive lessons, including for a few of the packets in this book. As much as possible, test prep should be affordable and accessible. By purchasing this book, you're supporting my efforts to create more free content. I also offer a limited amount of private online tutoring for students who need help with particular packets or want a personalized program for all subjects on the SAT or ACT. Please visit my website to book sessions.

Once again, thank you for purchasing this book. I wish you the best of luck in your studying and on the test!

Sincerely,

Mike Settele
Settele Tutoring
mike@setteletutoring.com
www.setteletutoring.com

Table of Contents

Introduction

This study guide is a little different than other practice materials, so don't just dive into the lessons. Take a few minutes to read this introduction so that you know what you're getting into. It's better to have a plan!

What are "Packets"?

The Basics

Think of this book as a collection of tiny "packets" of SAT Math information. Each packet is designed to be a miniature lesson on one very specific math topic. Here's how you should work on each packet:

1. Read **The Basics** to learn the most essential information that you'll need for that topic.

2. Work on the basic **Examples**, which will help you practice that topic with relatively straightforward questions.

3. Read **The Twists** to learn how the SAT makes that topic more difficult.

4. Work on the twisted **Examples**, which will help you practice avoiding the SAT's tricks and traps.

5. Compare the basic and twisted Examples to find the **patterns** for that topic. What makes the questions similar? How did the SAT try to disguise the topic so that you'd be more confused? How did you "untwist" the hard questions to get back to basics?

6. Use the **Exercise** to continue practicing. Keep looking for patterns that make the questions similar, even when they seem very different.

Narrow Your Focus

The whole point of these packets is to help you NARROW YOUR FOCUS as much as possible. Each packet lets you see several questions of the same type in a row, which means that you can practice one topic without interruption. You're much more likely to learn a pattern for a topic when you're not distracted by everything else on the SAT.

In general, NARROW YOUR FOCUS is an important idea on the SAT. If studying is stressing you out, NARROW YOUR FOCUS to one packet at a time. If a question is confusing you, NARROW YOUR FOCUS to the most important information.

The Twists

In some ways, the packets in this book are similar to the chapters that you'd find in any other test prep guide — they break the test down into more manageable pieces. However, there are two key differences between this book and most others:

1. **Much Less Reading** — Most test prep guides have a lot of text, which can be overwhelming. My packets only have a few sentences of guidance before the Examples. That's because you need to get in the habit of trusting yourself. You're smarter than you think you are! Through math class in school, you've already learned pretty much everything you need for the SAT, so use the Examples to see how much you remember. These are just practice questions, so don't be afraid to try something and fail. When you've found an answer, go to the **detailed Lesson in the back of the book** to see if you're right and to learn the best way to solve the question. Many students struggle with the SAT because they have a bad habit of giving up on questions without really trying them. My packets are designed to help you form the good habit of trying something — anything! — on questions that seem confusing.

2. **Much Less Math** — As you practice, you'll discover that you're better at math than you thought you were. Still, some questions are just hard. If you struggled with a topic when you first learned it in school, you'll probably struggle with it again on the SAT. Most study guides just repeat the same-old, complicated, mathematical explanations that you've already heard from your teachers. This book understands that you need alternatives. **The first section of this guide covers four SAT-specific strategies** that will make some of the questions easier. My Lessons and explanations will tell you when a question is more easily solved using one of the strategies.

The Packets

free points		
grph	read the graph
chrt	read the chart
COP	chart of points

arithmetic		
arith	basic arithmetic
ratio	ratios and units
perc	percentages
stat	statistics

algebra		
CAM	common algebra mistakes
rad	radicals
exp	exponent rules
abs	absolute value
MBT	must be true
POI	point of intersection
alg+	advanced algebra
div	dividing polynomials
imag	imaginary numbers

properties		
LP	linear properties
QP	quadratic properties
FP	function properties
CP	circle properties

models		
LM	linear models
QV	quantity & value
GM	geometry models
XM	exponential models
RF	rearrange formulas
WTF	"unusual" models

geometry		
POW	part over whole
ang	angle rules
ST	similar triangles
cyl	cylinders
trig	trigonometry
geo+	advanced geometry

Typical SAT

No two SATs will be exactly the same, but there are still general trends. The chart below represents the average breakdown of the 58 questions on the Math section of the SAT.

As you can see, some packets are more important than others. Still, **each question is worth about 10 points**, so even the minor topics can add up. For example, if you study the Part Over Whole (POW) questions enough that you always get them right, you're essentially guaranteeing yourself those 10 points on every SAT. That's how you improve your scores — one question at a time!

Math	grph	grph	grph	chrt
arith	arith	ratio	ratio	ratio	COP
perc	perc	stat	stat	stat	imag
CAM	CAM	CAM	CAM	CAM	rad/abs
exp	POI	POI	POI	alg+	MBT/div
LP	LP	LP	QP	QP	QP
FP	FP	CP	RF	XM	XM
LM	LM	LM	WTF	WTF	WTF
LM	LM	QV	WTF	WTF	WTF
GM	POW	ang	ST/cyl	trig	geo+

Practice Tests

introduction

The Basics

These packets are comprehensive, but they're not meant to be the only study tool that you use. I strongly recommend that you purchase *The Official SAT Study Guide*. It contains 8 practice tests made by the same people who make the real SAT. Most of the tests are also available for free on The College Board and Khan Academy websites, but you should print them out if you can. The real SAT is a pencil-and-paper exam, and you should take practice tests the same way so that you can show your work and cross off answers.

But don't just dive into the practice tests without a plan. They are a limited resource, so use them sparingly! Use my packets to learn and practice specific topics, and save the official exams to diagnose weaknesses and to practice enduring a 4-hour test. Here's my recommendation:

The 2 to 3 Plan

- Start practicing 2-3 months before test day.
- Take a practice test every 2-3 weeks.
- Practice for an additional 2-3 hours per week.

It's important that you create a test prep schedule and stick to it. I know that full-length practice tests are long and boring, but you have to do them. You have to build your endurance. Every 2 to 3 weeks, you need to set aside several hours to take a practice test in one sitting, just like the real SAT. To make it easier, I've made a timer video that will proctor the test for you. It will announce the time remaining in the sections and give you breaks so that you can focus on taking the test. Subscribe to my YouTube channel or visit my website for the timers:

www.setteletutoring.com/SATtimer

www.youtube.com/SetteleTutoring

The Twists

After you take a practice test, you need to make sure that you're learning from your mistakes. You can use Khan Academy or the College Board's SAT phone app to score the tests and get feedback. But you should also use these packets! Here's how:

Start your prep with a full-length practice test. Don't worry about the scores. Think of it like the PSAT — it's just to see where you're starting from. Compare your answers to the charts on the next page, which give the packet category for every question on the 10 official practice tests that have been released by the College Board. Choose the 5 topics that you had the most difficulty with and work on the corresponding packets. Don't try to do too much. NARROW YOUR FOCUS and you're more likely to learn from your mistakes.

Take another full-length practice test 2 to 3 weeks later. Review your answers the same way. Compare your answers to the charts, and work on the 5 packets that you had the most difficulty with. Repeat this process right up until the real test. If you need more practice with a packet that you've already completed, use the Khan Academy website.

Notes on the Test Numbers

As of August 2019, the College Board has released 10 official practice exams. However, they are not all found in the same places. Here's where to find each test, as of August 2019:

Test #	Official SAT Study Guide		Online	
	2018 edition	2020 edition	CB website	Khan Academy
1	✔	✔	✔	✔
2	✔		✔	✔
3	✔	✔	✔	✔
4	✔		✔	✔
5	✔	✔	✔	✔
6	✔	✔	✔	✔
7	✔	✔	✔	✔
8	✔	✔	✔	✔
9		✔	✔	
10		✔	✔	

Scoring Your Test

Unfortunately, the College Board does not make scoring tests easy. They want you to use their *Daily Practice for the New SAT* app. I do recommend downloading the app on your phone since it works pretty well. You can take pictures of your practice test answer forms, and the app will automatically score the test for you. However, there are a lot of reasons you might want to score your practice tests manually. For one, the app can be glitchy, and it might not accept the pictures if they're not great quality. But also, many students like to ask, "what if?" You might check over a Math section and notice that you made 5 careless mistakes. What if you had gotten those five questions right? The app doesn't let you easily understand how your mistakes can improve your score. For comprehensive scoring tables, visit:

https://collegereadiness.collegeboard.org/sat/practice/full-length-practice-tests

SAT Practice Test 1

Sect. 3	#	Sect. 4
CAM	1	grph
imag	2	CAM
WTF	3	ang
LM	4	CAM
CAM	5	grph
LM	6	ratio
RF	7	grph
CAM	8	abs
POI	9	RF
alg+	10	LM
WTF	11	CAM
LP	12	stat
alg+	13	perc
exp	14	stat
QP	15	LM
CAM	16	LM
ST	17	FP
POI	18	MBT
trig	19	QV
rad	20	WTF
	21	chrt
	22	chrt
	23	ratio
	24	CP
	25	QP
	26	perc
	27	ratio
	28	LP
	29	FP
	30	QP
	31	arith
	32	WTF
	33	grph
	34	arith
	35	cyl
	36	FP
	37	XM
	38	XM

SAT Practice Test 2

Sect. 3	#	Sect. 4
CAM	1	WTF
POI	2	ratio
LM	3	LM
CAM	4	ratio
rad	5	perc
LP	6	CAM
exp	7	QP
GM	8	WTF
LP	9	QV
FP	10	FP
imag	11	ratio
RF	12	LM
QP	13	stat
XM	14	grph
div	15	ratio
arith	16	chrt
CAM	17	perc
ST	18	stat
geo+	19	stat
LP	20	stat
	21	WTF
	22	RF
	23	RF
	24	CP
	25	LP
	26	FP
	27	grph
	28	LP
	29	QP
	30	geo+
	31	ratio
	32	arith
	33	QP
	34	WTF
	35	LM
	36	POW
	37	WTF
	38	WTF

SAT Practice Test 3

Sect. 3	#	Sect. 4
WTF	1	grph
CAM	2	chrt
exp	3	grph
WTF	4	COP
CAM	5	perc
POI	6	CAM
FP	7	CAM
LP	8	LM
LP	9	ratio
POI	10	LM
ang	11	LM
QP	12	FP
div	13	RF
QP	14	WTF
LM	15	stat
alg+	16	FP
CAM	17	LM
ang	18	WTF
WTF	19	ratio
trig	20	grph
	21	XM
	22	WTF
	23	trig
	24	arith
	25	cyl
	26	LP
	27	GM
	28	XM
	29	WTF
	30	alg+
	31	arith
	32	stat
	33	CAM
	34	POW
	35	stat
	36	LP
	37	WTF
	38	WTF

SAT Practice Test 4

Sect. 3	#	Sect. 4
abs	1	LM
alg+	2	LM
POI	3	ratio
alg+	4	perc
CAM	5	WTF
MBT	6	WTF
LM	7	chrt
LP	8	LP
rad	9	chrt
CAM	10	grph
POI	11	grph
WTF	12	FP
QP	13	XM
imag	14	XM
QP	15	XM
arith	16	WTF
trig	17	LM
alg+	18	cyl
POI	19	CAM
ratio	20	XM
	21	WTF
	22	perc
	23	stat
	24	POW
	25	alg+
	26	MBT
	27	LM
	28	QP
	29	stat
	30	FP
	31	arith
	32	LM
	33	ratio
	34	WTF
	35	RF
	36	POW
	37	XM
	38	XM

Note on Tests 1-4: These were the first four tests released by the College Board ahead of the new SAT in 2016. In my opinion, they are not as perfectly polished as Tests 5-10. Test 4, in particular, has a lot of quirky questions and a highly unusual emphasis on Exponential Models. **If you want to practice taking sections without timing yourself, I recommend using Tests 1-4.**

Sect. 3	#	Sect. 4	Sect. 3	#	Sect. 4	Sect. 3	#	Sect. 4
LP	1	grph	LM	1	CAM	WTF	1	chrt
POW	2	COP	WTF	2	LM	CAM	2	CAM
QP	3	ratio	imag	3	grph	POI	3	ratio
QP	4	CAM	CAM	4	LM	imag	4	stat
rad	5	arith	LP	5	CAM	alg+	5	COP
CAM	6	QV	CAM	6	perc	LM	6	alg+
QV	7	XM	RF	7	stat	QP	7	grph
LM	8	CAM	COP	8	chrt	arith	8	grph
POI	9	ratio	rad	9	ratio	QV	9	alg+
CAM	10	RF	WTF	10	WTF	FP	10	ratio
cyl	11	LP	QP	11	POI	exp	11	QV
exp	12	POI	div	12	grph	QP	12	perc
LM	13	POI	QP	13	LM	div	13	grph
FP	14	chrt	WTF	14	COP	GM	14	ang
WTF	15	stat	CAM	15	COP	alg+	15	ratio
arith	16	LM	exp	16	ST	CAM	16	CAM
CAM	17	LM	CAM	17	RF	geo+	17	LM
POI	18	LM	ST	18	WTF	trig	18	grph
alg+	19	geo+	WTF	19	WTF	LP	19	RF
ang	20	WTF	POW	20	QP	CAM	20	RF
	21	MBT		21	stat		21	LM
	22	perc		22	stat		22	stat
	23	COP		23	grph		23	cyl
	24	perc		24	perc		24	QP
	25	WTF		25	LP		25	COP
	26	geo+		26	ratio		26	WTF
	27	stat		27	CP		27	XM
	28	LP		28	abs		28	LP
	29	CP		29	WTF		29	CP
	30	CAM		30	QP		30	perc
	31	ratio		31	arith		31	ratio
	32	ratio		32	CAM		32	LP
	33	GM		33	cyl		33	WTF
	34	alg+		34	POI		34	POW
	35	GM		35	LP		35	POI
	36	geo+		36	stat		36	trig
	37	WTF		37	XM		37	stat
	38	WTF		38	perc		38	chrt

Note on Tests 5-8: These four tests were added to *The Official SAT Study Guide* in 2018. They are actual SAT exams that were given to real students just like you. Those students took these exams under proctored conditions, got official scores, sent those scores to colleges, and received acceptances based on those scores. For that reason, I trust Tests 5-8 more than Tests 1-4. **Save Tests 5-8 for when you need to take full exams under proctored conditions to receive reliable practice scores.**

SAT Practice Test 8			SAT Practice Test 9			SAT Practice Test 10		
Sect. 3	#	Sect. 4	Sect. 3	#	Sect. 4	Sect. 3	#	Sect. 4
CAM	1	WTF	POI	1	CAM	CAM	1	LM
LM	2	grph	CAM	2	ratio	LM	2	grph
RF	3	ratio	LP	3	CAM	COP	3	grph
ang	4	LM	LM	4	rad	grph	4	CAM
GM	5	ang	LM	5	grph	rad	5	alg+
POI	6	QV	POW	6	grph	CAM	6	CAM
rad	7	LP	CAM	7	ang	FP	7	stat
alg+	8	alg+	LP	8	LM	ang	8	grph
CP	9	WTF	POI	9	chrt	LP	9	alg+
QV	10	WTF	alg+	10	arith	QP	10	stat
FP	11	ratio	CAM	11	ratio	CP	11	stat
CAM	12	QV	div	12	ratio	trig	12	perc
LM	13	exp	QP	13	QV	QP	13	grph
POI	14	FP	POI	14	LM	alg+	14	ratio
alg+	15	GM	rad	15	LP	LP	15	geo+
QP	16	chrt	GM	16	alg+	WTF	16	perc
CAM	17	stat	CAM	17	POI	abs	17	RF
POI	18	grph	FP	18	WTF	XM	18	chrt
LM	19	QP	trig	19	WTF	POI	19	QP
POW	20	WTF	LP	20	LM	CAM	20	stat
	21	LM		21	XM		21	WTF
	22	perc		22	stat		22	XM
	23	XM		23	stat		23	LP
	24	stat		24	alg+		24	LM
	25	LM		25	trig		25	POI
	26	stat		26	QP		26	XM
	27	LP		27	FP		27	CAM
	28	stat		28	QP		28	QP
	29	WTF		29	LM		29	LM
	30	FP		30	LM		30	geo+
	31	ratio		31	CP		31	arith
	32	CAM		32	LP		32	ang
	33	LP		33	chrt		33	stat
	34	ratio		34	stat		34	CAM
	35	POI		35	perc		35	LP
	36	trig		36	LP		36	QP
	37	COP		37	stat		37	ratio
	38	XM		38	perc		38	ratio

Note on Tests 9-10: Like Tests 5-8, these tests were official exams given to students just like you. Since they are the most recent official tests, I believe they are the most representative of the content and difficulty that you're likely to see on your own SAT. **Since I trust Tests 9-10 the most, I recommend saving them for big moments in your test prep schedule, like the halfway point and your final practice test before the real SAT.**

Additional Practice

Khan Academy

The Basics

Khan Academy is a great free resource for more practice. You can sync your PSAT and practice test scores with your account, and the website will tell you which topics to practice. The exercises will get easier or harder, depending on your skill level.

The Twists

Unfortunately, *Khan Academy*'s topic categories aren't great. They mix a lot of different kinds of questions together, so it's harder to NARROW YOUR FOCUS to very specific ideas. Also, the questions don't always capture the style of SAT questions. They don't involve as many twists or tricks.

Still, *Khan Academy* is very useful if you need more practice with The Basics. Sometimes you just need to practice simple things like factoring and FOILing. What follows is a list of the packets from this book and the *Khan Academy* categories that include similar questions.

Khan Academy Categories

- ## Free Points
  - **read the graph**
    - Scatterplots
  - **read the chart**
    - Units
    - Table data
  - **chart of points**
    - Linear and exponential growth
    - Function notation
- ## Arithmetic
  - **basic arithmetic**
    - Linear equation word problems
    - Linear inequality word problems
    - Units
  - **ratios and units**
    - Ratios, rates, and proportions
    - Units

- **percentages**
  - Percents
- **statistics**
  - Data inferences
  - Center, spread, and shape of distributions
  - Data collection and conclusions

- ## Algebra
  - **common algebra mistakes**
    - Solving linear equations and linear inequalities
    - Solving quadratic equations
    - Operations with rational expressions
    - Operations with polynomials
    - Structure in expressions
  - **radicals**
    - Radicals and rational exponents
    - Radical and rational equations
  - **exponent rules**
    - Radicals and rational exponents
    - Structure in expressions
  - **absolute value**
    - Solving linear equations and linear inequalities
    - Linear equation word problems
  - **must be true**
    - Interpreting nonlinear expressions
    - Structure in expressions
  - **point of intersection**
    - Solving systems of linear equations
    - Linear and quadratic systems
  - **advanced algebra**
    - Radical and rational equations
    - Operations with rational expressions
    - Operations with polynomials
    - Polynomial factors and graphs
    - Function notation
  - **dividing polynomials**
    - Operations with rational expressions
    - Polynomial factors and graphs
  - **imaginary numbers**
    - Complex numbers

- Properties
  - **linear properties**
    - Graphing linear equations
    - Solving systems of linear equations
  - **quadratic properties**
    - Interpreting nonlinear expressions
    - Manipulating quadratic and exponential expressions
    - Polynomial factors and graphs
    - Nonlinear equation graphs
  - **function properties**
    - Polynomial factors and graphs
    - Nonlinear equation graphs
    - Function notation
  - **circle properties**
    - Circle equations

- Models
  - **linear models**
    - Interpreting linear functions
    - Linear equation word problems
    - Linear inequality word problems
    - Linear function word problems
    - Scatterplots
    - Linear and exponential growth
  - **quantity & value**
    - Systems of linear inequalities word problems
    - Systems of linear equations word problems
  - **geometry models**
    - Linear function word problems
    - Systems of linear equations word problems
    - Quadratic and exponential word problems
    - Volume word problems
  - **exponential models**
    - Linear and exponential growth
    - Interpreting nonlinear expressions
    - Quadratic and exponential word problems
    - Manipulating quadratic and exponential expressions

- **rearrange formulas**
  - Interpreting nonlinear expressions
  - Manipulating quadratic and exponential expressions
  - Structure in expressions
  - Isolating quantities
- **WTF models**
  - Systems of linear inequalities word problems
  - Systems of linear equations word problems
  - Scatterplots
  - Key features of graphs
  - Linear and exponential growth
  - Interpreting nonlinear expressions
  - Quadratic and exponential word problems
  - Manipulating quadratic and exponential expressions

- Geometry
  - **part over whole**
    - Circle theorems
  - **angle rules**
    - Congruence and similarity
  - **similar triangles**
    - Congruence and similarity
  - **cylinders**
    - Quadratic and exponential word problems
    - Volume word problems
  - **trigonometry**
    - Right triangle trigonometry
  - **advanced geometry**
    - Volume word problems
    - Right triangle word problems
    - Circle theorems

Social Media

Settele Tutoring

The Basics

So many students start their SAT prep with high ambitions — "I'll practice everyday!" But life gets in the way, and SAT studying tends to fall to the bottom of the to-do list. Suddenly, two weeks before test day, you remember that you should probably do some practice tests or something. **The problem is that you cannot cram for the SAT**. That's why I recommend that you start consistently practicing 2 to 3 months before test day. Set a schedule and stick to it.

But without a structured prep course or regular tutoring sessions, it can be difficult to know what to do. And it's hard to get motivated on your own. That's why **I post a Daily Test Prep question or strategy every single day.** One question a day isn't much, but it's enough to remind you to do a little more on your own. And if you have trouble with that day's topic, you can use this book to seek out more practice. So use the links below to follow me!

 YouTube.com/SetteleTutoring

 Instagram @SetteleTutoring

 Twitter @SetteleTutoring

Facebook @SetteleTutoring

Daily Test Prep Schedule

Mondays — *short FAQ videos*
Tuesdays — *Reading questions*
Wednesdays — *Writing questions*
Thursdays — *Math questions*
Fridays — *ACT-only questions*
Saturdays — *Reading vocabulary words*
Sundays — *Math vocabulary words*

The Twists

One of the benefits of social media is that it's social! If you have questions, you have lots of ways to reach out to me. My Minute Movie Monday videos are meant to concisely answer the most common SAT and ACT questions. But if you have another, ask it. Who knows? Maybe I'll turn the answer into my next video!

I also love feedback. I only have so much time to make new materials, and I want to spend it making things that you find useful. So if there's a topic you want more practice with, let me know! If there's a resource that you think is missing from the test prep world, let me know!

I've already made a video series that can help you with the packets in this book and with the SAT in general. Subscribe to my YouTube channel to get 5 free lessons:

---

5 Test Prep Problems
(5 videos total)

Problem #1: the SAT and ACT are different
Lesson: change how you think, change how you score

Problem #2: you're overwhelmed
Lesson: Part Over Whole packet

Problem #3: you're intimidated
Lesson: Imaginary Numbers packet

Problem #4: you're inflexible
Lesson: Linear Properties packet

Problem #5: you're confused
Lesson: Linear Models packet

find all of these videos and more on the
Settele Tutoring YouTube channel!

Frequently Asked Questions

introduction

Can I Use a Calculator?

Try not to. The real SAT will be divided into a No Calculator and a Calculator section, but this book does not make a distinction between these questions, mostly because it doesn't matter. **Most question types can appear in either section, so you need to know how to answer them without a calculator.** Also, you won't even need a calculator for the vast majority of questions in the Calculator section.

My advice is to have your calculator handy, but only reach for it if you absolutely need to. You should not be doing "8 times 7" in your calculator. You should not be doing "180 minus 43" either. You'll know when you're working on a true Calculator section question because the numbers will be huge or involve complicated decimals.

You're using this book to practice your SAT Math skills, so why not take the opportunity to also practice your arithmetic skills? Students who rely too much on their calculators tend to make a lot of careless mistakes. Challenge yourself as you practice. It will pay off on test day!

Is there a Guessing Penalty?

No. You do not lose points for wrong answers on the SAT. That's why **you should never leave an SAT question blank.**

On the Multiple Choice questions, guess B for questions where you have no idea. On the Free Response/Grid-in questions, guess 2 instead of leaving questions blank.

Are the Questions in Order of Difficulty?

For the most part, yes. Remember that **the Math sections on the real SAT will be roughly in order of difficulty**—easy questions at the beginning, hard questions at the end. Each packet in this book roughly goes in the same order.

But one very important thing to note is that the Free Response/Grid-in questions at the end of the sections are NOT necessarily harder than the Multiple Choice questions. In fact, the difficulty "resets" when you get to the Grid-ins. The No Calculator section is basically two sections in one:

- #1 to #15 — Multiple Choice
- #16 to #20 — Grid-in

Question #1 is usually very easy, and #15 is usually very difficult. However, #16 is usually an easy question! In these packets, this just means that you should not assume a Grid-in question is hard just because it doesn't have answer choices. On the SAT, it's important to know that the first few Grid-ins will be easy. **If you're running out of time, guess B on the hard Multiple Choice questions and go straight to the Grid-ins to pick up those easy points.**

What's the SAT's format?

The SAT Math has a 25-minute, 20-question No Calculator section and a 55-minute, 38-question Calculator section. If you have more questions, just go online and look them up. It's super easy to find information about the SAT! My YouTube channel has short FAQ videos, and *The Official SAT Study Guide* will answer all of your formatting questions. You didn't buy this book to learn SAT trivia. You bought it to practice the SAT Math. Get to work!

SAT-Specific Strategies

The SAT is a little different from the math tests you take in school. These strategies will make you faster and more accurate. Use them when you can!

Guess & Check

SAT-specific strategies

The Basics

You've definitely used **Guess & Check** before. Use the answer choices to work backwards. It's much easier to test the numbers than to solve a complex equation. Plug the values from the choices in for x:

Example 1

$$\sqrt{10 - 3x} - 7 = x - 9$$

What is the solution set of the equation above?

A) {–2}

B) {3}

C) {–2, 3}

D) {–9, –2, 3}

Sometimes **Guess & Check** is helpful because it lets you do slightly easier algebra. In this case, FOILing is easier than factoring, so plug an answer choice in for *k* and see if it gets you back to the original expression:

Example 2

The expression $\frac{1}{2}x^2 - 8$ can be rewritten as $\frac{1}{2}(x + k)(x - k)$, where *k* is a positive constant. What is the value of *k* ?

A) 2

B) 4

C) 8

D) 16

The Twists

If there's a lot of information in the question, **Guess & Check** can still be confusing. But picking an answer choice at least gives you a starting point. Test Choice B first. If B is wrong, you can guess A or C next, depending on whether you need a bigger or smaller number.

Example 3

Veronica is organizing the carpool for her family reunion. Some of the cars seat 5 people each, and the rest seat 7 people each. If she organizes the carpool so that 55 people ride in 9 cars and each car is filled to capacity, how many of the cars seat 7 people each?

A) 3

B) 4

C) 5

D) 6

Arithmetize
SAT-specific strategies

The Basics

Arithmetize is a very valuable tool. However, it's not something that helps all that much for math class in school. It's very specific to the SAT. Even if you're amazing at algebra, there will be times when it's easier to work with actual numbers, just like with Guess & Check. But instead of using the numbers in the answer choices, **Arithmetize lets you pick your own numbers.** If you NARROW YOUR FOCUS to just one value, you're more likely to understand how an equation changes that value. You're also less likely to make the common algebra mistakes that the SAT is setting you up for. What happens if you make x equal to 1 in the example below?

Example 1

$$y = \frac{2x^2(3x)^2}{6x^4}$$

In the equation above, $x \neq 0$. What is the value of y ?

A) 0

B) 1

C) 2

D) 3

The Twists

Some tutors will tell you to never Arithmetize with 0 or 1, but that's nonsense. Even if those numbers don't work, they might eliminate some answer choices. At the least, the math is quick and less likely to cause mistakes. If you do end up with multiple choices that work, just choose a new number and try it in the choices you couldn't eliminate. This is why you should **always test all of the answer choices when you Arithmetize.** What happens when you make x equal to 0 in the example below?

Example 2

$$x^2 - 2x + 5$$

Which of the following is equivalent to the expression above?

A) $(x + 1)^2 + 4$

B) $(x + 1)^2 - 4$

C) $(x - 1)^2 + 4$

D) $(x - 1)^2 - 4$

Sometimes you can't **Arithmetize** for all the variables in a question. In this example, pick values for x and y, but not for a and b. Use your x and y to find a and b:

Example 3

If $x^2 + y^2 = a$ and $xy = b$, which of the following is equivalent to $2a + 4b$?

A) $(x + y)^2$

B) $2(x + y)^2$

C) $(x + 2y)^2$

D) $2(x + 2y)^2$

Plug Points Into Equations
SAT-specific strategies

The Basics

You might think of this strategy as a version of Guess & Check. But it deserves its own page because it's often overlooked. Questions that seem like they require a thorough knowledge of algebra and the properties of equations might actually be solved easily by just testing a point. A point that "works" in an equation will produce a valid result, like 2 = 2. A point that does not "work" will end with an equation that doesn't make sense, like 2 = 5. **When you Plug Points Into Equations, start with easy points:**

Example 1

x	$\dfrac{1}{2}$	1	$\dfrac{3}{2}$	2	$\dfrac{5}{2}$
$f(x)$	$\dfrac{13}{4}$	$\dfrac{7}{2}$	$\dfrac{15}{4}$	4	$\dfrac{17}{4}$

Some of the values of the function f are shown in the table above. Which of the following defines f?

A) $f(x) = \left(\dfrac{7}{2}\right)^x$

B) $f(x) = 4^x + \dfrac{5}{4}$

C) $f(x) = \dfrac{5}{2}x + 2$

D) $f(x) = \dfrac{1}{2}x + 3$

The Twists

It's easy to forget that lines and other graphs are just collections of points. Instead of trying to figure out equations by looking at the whole line, take one point and plug it into the possible equations. This is especially helpful on the SAT because they design the graphs to trick you. Usually, the boxes don't mean what you think they mean:

Example 2

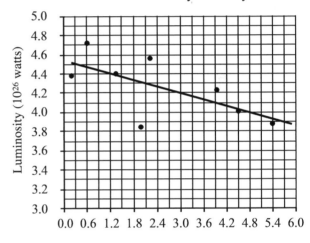

The scatterplot above shows the luminosity of 8 nearby stars, in 10^{26} watts, with respect to their solar masses in 10^{30} kilograms. The line of best fit is also shown. Based on the data in the scatterplot, which of the following equations best models the line of best fit, where m is the mass of the star, in 10^{30} kg, and $L(m)$ is the luminosity of the star, in 10^{26} watts?

A) $L(m) = \dfrac{9}{2} - \dfrac{9}{80}m$

B) $L(m) = \dfrac{9}{2} + \dfrac{9}{80}m$

C) $L(m) = \dfrac{9}{2} - \dfrac{1}{3}m$

D) $L(m) = \dfrac{9}{2} + \dfrac{1}{3}m$

Get Back to Basics

SAT-specific strategies

The Basics

The SAT is going to take the math concepts that you know from school and "twist" them up so that they're barely recognizable. On many questions, you won't know where to start, or you'll be so intimidated by a crazy equation or graph that you'll just give up. Try to use that feeling to your advantage. What is it about the question that confuses you the most or makes it difficult? **Get Back to Basics** by fixing that problem first. You might find that the main part of the question isn't so bad once you untwist the thing that makes it look hard. It might also make it less likely that you make a careless mistake.

In this example, the fractions complicate the equations. **Get Back to Basics by multiplying the first equation by a number that eliminates the fractions.** You can absolutely answer this without eliminating the fractions, but why take the risk? The SAT knows where you're most likely to make careless mistakes — fractions, negatives, distribution, etc. Take steps to prevent errors before they happen!

Example 1

$$\frac{1}{2}x + \frac{1}{4}y = 9$$
$$y = 6x$$

The system of equations above has solution (x, y). What is the value of x ?

The Twists

Sometimes it's hard to know what The Basics of a question are. The SAT can disguise things well. As you go through the packets, you'll get better at recognizing what the questions are testing. Stories make things even more confusing, but remember that the algebra is still the same algebra that you learned in school. **Get Back to Basics** by changing equations into the familiar ones that you're used to — lines, quadratics, and exponential functions. Which type is this?

Example 2

$$h = \frac{5t + 51}{2}$$

The equation above is used to estimate the height h, in inches, of an oak tree t years after it was planted. Based on the equation, which of the following must be true?

A) An oak tree's height increases by 51 inches every year.

B) An oak tree's height increases by 25.5 inches every year.

C) An oak tree's height increases by 5 inches every year.

D) An oak tree's height increases by 2.5 inches every year.

Math
Packets

I recommend that you start with a plan. Take a full practice test and pick the packets for the questions you got wrong. If you are just diving in, remember that there are detailed lessons and explanations in the back of the book.

Free Points

The Basics

Well, they're not exactly free. But in general, Free Points questions tend to be relatively easy. Almost all of them will be in the Calculator section, but very few will actually require you to calculate anything. Most are just about correctly reading a graph or chart. In order to do that, you also need to read the question carefully, so underline key words to help you NARROW YOUR FOCUS.

The Twists

If a Free Points question appears near the beginning of a section, there probably won't be many twists. You might need to find a particular point or understand a trend (is it increasing or decreasing). More difficult Free Points questions will mess with the graph so it's harder to read. **Pay attention to the units on the axes.** One box might not be one unit. For that matter, make sure you're looking at the correct axis. Sometimes they'll ask for the *y*-value of a point, but the *x*-value will be an answer choice to trick you if you're not careful.

Some of the charts will be lists of points, usually using function notation instead of *y*. Even if you haven't worked with functions in math class in school, you should still be able to get these right. **Just think of *f(x)* as *y*.**

If the chart seems like the result of a survey, then things might be more complicated. Often, they ask about probability, but it's never the complex probability you might have learned in school (combinations, permutations, and factorials). You're almost always looking for a fraction, where the numerator is the specific thing they're asking for and the denominator is the group that they're asking you to pick from. Sometimes the group is the entire chart, but sometimes it's only a column or two. Once again, read carefully and you should be okay.

Packets

- read the graph
- read the chart
- chart of points

approximately 5 questions per test

worth approximately 50 points total

Math	grph	grph	grph	chrt
arith	arith	ratio	ratio	ratio	COP
perc	perc	stat	stat	stat	imag
CAM	CAM	CAM	CAM	CAM	rad/abs
exp	POI	POI	POI	alg+	MBT/div
LP	LP	LP	QP	QP	QP
FP	FP	CP	RF	XM	XM
LM	LM	LM	WTF	WTF	WTF
LM	LM	QV	WTF	WTF	WTF
GM	POW	ang	ST/cyl	trig	geo+

Important Ideas

Graphs

Pay attention to:
- axis labels
- units for each axis
- x-axis is horizontal (left and right)
- y-axis is vertical (up and down)

When they're talking about "greatest change" or "rate of change," they're probably talking about the slope of the line. **Steeper slopes mean greater rates of change**. Flat lines mean there is no change.

Most graphs will be linear or composed of lines. In other words, the rate of change will be constant over a certain interval. Here's a very basic example:

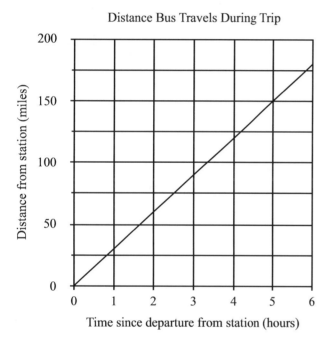

Distance Bus Travels During Trip

Since this graph is a line, we know that the bus traveled at a **constant speed**. In fact, the speed is given by the slope of the line.

Use known points to calculate slope or to test equations. We know this bus travels 150 miles in 5 hours, which means it travels at a constant rate of 30 miles per hour.

Scatterplots

A scatterplot shows two things: the actual data collected (the dots) and the predicted trend (the line of best fit).

When a graph question asks you to compare the actual and estimated values, find the difference between the data point and the line of best fit at whatever value they ask for. Just make sure you're looking at the right axis.

Charts

Read the question carefully, and underline key words that tell you which columns and rows are important.

If they don't give you totals, you may need to calculate them yourself.

But sometimes, the totals are misleading. If a chart question wants you to NARROW YOUR FOCUS to just a few rows or columns, you may need to adjust the totals to reflect the narrower range.

Usually, the "of" portion of the question tells you the denominator of the fraction.

f(x)

Remember that *f(x)* is just a fancy way of saying *y*.

In other words, most *f(x)* charts are just lists of points that are in the format you're used to: (*x*, *y*).

Know how to translate from function notation to regular algebra:

"What is the value of *f(3)* ?"

is just another way of saying:

"What is the *y*-value when *x* is 3 ?"

Read the Graph

free points

The Basics

You can't get these wrong! Pay attention to slopes. Read all the choices.

Example 1

The graph below shows the number of digital movie rentals, in millions, from 2002 to 2015.

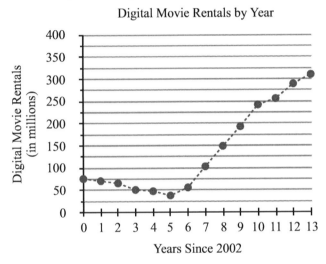

Digital Movie Rentals by Year

Based on the graph, which of the following best describes the general trend in digital movie rentals from 2002 to 2015?

A) Sales generally increased each year since 2002.

B) Sales generally decreased each year since 2002.

C) Sales generally decreased until 2005 and then increased.

D) Sales generally decreased until 2007 and then increased.

Example 2

Based on the graph, during which of the following periods was there the greatest change in the number of digital movie rentals?

A) 2006–2008

B) 2008–2010

C) 2011–2013

D) 2013–2015

The Twists

Don't let scatterplots or weird stories throw you off. It's still about slopes and points.

Example 3

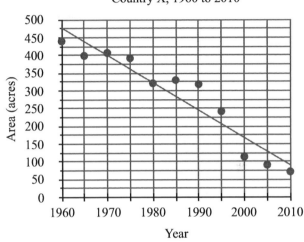

Area of Wetlands in Country X, 1960 to 2010

According to the line of best fit in the scatterplot above, which of the following best approximates the year in which the area of the wetlands in Country X was estimated to be 150 acres?

A) 1998

B) 2002

C) 2005

D) 2010

Example 4

For the year 1990, the actual area of the wetlands was approximately how much greater than the area predicted by the line of best fit?

A) 70

B) 140

C) 200

D) 250

Exercise: Read the Graph

Games Played versus Goals Scored

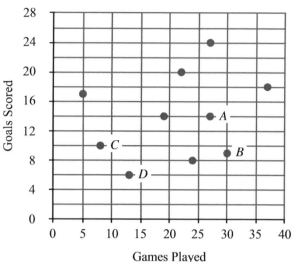

A statistician created the scatterplot above to analyze the relationship between games played and goals scored for 10 different soccer players.

1

How many goals were scored by the player who played in the most games?

A) 18

B) 24

C) 27

D) 37

2

Of the labeled points, which represents the player with the most goals scored per game played?

A) *A*

B) *B*

C) *C*

D) *D*

Rodrigo's Distance from Home

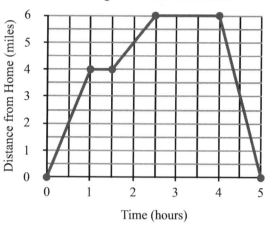

Rodrigo left home in his car and went to the dry cleaner to pick up his clothes. He then drove to a restaurant and ate dinner. Finally, he drove home on the same route after he finished dinner. The graph above shows Rodrigo's distance from home during the 5 hours he spent away from home.

3

According to the graph, which of the following statements is NOT true?

A) Rodrigo drove at a constant speed from his home to the dry cleaner.

B) Rodrigo was 2 miles away from home twice during the drive.

C) Rodrigo spent 3 hours at dinner.

D) Rodrigo spent 30 minutes at the dry cleaner.

4

According to the graph, how many total miles did Rodrigo drive during his trip?

A) 5

B) 6

C) 12

D) 30

Read the Chart

free points

The Basics

Focus on the end of the question. Make sure you select the right boxes for the numerator and denominator. **The "of" statement usually tells you the denominator.**

Example 1

	Trains	Buses	Total
Late	36	98	134
On-time	114	52	166
Total	150	150	300

The table shows the results of a study conducted by a transit agency that investigated whether trains or buses were more likely to arrive late to a certain mass transit stop. A random sample of 300 train and bus arrivals were selected for the study. What proportion of the arrivals were trains that were late?

A) $\frac{3}{25}$

B) $\frac{6}{25}$

C) $\frac{18}{67}$

D) $\frac{49}{150}$

Example 2

What fraction of the on-time arrivals were buses?

A) $\frac{52}{98}$

B) $\frac{52}{166}$

C) $\frac{52}{150}$

D) $\frac{52}{300}$

The Twists

Don't be confused by probability. They are still asking for the fraction. Use your calculator to find the decimal equivalent. Just be careful when they start asking for numbers from multiple boxes.

	Number of Stars			
	0	1	2	3
Comedy	3	8	6	8
Horror	4	5	9	7
Drama	1	10	7	7

A movie critic rates movies by giving them from 0 to 3 stars. The table above shows the critic's ratings for 75 movies in three genres.

Example 3

If one of the movies is selected at random, what is the probability that the selected movie is a drama that received 1 star?

A) 0.10

B) 0.13

C) 0.40

D) 0.43

Example 4

If a movie that received at least 2 stars is chosen at random, which of the following is closest to the probability that the movie was a comedy?

A) 0.19

B) 0.27

C) 0.32

D) 0.56

Exercise: Read the Chart

	Bought product	Did not buy product
Saw advertisement	52	94
Did not see advertisement	32	122

The table above provides the results of an advertising survey of 300 people. The respondents were asked whether they bought a certain product and whether they had previously seen an advertisement for that product. If one of the people who bought the product is chosen at random for a follow-up survey, what is the probability that the person chosen saw the advertisement?

A) $\frac{32}{84}$

B) $\frac{52}{84}$

C) $\frac{52}{300}$

D) $\frac{84}{300}$

2

	Saw movie	Did not see movie	Total
Men	41	39	80
Women	22	58	80
Total	63	97	160

A marketing company gave 160 people a free ticket to see a certain movie. The table above shows the number of men and women who used the free ticket to see the movie. Which of the following is closest to the probability that a person who saw the movie is a woman?

A) 0.15

B) 0.35

C) 0.55

D) 0.65

Project	2005	2006	2007	2008
A	$1,200	$1,345	$1,512	$1,603
B	$3,378	$4,598	$4,622	$4,870
C	$916	$1,040	$1,155	$1,321
D	$2,040	$3,916	$5,008	$6,775
Total	$7,534	$10,899	$12,297	$14,569

The table above gives the annual budgets for four projects run by the Parks and Recreation Department of City X from 2005 to 2008.

3

Which of the following projects accounted for approximately one third of the money spent on all projects in the given year?

A) Project A in 2006

B) Project B in 2008

C) Project C in 2008

D) Project D in 2007

4

Which of the following best approximates the average rate of change in the annual budget for Project C from 2006 to 2008 ?

A) $140

B) $165

C) $240

D) $280

Chart of Points

free points

The Basics

It's literally a chart of points! **Plug Points Into Equations** until you find one that fits. As you can see, f(x) is just a fancy way of saying y.

Example 1

x	f(x)
1	−1
3	−7
5	−13

Some values of the linear function f are shown in the table above. Which of the following defines f?

A) $f(x) = 1 - 2x$

B) $f(x) = 2 - 3x$

C) $f(x) = 3 - 2x$

D) $f(x) = 7 - 4x$

Example 2

x	g(x)	h(x)
0	5	6
1	3	2
2	1	1
3	−1	2
4	−3	6

The table above shows some values of the functions g and h. For which value of x is $g(x) - h(x) = x$?

A) 0

B) 1

C) 2

D) 3

The Twists

Sometimes there's a story. You should still **Plug Points Into Equations**. It doesn't matter whether those points are listed in a chart or shown as a line on a graph.

Example 3

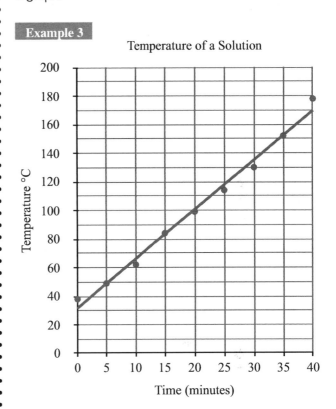

Temperature of a Solution

A chemist conducts an experiment by measuring the temperature T of a solution, in degrees Celsius, m minutes after a reactive agent has been added. Over the interval in the graph, the change in temperature is nearly linear. Which of the following equations best models the line of best fit?

A) $T(m) = 2m + 31$

B) $T(m) = 3.45m + 32$

C) $T(m) = 4.24m + 38$

D) $T(m) = 5m - 40$

Exercise: Chart of Points

1

x	1	2	3	4
$g(x)$	–4	1	6	11

The table above shows some values of the linear function g. Which of the following defines g ?

A) $g(x) = 2x - 6$

B) $g(x) = 3x - 7$

C) $g(x) = 5x - 9$

D) $g(x) = 7x - 11$

2

x	0	1	2	3	4
y	$\dfrac{12}{5}$	$\dfrac{19}{5}$	$\dfrac{26}{5}$	$\dfrac{33}{5}$	8

Which of the following equations relates y to x for the values in the table above?

A) $y = \left(\dfrac{7}{5}\right)^x + 1$

B) $y = \left(\dfrac{12}{5}\right)^x + \dfrac{7}{5}$

C) $y = \dfrac{19}{5}x + \dfrac{12}{5}$

D) $y = \dfrac{7}{5}x + \dfrac{12}{5}$

3

Weight of Different Finches

Finch	Ounces	Grams
grey-warbler finch	0.28	8.0
cocos finch	0.53	15.0
large cactus finch	0.95	27.0
mangrove finch	0.64	18.0

The table above gives the typical weights for four different Galapagos finches, expressed in both ounces and grams. If x ounces is equivalent to g grams, which of the following best represents the relationship between x and g ?

A) $x = 28.3g$

B) $g = 28.3x$

C) $g = 0.35x$

D) $g + x = 28.3$

4

Which of the following ordered pairs (x, y) satisfies the inequality $4y - 3x < 9$?

    I. $(1, -2)$

    II. $(3, 2)$

    III. $(-3, 1)$

A) II only

B) I and II only

C) II and III only

D) I, II, and III

Arithmetic

The Basics

Arithmetic questions are almost entirely in the Calculator section, which is good because the math can involve lots of numbers and lots of steps. This means that **staying organized is very important**. Showing your work can be the difference between right and wrong on Arithmetic questions. In fact, even if you're doing the work in your calculator, you should take the time to write down the steps on the page. The calculator isn't foolproof, and if you make a mistake, you're more likely to catch it if you write your steps down as you go.

The Twists

You know that warm, fuzzy feeling you get when you finish a math problem and your answer is also one of the choices? Unfortunately, the SAT loves to take advantage of your confidence. Don't rely on that feeling too much!

Many Arithmetic questions only involve three numbers. Subtract, then divide. Or is it divide, then subtract? Or is it multiply, then subtract? All three will be answer choices, so you won't notice if you've done the wrong thing. You'll be confident but wrong. Showing your work will help, as will taking the time to write out your units. But you should also make sure that you're always following the order of operations — PEMDAS.

For Statistics questions, you need to memorize a lot of definitions. Again, the incorrect answer choices will be purposely misleading, so if you confuse median and mean, you will be lured into the wrong answer. Statistics questions also involve a lot of reading, so take the time to underline problem words. Sometimes, it only takes one word to make a long answer choice wrong.

Packets

- basic arithmetic
- ratios and units
- percentages
- statistics

approximately 10 questions per test

worth approximately 100 points total

Math	grph	grph	grph	chrt
arith	arith	ratio	ratio	ratio	COP
perc	perc	stat	stat	stat	imag
CAM	CAM	CAM	CAM	CAM	rad/abs
exp	POI	POI	POI	alg+	MBT/div
LP	LP	LP	QP	QP	QP
FP	FP	CP	RF	XM	XM
LM	LM	LM	WTF	WTF	WTF
LM	LM	QV	WTF	WTF	WTF
GM	POW	ang	ST/cyl	trig	geo+

Important Ideas

PEMDAS

Remember to follow the order of operations:
- parentheses
- exponents
- multiplication/division
- addition/subtraction

But more importantly, follow the instructions in the question. Reading is half the battle on Arithmetic questions.

Ratios and Units

Rates usually mean you need to multiply or divide. For example, "cookies cost $2 each" means you need to multiply the number of cookies by 2.

But they can also be written as fractions, or ratios. For example, "a bakery makes 36 cookies in 90 minutes" can be expressed as:

$$\frac{36 \text{ cookies}}{90 \text{ minutes}}$$

Mismatched units are the most common mistake on ratios questions, so **taking a second to write out the units could save you 10 points!** Start with a ratio and compare the units. If they don't match up, you can multiply by additional fractions to get the correct units. You'll know you're done when the units cancel so that the top units on both sides are the same and the bottom units on both sides are the same.

If a car is traveling at 30 miles per hour, how many minutes does it take for the car to travel 2 miles?

$$\frac{30 \text{ miles}}{1 \text{ hour}} = \frac{2 \text{ miles}}{x \text{ minutes}} \cdot \frac{60 \text{ minutes}}{1 \text{ hour}}$$

$$\frac{30}{1} = \frac{120}{x} \rightarrow 30x = 120$$

$$x = 4 \text{ minutes}$$

Percentages

The SAT loves to twist percentages questions, so use the **OPEN** formula to make sure everything is in the right place.

$$(\text{Original})(\text{Percent}) = \text{New}$$

When the question references percent change or uses phrases like "20% less than", modify the OPEN formula to represent a change from 100%.

$$(O)(1 \pm P) = N$$

Statistics

The **mean** (or arithmetic mean) is the same as the average. Memorize the formula:

$$\text{average} = \frac{\text{sum of the numbers}}{\text{how many numbers}}$$

The **median** is the middle number in a set when the numbers are arranged from least to greatest.

The **mode** is the most common number in a set.

The **range** of a set is the biggest number minus the smallest number.

Standard deviation refers to how spread out the data is. If the numbers are all close to a clear middle, the set has a low standard deviation. If the numbers are spread out, the set has a high standard deviation.

Sample size refers to the number of people involved in a survey.

Bias refers to factors that might make the results of a survey inaccurate.

Margin of error is a measure of the accuracy of a survey. The higher the margin of error, the less reliable the survey.

The most accurate surveys will have large sample sizes. More importantly, the survey will be given to a **random sample** of the population.

Basic Arithmetic

arithmetic

The Basics

The SAT loves to mess with your head. One common trick involves the Free Response/Grid-in questions. You're probably aware that the Math questions are generally in order from easiest to hardest. Actually, each Math section is really two sections in one — multiple choice and grid-in — which means two sets of easy to hard. In other words, **the first Grid-in is generally pretty easy.** Unfortunately, they make you think it's hard by giving you a complicated story. Just follow instructions, and Guess & Check when you can.

Example 1

A cupcake store sold a total of 50 cupcakes on Tuesday. The store sells cupcakes in small packages of 4 and large packages of 6. If the store sold at least one large package of 6 cupcakes on Tuesday, what is one possible number of small packages of 4 cupcakes sold on Tuesday?

The Twists

It may not be immediately obvious, but a lot of Basic Arithmetic questions involve **remainders**. Remember that a remainder is what's leftover when you can't divide a number evenly. Sometimes they ask for the remainder. Sometimes they want you to ignore it and focus on the division. Other times, you have to eliminate answers that don't divide evenly:

Example 2

Betsy is going to an amusement park. The park entrance fee is $15, and tickets for the rides cost $4 each. If Betsy wants to spend no more than $42 at the amusement park, what is the maximum number of ride tickets she can buy after paying the entrance fee?

Exercise: Basic Arithmetic

1

An airplane has already flown 1,400 miles from its starting airport. If the airplane continues to fly at a constant speed of 550 miles per hour, how far will it be from its starting airport after another 5 hours of flying?

2

A car wash can clean at least 8 cars per hour and at most 14 cars per hour. Based on this information, what is one possible amount of time, in hours, that it could take the car wash to clean 112 cars?

3

A restaurant sells appetizers for $8 and entrees for $10. Mike orders 1 entree and a appetizers. If he spends at least $49 but no more than $59, what is one possible value of a ?

4

A group of workers in a factory must inspect a total of 150 widgets, and they decide that each of them will inspect the same number of widgets. When two of the workers called out sick, the remaining workers still had to inspect a total of 150 widgets, but each worker had to inspect an additional 20 widgets. How many workers were in the group originally?

5

Fletcher has m mice to feed to his pet snakes. If he feeds each snake 3 mice, he'll have 5 extra mice left over. In order to feed each snake 4 mice, he would need an additional 8 mice. How many pet snakes does Fletcher have?

Ratios and Units

arithmetic

The Basics

A ratio is a comparison of two values that takes the form of a fraction. Typically, you will set two ratios equal to each other by setting up a proportion. This lets you scale a rate up or down:

Example 1

A waiter makes $23 in tips during a 2-hour shift. At this rate, how much will the waiter make in tips during a 7-hour shift?

A) $6.57

B) $80.50

C) $115.00

D) $161.00

Sometimes they'll use more complicated words, like "directly proportional", but the idea is the same. The rate is consistent, so you can use fractions to compare two situations:

Example 2

The number of apples produced by a certain apple tree is directly proportional to the tree's age. If a 15-year-old tree produces 65 apples, how many apples will a 21-year-old tree produce?

The Twists

The most common twist by far is that the SAT will mess with the units. **Take 10 seconds to write out the units when you set up your ratios, and you could could easily save yourself 10 points.** This is a fully preventable careless mistake!

Example 3

A truck traveled 4 miles in 7 minutes. To the nearest tenth, what was the truck's average speed in miles per hour?

Most people solve the above example using two steps, but can you use ratios to do all of the work at once? Hint: you can convert units with more fractions!

$$\frac{4 \text{ miles}}{7 \text{ minutes}} = \frac{x \text{ miles}}{1 \text{ hour}} \cdot \underline{}$$

As the questions get more complicated, keeping track of your units will become even more important. But the best part is that the units themselves allow you to check your work as you go:

Example 4

Angela spends $95 to buy 7 cakes for the office holiday party. She cuts each cake into quarters, then cuts each quarter into 3 pieces. If Kevin eats 5 pieces of cake during the party, how much did Angela spend on just Kevin's share of cake? (Round your answer to the nearest cent.)

Exercise: Ratios and Units

1

If a factory produces 550 shirts in 2 days, how many shirts does it produce in 7 days?

2

A fruit basket contains 2 apples for every 5 oranges. How many oranges are in the basket if it contains 10 apples?

A) 4

B) 13

C) 20

D) 25

3

A certain class contains 3 girls for every 2 boys. If there are 30 students in the class, how many girls are in the class?

A) 10

B) 18

C) 20

D) 45

4

The typical smartphone contains 34 milligrams of gold. What is the maximum number of smartphones that can be made with 5 grams of gold? (1 gram = 1000 mg)

5

States Daphne plans to visit	15
Hours Daphne plans to drive each day	6
Average speed in miles per hour	45
Number of rest stops along the route	214
Number of highways along the route	36
Length of the route in miles	2,416

Daphne is going on a roadtrip. Based on the information in the table above, how many days will it take for Daphne to complete her roadtrip? (Round your answer to the nearest whole day.)

2014 MLB Standings, AL West Division

Team	Home		Away	
	Wins	Losses	Wins	Losses
Dodgers	45	36	49	32
Giants	45	36	43	38
Padres	48	33	29	52
Rockies	45	36	21	60
D-backs	33	48	31	50

The table above shows the wins and losses for the 5 teams in the American League West Division of Major League Baseball during the 2014 season. Each team played a total of 162 games. Each team played 81 games at its home stadium and 81 games away (at another team's stadium).

6

To the nearest hundredth, what is the ratio of the first place team's total wins to the last place team's total wins?

7

If the Giants had only played 45 home games in 2014, how many home games would they have been expected to win, assuming they win home games at the same rate?

8

A team's Consistency Ratio compares the number of wins at home to the number of wins away. A team that is perfectly consistent will win 1 home game for every 1 away game and have a Consistency Ratio of 1. Based on the table, which team was the most consistent in 2014?

A) Dodgers

B) Giants

C) Padres

D) D-backs

9

Mike's bank account contained $1,000 in 2013. Exactly 4 years later, in 2017, the same account contained $2,056. If the amount of money in Mike's bank account increased by c dollars every 5 months, where c is a constant, what is the value of c ?

10

An ecologist calculates that a certain forest is growing at a rate of $2\frac{3}{5}$ of an acre every two years. Based on this ecologist's calculation, how many years will it take for this forest to grow 39 acres?

Jim walks 18 feet in 13.9 seconds. At this rate, how many feet will Jim walk in 2 hours? (Round your answer to the nearest whole number of feet.)

In a different galaxy, aliens use a unit of weight called a *snark*, which is equivalent to 14.1 ounces. Those aliens also use a larger unit called a *blerg*, which is composed of 7 *snarks*. Based on these relationships, 30 *blergs* is equivalent to approximately how many pounds? (1 pound = 16 ounces)

A) 185

B) 238

C) 2,961

D) 3,360

A local concert venue can hold up to 1,200 people. The cost to put on a concert at the venue is $24,000, regardless of the number of people who attend. If the event organizers expect to sell only 85 percent of the tickets to a certain concert at the venue, what is the minimum amount they should charge per ticket so that they at least cover the cost of the concert?

A) $14.12

B) $17.00

C) $20.00

D) $23.53

A groundskeeper at a football stadium buys grass seed for the field. One bag of seed can plant $\frac{1}{5}$ of the field with grass. If a football field is approximately $1\frac{1}{3}$ acres, how many acres can be planted with 72 bags of seed? (Round your answer to the nearest tenth of an acre.)

A bus traveled 4 miles in 14 minutes. To the nearest tenth, what was the bus's average speed in meters per second? (Note: 1 mile is approximately 1,609 meters.)

Arithmetic

Percentages

arithmetic

The Basics

Get used to thinking of percentages as decimals:

What is 12% of 275?

What is 4% of 340?

What is 200% of 68?

What is 1.9% of 320?

42 is what percent of 175?

63.84 is 76% of what number?

Were the last two questions difficult? The problem is that your brain associates percentages with multiplication. The SAT takes advantage of this habit by creating situations where you actually need to divide. To combat this twist, you need to be "**OPEN**" to a new formula:

Original times Percentage Equals New

(O)(P) = N

Example 1

An ecologist discovered that 21.4% of the trees in a small grove were infected with a certain fungus. If 199 of the trees in the small grove were infected with the fungus, approximately how many total trees are in the grove? (Round your answer to the nearest whole number of trees.)

The Twists

Unfortunately, things still get complicated when the question asks about percent increase or decrease. What happens when you use the **OPEN** formula on this Example?

Example 2

Last year, 916 babies were born in a certain hospital. This year, 958 babies were born in the same hospital. To the nearest tenth of a percent, what was the percent increase in the number of babies born in the hospital?

A) 1.0 %

B) 4.2 %

C) 4.4 %

D) 4.6 %

You need to start thinking of percent change as it relates to 100%. (This will be essential for Exponential Models questions.) When you're dealing with percent change, adjust the **OPEN** formula to reflect the increase (+) or decrease (–) from the original:

(O)(1 ± P) = N

Example 3

Kim has 30% more french fries than Todd. If Kim has 65 french fries, how many french fries does Todd have?

A) 35

B) 45

C) 50

D) 85

Exercise: Percentages

1

A cable company charges $63.13 for television service after a 7% fee is added. What is the price of the television service before the fee was added?

A) $58.71

B) $59.00

C) $61.43

D) $62.06

2

A farmer sells watermelons and apples at a market. At the end of the day, approximately 6% of the watermelons and 3% of the apples remain unsold. If he started the day with 129 watermelons and 369 apples, which of the following is closest to the total number of fruits that remain unsold?

A) 15

B) 19

C) 26

D) 30

3

The weight of a person on Mars is approximately 60% less than his weight on Earth. If a person weighs 160 pounds on Earth, how much does he weigh on Mars, in pounds?

A) 60

B) 64

C) 96

D) 100

Questions 4 and 5 refer to the following information.

	Car Color		
	Red	Green	Total
2010	197	168	365
2015	217	128	345
Total	414	296	710

The table shows the number of red and green cars sold by a car dealership during 2010 and 2015.

4

Approximately what percentage of the cars sold in 2010 were red?

A) 28 %

B) 46 %

C) 48 %

D) 54 %

5

What was the approximate percent decrease in green cars sold from 2010 to 2015?

A) 24 %

B) 31 %

C) 40 %

D) 76 %

Statistics

arithmetic

The Basics

Statistics questions vary widely, but there isn't usually much math involved. Mostly, you need to know these essential definitions:

mean

$$\text{average} = \frac{\text{sum of the numbers}}{\text{how many numbers}}$$

median

middle number when the set is arranged from least to greatest

mode

most common number in the set

range

maximum – minimum

standard deviation

measures deviation of the data; how much does it wander from the middle?

Example 1

Which dot plot shows the greater standard deviation?

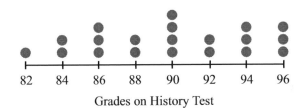

Grades on History Test

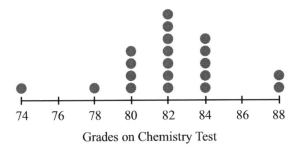

Grades on Chemistry Test

The Twists

For whatever reason, the SAT loves presenting data not as a list of values but as a list of frequencies:

Example 2

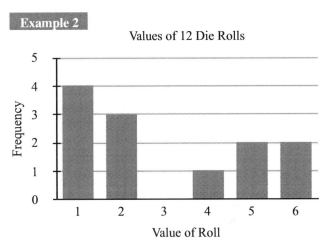

Values of 12 Die Rolls

mode =

median =

mean =

Example 3

Ages of Softball Team Members

Age	Frequency
19	1
23	1
25	2
28	1
29	2
30	4
32	1
33	1
35	1
48	1

mode =

median =

mean =

Exercise: Basic Statistics

1

Number of States Visited by Seven Travel Bloggers

Blogger	States Visited
John	36
Rick	48
Marion	25
Tom	41
Susanne	37
Lillian	48
Amy	32

A survey was given to seven travel bloggers asking how many states each had visited. The results of the survey are given in the table above. What is the median number of states visited by these seven travel bloggers?

2

Sick Days Used by a Random Sample of Employees

Sick Days	Frequency
0	4
1	12
2	17
3	14
4	18
5	8
6	3
23	1

The table above gives the results of a survey of a random sample of employees at Company A who were asked to report the number of sick days they used during a 12-month period. If the employee who took 23 sick days were removed from the data set, which of the following would change the most?

A) median

B) mean

C) mode

D) range

3

The tables below give the distribution of the average hours of sleep per night for 20 people in East Springfield and West Springfield.

East Springfield

Average Hours of Sleep	Frequency
5	3
6	4
7	4
8	5
9	4

West Springfield

Average Hours of Sleep	Frequency
5	1
6	2
7	4
8	10
9	3

Which of the following is true about the data shown above?

A) The standard deviation of hours of sleep in East Springfield is greater than the standard deviation of hours of sleep in West Springfield.

B) The standard deviation of hours of sleep in East Springfield is less than the standard deviation of hours of sleep in West Springfield.

C) The standard deviation of hours of sleep in East Springfield is the same as the standard deviation of hours of sleep in West Springfield.

D) The standard deviation of hours of sleep in East Springfield and West Springfield cannot be calculated with the data provided.

Arithmetic

Number of Stars Awarded by Group

Team	4 stars	3 stars	2 stars	1 star	0 stars
Group A	12	23	19	3	3
Group B	47	8	2	0	3
Group C	11	16	28	4	1
Group D	17	19	4	8	12
Total	87	66	53	15	19

A new movie was shown to four different test groups of 60 people each. After the movie, each person was asked to rate the movie on a scale of 0 to 4 stars. The number of people in each group who awarded different numbers of stars is shown in the table above.

4

What was the mean number of stars awarded by Group B ?

5

The median number of stars awarded by Group A was how much greater than the median number of stars awarded by Group C?

6

Which of the following box plots could represent the number of stars awarded by Group D ?

A)
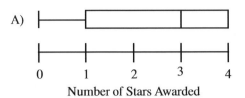
Number of Stars Awarded

B)
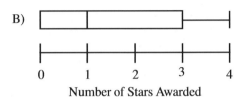
Number of Stars Awarded

C)
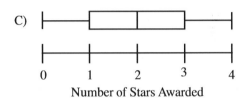
Number of Stars Awarded

D)
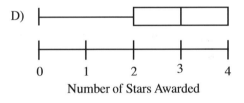
Number of Stars Awarded

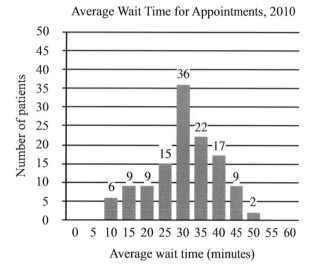

Average Wait Time for Appointments, 2010

In 2010, a doctor's office with 2,000 total patients wanted to improve efficiency by lowering wait times. Roger surveyed 125 patients to determine how long they had spent in the waiting room before their appointment, rounded to the nearest 5 minutes. The results from Roger's survey are shown above.

In 2011, Roger conducted a similar survey at the same doctor's office. He asked 250 patients about their wait times and found that 6 patients had a wait time of 10 minutes. The office continued to serve 2,000 total patients.

7

Which of the following represents the range of the average wait times for Roger's 2010 survey?

A) 36

B) 40

C) 50

D) 60

8

Based on Roger's two surveys, which of the following most accurately compares the expected total number of patients with 10-minute wait times in each year?

A) The total number of patients with a 10-minute wait time in 2010 was expected to be equal to the total number of patients with a 10-minute wait time in 2011.

B) The total number of patients with a 10-minute wait time in 2010 was expected to be 2 times larger than the total number of patients with a 10-minute wait time in 2011.

C) The total number of patients with a 10-minute wait time in 2011 was expected to be 2 times larger than the total number of patients with a 10-minute wait time in 2010.

D) The total number of patients with a 10-minute wait time in 2011 was expected to be 125 times larger than the total number of patients with a 10-minute wait time in 2010.

9

Which of the following box plots could represent Roger's 2010 survey data?

A)

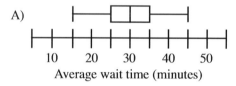

Average wait time (minutes)

B)

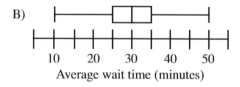

Average wait time (minutes)

C)

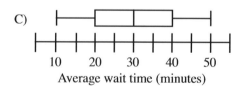

Average wait time (minutes)

D)

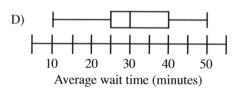

Average wait time (minutes)

Mystery Averages

Occasionally, you'll need to calculate an average that's missing a value or that changes when a value is added or removed. Basically, you just need to **use the average formula twice**. It's very helpful to write the average formula on your page whenever you encounter a question that asks about it:

Example 4

	Weight of Cats (pounds)			
Meg	9.8	10.4	10.1	9.5
AJ	x	8.7	9.3	9.0

Meg and AJ each have four cats, and the weights of their cats are given in the table above. The mean weight of Meg's cats is 0.9 pounds greater than the mean weight of AJ's cats. What is the value of x?

Example 5

Josephine has an average of 86% on five History exams. What is the minimum score she must earn on a sixth exam so that her overall average is at least 88%?

1

A baseball pitcher averages 8 strikeouts per game over his first 4 games and 12 strikeouts per game over his next 2 games. To the nearest tenth, what is his average strikeouts per game for his first 6 games?

2

Hans is playing a game where players write a number from 1 to 50 on a blank card. He is playing with 5 other people, and the average of the first 3 players' cards is 9. If no two players write the same number, what is the maximum value that Hans can write on his card so that the average for all 6 players is still 9?

3

The average of x and 7 is a. The average of 4 and $3x$ is b. The average of $2x - 1$ and 8 is c. What is the average of a, b, and c in terms of x?

A) $x + 3$

B) $2x + 6$

C) $3x + 9$

D) $6x + 18$

Surveys

Don't be intimidated by questions with a lot of text. You can Arithmetize or, like in Reading, avoid strong words and pick the weakest answer.

Example 6

A car dealership took a survey of the value of the cars on its lot. The survey showed that the mean car value was $10,000 and the median car value was $16,000. Which of the following situations could explain the difference between the mean and median car values?

A) The cars have values that are close together.

B) There are a few cars that are much more valuable than the rest.

C) There are a few cars that are much less valuable than the rest.

D) Many of the cars are valued between $10,000 and $16,000.

Example 7

An ice cream manufacturer surveys a small town of 10,000 people to determine whether the residents prefer chocolate or vanilla ice cream. They surveyed 250 people over the age of 30 and found that 68% of them preferred chocolate ice cream. Which of the following must be true?

A) Exactly 68% of all the town's residents prefer chocolate ice cream.

B) Approximately 32% of all the town's residents prefer vanilla ice cream.

C) Approximately 68% of the town's residents over the age of 30 prefer chocolate ice cream.

D) Approximately 68% of the town's residents over the age of 30 like ice cream.

Exercise: Surveys

1

Sally conducts two surveys to determine the mean income in similarly-sized Floraltown and Parkville. She surveys 100 people in Floraltown and finds the mean income is $55,000. She surveys 200 people in Parkville and finds the mean income is $60,000. Which of the following must be true?

A) The majority of people in Parkville earn more than the majority of people in Floraltown.

B) Some people in Floraltown earn more than some people in Parkville.

C) The survey of Floraltown has a greater margin of error than the survey of Parkville.

D) The survey of Parkville has a greater margin of error than the survey of Floraltown.

2

A grocery store owner is debating whether to move his store to a new location 10 miles away. He conducts a survey at his current grocery store on a Tuesday morning, asking 150 of his customers whether they want the store to move. Which of the following factors makes it least likely that a reliable conclusion can be drawn from the survey?

A) Sample size

B) Population size

C) The time the survey was given

D) The distance the store would move

3

A small city wants to determine whether all city residents believe that a particular factory in the city should be taxed for emitting excess pollution. The city council conducts a survey of 300 people who work at the factory. The majority of those who were sampled were opposed to taxing the factory. Which of the following is true about the city council's survey?

A) It should have included more factory workers in its sample.

B) It shows that the majority of city residents oppose increasing taxes.

C) It shows that the majority of city residents oppose increasing taxes on this particular factory.

D) The survey is biased because its sample is not representative of all city residents.

Algebra

The Basics

Algebra makes up the vast majority of the SAT math section. The Properties and Models categories also test algebra, but they're separated out because they tend to test it in a different way. (More on that later.) This category is algebra stripped down to its most essential feature—solving for a variable.

The Twists

The **Common Algebra Mistakes** packet is actually 5 packets in one (Essential Algebra, Distribution, Fractions, Inequalities, and Factor & FOIL). They're meant to highlight the most basic algebra concepts. But also, the SAT knows the algebra mistakes that you're most likely to make, and the answer choices will reflect that. If you lose a negative, distribute incorrectly, or forget how to add fractions, you'll still get an answer that matches one of the choices. Be as careful as possible, and take note of the mistakes that you make most often. Self-awareness will help you prevent them. So will showing your work.

Some of the Algebra questions will involve some clever maneuvers, like manipulation of exponential bases, long division of polynomials, and multiplication by the conjugate. That might sound scary if you're not confident with algebra, but practice makes perfect. The rules of algebra don't change, so the more questions you see, the better you'll be at applying the rules in the correct situation. Khan Academy is a great resource to help you see a ton of Algebra questions.

If you haven't taken Algebra 2, factoring and functions will probably be difficult. But you shouldn't give up. The test-taking strategies can help. **Guess & Check** when the answer choices can be easily plugged back into an equation. **Arithmetize** when the value of x doesn't really matter. Use simple numbers like 0, 1, and 2 so that the math is easy. Arithmetizing can be strange at first, but it becomes more natural with practice.

Packets

- common algebra mistakes
- radicals
- exponent rules
- absolute value
- must be true
- point of intersection
- advanced algebra
- dividing polynomials
- imaginary numbers

approximately 13 questions per test

worth approximately 130 points total

Math	grph	grph	grph	chrt
arith	arith	ratio	ratio	ratio	COP
perc	perc	stat	stat	stat	imag
CAM	CAM	CAM	CAM	CAM	rad/abs
exp	POI	POI	POI	alg+	MBT/div
LP	LP	LP	QP	QP	QP
FP	FP	CP	RF	XM	XM
LM	LM	LM	WTF	WTF	WTF
LM	LM	QV	WTF	WTF	WTF
GM	POW	ang	ST/cyl	trig	geo+

Important Ideas

Common Algebra Mistakes

Here's where most students tend to lose points:

negatives: $5 - (x - 2) = ?$

wrong: $3 - x$

right: $7 - x$

distribution: $6 + x(2x - 3) = ?$

wrong: $2x^2 + 3$

right: $2x^2 - 3x + 6$

greater/less than: "The cost, c, is at least \$4"

wrong: $c \leq 4$

right: $c \geq 4$

adding/subtracting fractions: $\dfrac{1}{2} + \dfrac{1}{4} = ?$

wrong: $\dfrac{1}{2} + \dfrac{1}{4} = \dfrac{2}{6}$

right: $\dfrac{2}{4} + \dfrac{1}{4} = \dfrac{3}{4}$

denominators: $\dfrac{x}{2y} = 12$

wrong: $\dfrac{x}{y} = 6$

right: $\dfrac{x}{y} = 24$

reducing: $\dfrac{2x + 6}{2x} = ?$

wrong: 6

right: $\dfrac{x + 3}{x}$

FOILing: $(x + 3)^2 = ?$

wrong: $x^2 + 9$

right: $x^2 + 6x + 9$

Use the Math Strategies

You might be able to **Guess & Check** if the choices are possible values of the variable. Look for questions like:
- which of the following could be the value of x?
- what value of x is a solution to the equation above?
- what is the least possible value of x?

You might be able to **Arithmetize** if you don't actually need to solve for the variables. Look for questions like:
- what is x in terms of y?
- which of the following is an equivalent form of the expression above?
- which of the following must be true?

Algebra Vocabulary

A **constant** is just a number. When they say that a letter is a constant, it means we don't know the number, so we're using a letter as a placeholder.

Sum means addition. **Difference** means subtraction. **Product** means multiplication.

"What is the value of **f(2)**?" means "What is the value of the equation when x equals 2?" so substitute 2 in for x.

Ways to Solve

If there's **one variable without an exponent**, try to get it by itself. Usually, x equals a number.

If there's **one variable with a squared exponent**, try to get everything equal to 0. Usually, you'll have to factor.

If there are **multiple variables and one equation**, move things around until you solve for what they want. Usually, "x in terms of y".

If there are **multiple variables and two equations**, substitute or "stack" to eliminate one of the variables. Usually, a point of intersection.

Essential Algebra

common algebra mistakes

The Basics

Show your work.

Example 1

If $6x + 15 = 27$, what is the value of $2x + 5$?

Example 2

If $2a = 14$, what is the value of $4a + 8$?

Example 3

If $x > 0$ and $x^2 - 16 = 0$, what is the value of x ?

The Twists

Follow instructions.

Example 4

When 2 times a number n is added to 8, the result is 6. What number results when 4 times n is added to 20?

A) -1

B) 4

C) 6

D) 16

Example 5

$$2x^2 - 6x + 1$$
$$4x^2 - 3x - 8$$

Which of the following is the sum of the two polynomials shown above?

A) $6x^2 - 9x - 7$

B) $6x^2 + 9x - 7$

C) $6x^4 - 9x^2 - 7$

D) $6x^4 + 9x^2 - 7$

Exercise: Essential Algebra

1

If $y = cx$, where c is a constant, and $y = 36$ when $x = 9$, what is the value of y when $x = 2$?

A) 4

B) 8

C) 18

D) 29

2

If $9 + 6t$ is 7 less than 28, what is the value of $3t$?

A) 2

B) 4

C) 6

D) 8

3

Which of the following is equivalent to the sum of the expressions $3 + y^2$ and $2y - 3$?

A) $y^2 + 2y$

B) $y^2 + 2y + 6$

C) $2y^3$

D) $3y^3$

4

If $5(a - b) = -8$, what is the value of $a - b$?

A) $-\dfrac{8}{5}$

B) $-\dfrac{5}{8}$

C) $\dfrac{5}{8}$

D) $\dfrac{8}{5}$

5

When 3 times n is added to 13, the result is 9. What is the value of $6n$?

A) -8

B) -4

C) $-\dfrac{4}{3}$

D) $\dfrac{3}{4}$

6

$$2x + x + 4 + x + 1 = x - 5 + x + 2$$

In the equation above, what is the value of x?

A) –6

B) –4

C) –1

D) 6

7

The sum of $5x^2 - 4x + 7$ and $-x^2 - 2x + 8$ can be written in the form $ax^2 + bx + c$, where a, b, and c are constants. What is the value of $a + b + c$?

8

If 2 times the number x is subtracted from 20, the result is 14. What number results when 8 times x is added to 5?

Distribution

common algebra mistakes

The Basics

Distribute to <u>all</u> parts.

Example 1

$$2(x + 5) + 6(x - 9) = 4x$$

What value of x is the solution of the equation above?

Example 2

Which of the following is equivalent to $4(x + 3) - 8$?

A) $12x - 8$

B) $4x + 4$

C) $4x - 5$

D) $4x - 20$

Example 3

$$(x^2 - 8) - (-5x^2 + 3)$$

Which of the following expressions is equivalent to the one above?

A) $6x^2 - 11$

B) $6x^2 - 5$

C) $-4x^2 - 11$

D) $-4x^2 - 5$

The Twists

Don't let weird instructions scare you. And don't lose negatives!

Example 4

$$(2ab^2 + 5a^2 - 4a^2b) - (-2ab^2 - a^2b + 5a^2)$$

Which of the following is equivalent to the expression above?

A) $4ab^2 - 3a^2b$

B) $4ab^2 - 3a^2b + 10a^2$

C) $4ab^2 - 5a^2b$

D) $4ab^2 - 5a^2b + 10a^2$

Example 5

$$3x(4x - 2) - 5(4x - 2) = ax^2 + bx + c$$

In the equation above, a, b, and c are constants. If the equation is true for all values of x, what is the value of $a + b$?

A) -14

B) -4

C) 12

D) 38

Exercise: Distribution

1

$$4(x^2y - 3xy^2) - (3x^2y + xy^2)$$

Which of the following is equivalent to the expression above?

A) $x^2y - 13xy^2$

B) $x^2y - 4xy^2$

C) $x^2y - 2xy^2$

D) $5x^2y$

2

$$x(x - 5) + 2(x + 5) - 5 = ax^2 + bx + c$$

In the equation above, a, b, and c are constants. If the equation is true for all values of x, what is the value of c?

A) –5

B) 0

C) 5

D) 10

3

$$5(t - 1) - 2(t + 2) = 2t$$

What value of t is the solution of the equation above?

A) –9

B) –1

C) 1

D) 9

4

$$(400x^2 + 1095) - 20(32 - 5x^2)$$

The equation above can be written in the form $ax^2 + c$, where a and c are constants. What is the value of $a + c$?

5

Which expression is equivalent to $(-x^2 - 9) - (6 + 3x - 3x^2)$?

A) $2x^2 - 3x - 15$

B) $2x^2 + 3x - 15$

C) $-4x^2 - 3x - 15$

D) $-4x^2 + 3x - 15$

6

$$2(x^2 - 4) - 3x(x + 1)$$

The expression above can be rewritten in the form $ax^2 + bx + c$, where a, b, and c are constants. What is the value of $a - b - c$?

Fractions

common algebra mistakes

The Basics

Eliminate fractions by multiplying. Even if it's not necessary, eliminating fractions first makes algebra easier.

Example 1

If $\dfrac{x+3}{4} = y$ and $y = 5$, what is the value of x ?

A) 2

B) 8

C) 17

D) 23

Example 2

If $\dfrac{2}{7}t = \dfrac{3}{2}$, what is the value of t ?

A) $\dfrac{21}{4}$

B) $\dfrac{7}{3}$

C) $\dfrac{3}{7}$

D) $\dfrac{4}{21}$

The Twists

Fractions can get messy. Know what you can and cannot do with them.

Example 3

If $\dfrac{x}{y} = 3$, what is the value of $\dfrac{12y}{x}$?

A) 3

B) 4

C) 9

D) 36

Example 4

If $\dfrac{3}{7}x + \dfrac{2}{7}x = \dfrac{3}{8} + \dfrac{1}{2}$, what is the value of x ?

A) $\dfrac{49}{40}$

B) $\dfrac{28}{25}$

C) $\dfrac{5}{8}$

D) $\dfrac{14}{25}$

Exercise: Fractions

1

If $a = \dfrac{3}{4}b$ and $b = 28$, what is the value of $2a + 1$?

A) 7

B) 15

C) 21

D) 43

2

$$x - \frac{c}{5} = 0$$

If $x = 2$ in the equation above, what is the value of c ?

3

If $x - y + 15 = 0$ and $\dfrac{y}{2} = 6$, what is the value of xy ?

A) −36

B) −3

C) 3

D) 36

4

If $\dfrac{a + 2}{a + 4} = 6$, what is the value of a ?

A) $-\dfrac{22}{5}$

B) $-\dfrac{9}{4}$

C) $-\dfrac{4}{5}$

D) $-\dfrac{1}{2}$

5

If $\dfrac{x}{3} = \dfrac{x + 12}{9}$, what is the value of $\dfrac{x}{3}$?

A) 1

B) 2

C) 3

D) 6

6

If $\dfrac{x}{y} = \dfrac{1}{2}$, what is the value of $\dfrac{16y}{x}$?

A) 4

B) 8

C) 16

D) 32

7

If $\dfrac{4}{9}h = \dfrac{3}{2}$, what is the value of h ?

Algebra

Inequalities

common algebra mistakes

The Basics

Most of these will be multiple choice. **Guess & Check** the answer choices.

Example 1

Which of the following numbers is NOT a solution of the inequality $2x + 1 \leq 5x - 2$?

A) −1

B) 1

C) 2

D) 4

Example 2

$$6 \leq 1 - x$$

Which of the following represents all of the solutions to the inequality above?

A) $x \leq 5$

B) $x \geq 5$

C) $x \leq -5$

D) $x \geq -5$

The Twists

Words like "least" and "greatest" sound scary, but you can usually pretend the inequality is an equals sign.

Example 3

If $3a - 1 \leq 5$, what is the greatest possible value of $3a + 1$?

A) 1

B) 2

C) 7

D) 8

Example 4

If $x + y \leq 10$ and $y \geq 3$, what is the greatest possible value of x ?

A) 6

B) 7

C) 11

D) 13

Exercise: Inequalities

1

$$2x - 7 < 11$$

Which of the following represents the solutions to the inequality above?

A) $x < 18$

B) $x > 18$

C) $x < 9$

D) $x > 9$

2

$$4x - 1 < 2x$$

Which of the following is a solution of the inequality shown above?

A) 0

B) 1

C) 2

D) 4

3

$$8x - 6y \le 26$$

Which of the following inequalities is equivalent to the inequality above?

A) $2x - y \le 6$

B) $3x - 4y \le 13$

C) $4x - 3y \le 13$

D) $4y - 3x \le 6$

4

If $5k - 2 \ge -12$, what is the least possible value of k ?

A) 2

B) 1

C) –2

D) –3

5

If $2x + 5 \le -1$, what is the greatest possible value of $4x + 15$?

A) –11

B) –2

C) 1

D) 3

6

$$5 - 4x > 2x - 1$$

Which of the following represents the solutions to the inequality above?

A) $x < -1$

B) $x > -1$

C) $x < 1$

D) $x > 1$

Algebra

Factor & FOIL

common algebra mistakes

The Basics

FOILing is easy since the instructions are in the name. Show your work, and don't forget the middle term. If you don't feel confident, **Arithmetize** to make most Factor & FOIL questions much easier.

Example 1

$$2(x + 1)(3x + 4)$$

Which of the following is equivalent to the expression above?

A) $6x^2 + 8$

B) $6x^2 + 11x + 4$

C) $6x^2 + 14x + 8$

D) $12x^2 + 28x + 16$

Example 2

Which of the following is equivalent to $\left(\dfrac{x}{2} + y\right)^2$?

A) $\dfrac{x^2}{2} + y^2$

B) $\dfrac{x^2}{4} + y^2$

C) $\dfrac{x^2}{4} + \dfrac{xy}{2} + y^2$

D) $\dfrac{x^2}{4} + xy + y^2$

The Twists

If you understand FOILing, factoring shouldn't be much harder. And you can always check your answer by FOILing it out.

Example 3

$$4x^4 - 4x^2y^2 + y^4$$

Which of the following is equivalent to the expression shown above?

A) $(2x^2 - y^2)^2$

B) $(2x^2 - y^2)^4$

C) $(4x^2 - y^2)^2$

D) $(4x^2 - y^2)^4$

Even stuff that doesn't look like Factor & FOIL might be if there are squared terms involved.

Example 4

If $a^2 - b^2 = x$ and $a + b = y$, which of the following is equivalent to $a - b$?

A) $x - y$

B) xy

C) $\dfrac{x}{y}$

D) $\dfrac{y}{x}$

Exercise: Factor & FOIL

1

$$3(5x - 2)(2x - 5)$$

Which of the following is equivalent to the expression above?

A) $10x^2 - 29x + 10$

B) $10x^2 + 29x - 10$

C) $30x^2 - 87x + 30$

D) $30x^2 + 87x - 30$

2

$$f(x) = x^2 - 4k$$

In the function f above, k is a positive constant. Which of the following is an equivalent form of f?

A) $f(x) = \left(x - 2\sqrt{k}\right)\left(x + 2\sqrt{k}\right)$

B) $f(x) = \left(x - \sqrt{2k}\right)\left(x + \sqrt{2k}\right)$

C) $f(x) = \left(x - 2k\right)\left(x + 2k\right)$

D) $f(x) = \left(x - 2\sqrt{k}\right)^2$

3

$$(p + 2q)^2$$

Which of the following is equivalent to the expression above?

A) $p^2 + 4q^2$

B) $p^2 + 2pq + 2q^2$

C) $p^2 + 2pq + 4q^2$

D) $p^2 + 4pq + 4q^2$

4

$$(4x + 9)(4x - 9) = a x^2 - b$$

In the equation above, a and b are constants. Which of the following could be the value of a?

A) 2

B) 4

C) 8

D) 16

5

Which of the following is an equivalent form of $(2x - 5)^2 - (2x^2 - 5)$?

A) $2x^2 + 20$

B) $2x^2 + 30$

C) $2x^2 - 20x + 20$

D) $2x^2 - 20x + 30$

6

If $a^2 + b^2 = 12$ and $a b = 4$, which of the following is equivalent to $(a + b)^2$?

A) 12

B) 16

C) 20

D) 24

Radicals

algebra

The Basics

Just follow instructions. Remember that you "undo" a square root by squaring both sides.

Example 1

$$\sqrt{a-1} - x = 1$$

In the equation above, a is a constant. If $x = 3$, what is the value of a ?

A) 3

B) 5

C) 17

D) 25

Example 2

If $x = 4\sqrt{3}$ and $3x = \sqrt{3y}$, what is the value of y ?

A) 4

B) 12

C) 16

D) 144

The Twists

Occasionally you need to worry about solutions that don't actually work when plugged back into the equation (extraneous solutions). These are usually multiple choice questions, so you can **Guess & Check** from the start so it's less of an issue:

Example 3

$$\sqrt{x+k} = x - 3$$

If $k = 3$, what is the solution set of the equation above?

A) $\{1, 6\}$

B) $\{1\}$

C) $\{3\}$

D) $\{6\}$

More importantly, don't get confused between squaring and square rooting. The SAT is counting on you to mess this up, so be careful!

Example 4

$$\sqrt{x} - \sqrt{16} = \sqrt{25}$$

In the equation above, what is the value of x ?

A) 3

B) 9

C) 41

D) 81

Exercise: Radicals

1

$$\sqrt{4x^2 + 28} - k = 0$$

If $x > 0$ and $k = 8$ in the equation above, what is the value of x ?

A) 1

B) 3

C) 5

D) 7

2

$$\sqrt{3x + 22} + 4 = x + 2$$

What is the solution set of the equation above?

A) $\{-2\}$

B) $\{9\}$

C) $\{-2, 9\}$

D) $\{-2, 2, 9\}$

3

If $9\sqrt{2} = x\sqrt{18}$, what is the value of x ?

A) 1

B) 2

C) 3

D) 9

4

If $\sqrt{2a} = b$, what is a in terms of b ?

A) $\dfrac{b^2}{2}$

B) $\dfrac{b^2}{4}$

C) $\sqrt{\dfrac{b^2}{2}}$

D) $\sqrt{\dfrac{b^2}{4}}$

5

$$x = 2 + \sqrt{k - x}$$

If $k = 4$, what is the solution set of the equation above?

A) $\{0\}$

B) $\{3\}$

C) $\{0, 3\}$

D) $\{-3, 0, 3\}$

Algebra

Exponent Rules

algebra

The Basics

Manipulating exponents is an essential part of algebra on the SAT. Some questions will incorporate the rules, but a few test them exclusively. You must memorize these!

Multiplication (add exponents)

$$x^6 \cdot x^2 = x^8$$

Division (subtract exponents)

$$\frac{x^6}{x^2} = x^4$$

Exponent to an Exponent (multiply exponents)

$$\left(x^6\right)^2 = x^{12}$$

Fractional Exponent (radical)

$$x^{\frac{1}{2}} = \sqrt{x} \qquad x^{\frac{2}{3}} = \sqrt[3]{x^2}$$

Negative Exponent (reciprocal)

$$x^{-1} = \frac{1}{x} \qquad \frac{1}{2x^{-3}} = \frac{x^3}{2}$$

The Twists

The hardest questions will incorporate multiple rules, so things can get tricky. In theory, you could Arithmetize, but in practice, there's just way too much going on. Knowing the rules is more efficient.

Example 1

Which of the following is equal to $\sqrt[4]{\dfrac{1}{b}}$, for $b > 0$?

A) b^{-4}

B) $b^{-\frac{1}{4}}$

C) $-b^4$

D) $-b^{\frac{1}{4}}$

Example 2

The expression $\dfrac{x^3 y^{-\frac{1}{2}}}{x^{-\frac{3}{2}} y^2}$, where $x > 1$ and $y > 1$ is

equivalent to which of the following?

A) $\dfrac{1}{x^2 \sqrt[4]{y}}$

B) $\dfrac{x\sqrt{x}}{y^2\sqrt{y}}$

C) $\dfrac{x^4\sqrt{x}}{y\sqrt{y}}$

D) $\dfrac{x^4\sqrt{x}}{y^2\sqrt{y}}$

Exercise: Exponent Rules

1

If $2x^{-\frac{1}{3}} = k$, where $x > 0$, what is x in terms of k ?

A) $\sqrt[3]{\dfrac{k}{2}}$

B) $-\sqrt[3]{\dfrac{k}{2}}$

C) $\dfrac{8}{k^3}$

D) $-\dfrac{8}{k^3}$

2

If $x^{\frac{y}{3}} = 81$ for positive integers x and y, and $x \le 81$ what is one possible value of y ?

3

Which of the following is equivalent to $4^{\frac{2}{3}}$?

A) $\sqrt[3]{4}$

B) $\sqrt{8}$

C) $2\sqrt{2}$

D) $2\sqrt[3]{2}$

4

Which of the following is equal to $a^{\frac{4}{3}}$, for all values of a ?

A) $\sqrt[4]{a^{\frac{1}{3}}}$

B) $\sqrt[4]{a^3}$

C) $\sqrt[3]{a^{\frac{1}{4}}}$

D) $\sqrt[3]{a^4}$

5

If $\left(x^{a^2}\right)\left(x^{-b^2}\right) = x^{12}$, $x > 1$, and $a - b = 4$, what is the value of $a + b$?

A) 3

B) 4

C) 6

D) 8

6

If $a - 2b = 24$, what is the value of $\dfrac{3^a}{9^b}$?

A) 3^{24}

B) 3^{12}

C) 9^8

D) The value cannot be determined from the information given.

Absolute Value

algebra

The Basics

Don't worry so much about the mathematical definition of absolute value. Just know that the <u>final</u> answer within the bars becomes positive.

Example 1

For what value of x is $|x - 2| - 2$ equal to 0?

A) –2

B) 0

C) 2

D) There is no such value of x.

The Twists

You should know what an absolute value graph looks like. It tends to show up on questions that ask about domain and range:

Example 2

Which of the following equations has a graph in the xy-plane for which y is always greater than or equal to 0 ?

A) $y = x - 3$

B) $y = x^2 - 3$

C) $y = x^3 - 3$

D) $y = |x - 3|$

Exercise: Absolute Value

1

If $x > 0$, which of the following expressions is equal to 0 for some value of x ?

A) $|x - 2| + x$

B) $|x - 2| - x$

C) $|2 - x| + x$

D) $|2 + x| + x$

2

$$|x - 5| = \frac{1}{2}$$

What is the least value of x that satisfies the equation above?

3

A point with coordinate n is plotted on a number line. Which of the following inequalities gives all of the values for x that are within 5 units of n ?

A) $|x + n| < 5$

B) $|x - n| < 5$

C) $|x| + n < 5$

D) $|x| - n < 5$

Must Be True

algebra

The Basics

These can be tough. You either need to be really comfortable with algebra or really good at **Arithmetizing**.

Example 1

$$x = \frac{a}{b - a}$$

In the equation above, if a is positive and b is negative, which of the following must be true?

A) $x > 0$

B) $x = 0$

C) $x < 0$

D) x is undefined.

The Twists

Remember that different types of numbers behave in different ways:

positive vs. negative

integer vs. fraction

Example 2

If $-1 < x < 0$, then which of the following must be true?

I. $x < x^2$

II. $x^2 < x^3$

III. $x < x^3$

A) I only

B) II only

C) I and III only

D) I, II, and III

Exercise: Must Be True

1

A parabola in the xy-plane has equation $y = ax^2 + bx + c$, where a, b, and c are constants. If the parabola has vertex $(-1, 0)$, which of the following must be true?

A) $a = b + c$

B) $b = a + c$

C) $c = a + b$

D) $a + b + c = 0$

2

If $a^2 = b^2$, then which of the following must be true?

I. $a = b$

II. $a^3 = b^3$

III. $a^{-2} = b^{-2}$

A) I only

B) III only

C) I and II only

D) I, II, and III

3

If $x + y > x$, which of the following must be true?

A) $x > 0$

B) $x < 0$

C) $y > 0$

D) $y < 0$

Algebra

Point of Intersection

algebra

The Basics

Point of Intersection questions are some of the most repetitive SAT questions. Each test has at least 2, and the method used to solve them doesn't change that much. You really need to get these right! If you're not comfortable with algebra, use **Guess & Check** when you can:

Example 1

$$4x - y = -12$$
$$2x + 3y = -34$$

What is the solution (x, y) to the system of equations above?

A) $(1, 16)$

B) $(-1, 8)$

C) $(-5, -8)$

D) $(-8, -6)$

Example 2

$$\frac{x}{3} = y$$
$$1 + 2(y + 2) = x$$

If (x, y) satisfies the system of equations above, what is the value of y?

A) 5

B) 10

C) 15

D) 20

The Twists

If there are no choices or if the question asks for a weird combination of the variables, you'll have to solve algebraically. Substitute when you can, and use the "stack" method when you can't. As always, try to make the algebra as easy as possible.

Example 3

$$\frac{1}{4}x + \frac{1}{2}y = 7$$
$$x - \frac{1}{4}y = 10$$

The system of equations above has solution (x, y).

What is the value of $\frac{x}{y}$?

Example 4

$$f(x) = x^2 - 8x + 16$$
$$g(x) = x - 2$$

The functions f and g are defined above. What is one possible value of a such that $f(a) = g(a)$?

Exercise: Point of Intersection

1

$$2x - y = 7$$
$$3x + 4y = 5$$

Which of the following ordered pairs (x, y) satisfies the system of equations above?

A) $(5, 3)$

B) $(5, -3)$

C) $(3, -1)$

D) $(-1, 2)$

2

$$x - y = -12$$
$$x + 2y = 24$$

According to the system of equations above, what is the value of x ?

3

$$y = x^2 + 1$$
$$2y - 5 = 9 - 2x$$

If (x, y) is a solution of the system of equations above and $x > 0$, what is the value of $x + y$?

4

$$y = \frac{3}{2}x + 1$$
$$y = (x - 6)(2x + 1)$$

How many ordered pairs (x, y) satisfy the system of equations shown above?

A) 0

B) 1

C) 2

D) Infinitely many

5

$$y > x - 6$$
$$4x > 12$$

Which of the following consists of the y-coordinates of all the points that satisfy the system of inequalities above?

A) $y > 6$

B) $y > 3$

C) $y > -3$

D) $y > -6$

6

$$y \leq 2x - 5$$
$$x - 2y > 4$$

Which of the following ordered pairs (x, y) satisfies the system of inequalities above?

A) $(3, 1)$

B) $(3, -2)$

C) $(2, 1)$

D) $(-1, -3)$

Advanced Algebra

algebra

The Basics

Most of these are just algebra with a lot of steps. There are more opportunities to accidentally make Common Algebra Mistakes, so be careful! Remember that **Arithmetizing** can make things easier.

Example 1

If $x \neq 4$ and $x \neq -1$, which of the following is equivalent to $\dfrac{1}{\dfrac{1}{x+1} + \dfrac{1}{x-4}}$?

A) $2x - 3$

B) $x^2 - 3x - 4$

C) $\dfrac{2x - 3}{x^2 - 3x - 4}$

D) $\dfrac{x^2 - 3x - 4}{2x - 3}$

Even when things look impossible, there's usually a convenient solution. Play around with the equation or **Guess & Check** a few numbers.

Example 2

$$x^3 - 4x^2 + 3x = 12$$

For what real value of x is the equation above true?

The Twists

You need to be comfortable working with functions. Try not to let the twists make you panic. **Plug Points Into Equations** when you can.

Example 3

$$h(x) = 2x^2 + c$$

For the function h defined above, c is a constant and $h(3) = 14$. What is the value of $h(-3)$?

A) 14

B) 4

C) –4

D) –14

Example 4

$$g(x) = x^2 - 4x + 3$$

The function g is defined above. If $g(k - 2) = 0$, what is one possible value of k ?

Exercise: Advanced Algebra

1

$$x - 2 = \frac{8}{x - 2}$$

In the equation above, which of the following is a possible value of $x - 2$?

A) 2

B) $2\sqrt{2}$

C) 4

D) 64

2

$$f(x) = 2 - x$$
$$g(x) = 5 - f(2x)$$

The functions f and g are defined above. What is the value of $g(4)$?

A) –3

B) –2

C) 7

D) 11

3

If $f(x) = \dfrac{x^2 - 4x + 9}{x + 2}$, what is $f(2)$?

4

$$f(x) = x^2 - x - 5$$
$$g(x) = 3x^3 - 3x^2 - 15x$$

The polynomials $f(x)$ and $g(x)$ are defined above. Which of the following polynomial functions is divisible by $2 - 3x$?

A) $p(x) = f(x) - g(x)$

B) $q(x) = f(x) - 2g(x)$

C) $r(x) = 2f(x) - g(x)$

D) $s(x) = 2f(x) - 3g(x)$

5

$$f(x) = ax - 3$$

In the function above, a is a constant. If $f(6) = -11$, what is the value of $f(-4)$?

Dividing Polynomials

algebra

The Basics

The SAT loves this type of question. This is difficult algebra, but if you know the process, the questions are fairly consistent. First, remember regular long division:

$$\frac{475}{3} = ?$$

You can also do long division with polynomials. If you're shooting for an 800, you need to know how to divide algebraically in case this comes up in the Grid-ins. But usually you can **Arithmetize**.

Example 1

$$\frac{x^3 - 4x^2 + 2x + 5}{x - 2}$$

Which of the following is equivalent to the expression above?

A) $x^2 - 2x - 2 + \dfrac{1}{x - 2}$

B) $x^2 - 2x + 6 - \dfrac{7}{x - 2}$

C) $x^2 - 6x - 10 + \dfrac{25}{x - 2}$

D) $x^2 - 6x + 14 - \dfrac{23}{x - 2}$

The Twists

Sometimes they ask for just a part of the whole process. Since the x carries through the whole equation, you can **Arithmetize**. Just stay organized.

Example 2

$$\frac{4x^2 - 3x + 7}{x + 2} = 4x - 11 + \frac{k}{x + 2}$$

If $x \neq -2$ above, what is the value of k ?

Exercise: Dividing Polynomials

1

$$\frac{2x^3 + 4x^2 - 5}{x + 3} = 2x^2 - 2x + 6 - \frac{A}{x + 3}$$

If $x \neq -3$ above, what is the value of A?

2

What is the remainder when $x^2 - 4x - 9$ is divided by $x - 7$?

A) –30

B) –2

C) 12

D) 68

3

The equation $\dfrac{20x^2 - 2x + 8}{kx + 2} = 5x - 3 + \dfrac{14}{kx + 2}$ is

true for all values of $x \neq -\dfrac{2}{k}$, where k is a constant.

What is the value of k?

4

The equation $\dfrac{18x^2 - 33x - 12}{6x + b} = 3x - 5 - \dfrac{17}{6x + b}$

is true for all values of $x \neq -\dfrac{b}{6}$, where b is a constant.

What is the value of b?

A) –5

B) –1

C) 1

D) 5

Imaginary Numbers

algebra

The Basics

Imaginary Numbers questions involve i, which is just a math constant, kind of like π.

$$i = \sqrt{-1}$$

Most of the time, this is an irrelevant fact meant only to confuse you. On easy questions, treat i like a variable and combine terms like you normally would.

Example 1

What is the sum of the complex numbers $7 + 4i$ and $3 + 8i$, where $i = \sqrt{-1}$?

A) 22

B) $22i$

C) $10 + 12i$

D) $21 + 32i$

If there's an i^2, replace it with –1.

Example 2

Which of the following complex numbers is equal to $(9 + 6i) - (4i^2 - 8i)$, for $i = \sqrt{-1}$?

A) $-13 - 14i$

B) $-5 + 2i$

C) $5 - 2i$

D) $13 + 14i$

The Twists

Harder questions will almost always involve the conjugate:

3 + 5i and 3 – 5i are conjugates

In math, it's bad to have radicals and imaginary numbers in the denominator of a fraction. Multiplying the numerator and denominator by the conjugate will solve the problem.

Example 3

Which of the following complex numbers is equivalent to $\dfrac{2}{3 + 5i}$? (Note: $i = \sqrt{-1}$)

A) $\dfrac{2}{3} + \dfrac{2i}{5}$

B) $\dfrac{2}{3} - \dfrac{2i}{5}$

C) $\dfrac{3}{17} + \dfrac{5i}{17}$

D) $\dfrac{3}{17} - \dfrac{5i}{17}$

Exercise: Imaginary Numbers

1

Which of the following complex numbers is equal to $(1 + 4i) - (5 - 2i)$, for $i = \sqrt{-1}$?

A) $-4 + 2i$

B) $-4 + 6i$

C) $4 + 2i$

D) $4 + 6i$

2

Which of the following complex numbers is equal to the product of $3 + 5i$ and $2 - i$, where $i = \sqrt{-1}$?

A) $1 + 7i$

B) $1 + 13i$

C) $5 + 4i$

D) $11 + 7i$

3

Which of the following complex numbers is equivalent to $\dfrac{5 - i}{4 + 6i}$? (Note: $i = \sqrt{-1}$)

A) $\dfrac{5}{4} - \dfrac{i}{6i}$

B) $\dfrac{5}{4} + \dfrac{i}{6i}$

C) $\dfrac{7}{26} - \dfrac{17i}{26}$

D) $\dfrac{7}{26} + \dfrac{17i}{26}$

4

$$\frac{10 - 3i}{2 - 5i}$$

If the expression above is rewritten in the form $a + bi$, where a and b are real numbers, what is the value of b ? (Note: $i = \sqrt{-1}$)

A) $\dfrac{3}{5}$

B) 1

C) $\dfrac{44}{29}$

D) $\dfrac{59}{29}$

5

Which of the following complex numbers is equivalent to $\dfrac{3 - 4i}{2i} + \dfrac{1 + 2i}{4}$? (Note: $i = \sqrt{-1}$)

A) $\dfrac{7}{4} + i$

B) $-\dfrac{7}{4} - i$

C) $\dfrac{3}{5} + \dfrac{4i}{5}$

D) $\dfrac{3}{5} - \dfrac{4i}{5}$

Algebra

Properties

The Basics

While Algebra questions test your math skills, Properties questions test your **math knowledge**. Some of these questions are about equations, but many also include graphs. In fact, Properties questions are mostly about how algebra "looks" when graphed in the xy-plane.

Most of the questions will involve lines and quadratics (parabolas), so you'll need to be comfortable with the standard forms of both types of equations. Some of the harder questions test circle equations and polynomial functions. If you haven't taken Algebra 2, these questions might be tough! But they only test a handful of properties, so you can learn the most essential rules just for the SAT.

The Twists

Pretty much everything you need to know for Geometry is included in the Reference Chart at the beginning of each section, but for some reason, the SAT expects you to memorize all of the formulas and rules for lines, quadratics, functions, and circles. The next page and the individual packets will list the properties, but it's up to you to **memorize them**!

The SAT also likes to twist the standard equations so that they're hard to recognize. A question might be worded in such a way that you have no idea it's asking about a line. Use the packets to learn the patterns that line questions share, even when they're well-disguised.

If the variables don't have exponents, you're probably working with a line, so try to get back to $y=mx+b$. If there's an x^2, it's probably a quadratic, but also remember that you might need to FOIL some terms in order to find the hidden x^2. Circles have an x^2 and a y^2. Once you figure out what you're working with, try to get back to the standard form. Also, don't forget that you can **Plug Points Into Equations**, even when they're not in the standard form.

Packets

- linear properties
- quadratic properties
- function properties
- circle properties

approximately 9 questions per test

worth approximately 90 points total

Math	grph	grph	grph	chrt
arith	arith	ratio	ratio	ratio	COP
perc	perc	stat	stat	stat	imag
CAM	CAM	CAM	CAM	CAM	rad/abs
exp	POI	POI	POI	alg+	MBT/div
LP	LP	LP	QP	QP	QP
FP	FP	CP	RF	XM	XM
LM	LM	LM	WTF	WTF	WTF
LM	LM	QV	WTF	WTF	WTF
GM	POW	ang	ST/cyl	trig	geo+

Important Ideas

Lines

Standard form: **y = mx + b**
- m = slope
- b = y-intercept
- (x, y) = points on the line

Memorize **slope formula**:

$$\text{slope} = \frac{\text{rise}}{\text{run}} = \frac{\Delta y}{\Delta x} = \frac{y_1 - y_2}{x_1 - x_2}$$

If you have **two points**, you can find the **slope** between them using slope formula.

Parallel lines have the same slope.

Perpendicular lines have negative reciprocal slopes.

Parallel lines will have **no solutions** because they never intersect.

Two lines have **infinitely many solutions** when they are the exact same line.

Often, you'll be explicitly told when you're working with a **line** or a **linear** function. Another clue is when the **x does not have an exponent.**

Functions

A **factor** is a term that divides evenly into a function. It also tells you where a function crosses the x-axis. Remember that if a function has an x-intercept at $x = 2$, then the term $(x - 2)$ will be a factor. Similarly, if $x = -2$ is an x-intercept, then $(x + 2)$ is a factor. Notice that the +/− sign changes!

When finding function values on a graph, do not confuse these two questions:

What is the value of f(3)? means "what is the y-value when x = 3?"

For what value of x does f(x) = 3? means "what is the x-value when y = 3?"

Quadratics

Standard form: **y = ax² + bx + c**
- a = smileyness/frownyness (opens up/down)
- b = not useful
- c = y-intercept
- (x, y) = points on the parabola

Root form: **y = (x − r)(x − s)**
- r = first root/solution/zero/x-intercept
- s = second root/solution/zero/x-intercept

Vertex form: **y = a(x − h)² + k**
- a = smileyness/frownyness (opens up/down)
- (h, k) = vertex

The **vertex** is also the **maximum or minimum** of the parabola. You can think of the vertex as the center, and parabolas are **symmetrical** over the vertex. In other words, the left side is the mirror image of the right side.

On very hard questions, you might not be able to factor, so you'll have to use quadratic formula:

$$x = \frac{-b \pm \sqrt{b^2 - 4ac}}{2a}$$

Circles

Standard form: **(x − h)² + (y − k)² = r²**
- (h, k) = center
- r = radius
- (x, y) = points on the circle

Complete the Square

To get a quadratic into vertex form or to get a circle into standard form, you might need to **complete the square:**

$$
\begin{aligned}
y &= x^2 + 10x + 4 & &\text{standard parabola} \\
y &= (x^2 + 10x) + 4 & &\text{group } a \text{ and } b \text{ terms} \\
y &= (x^2 + 10x + 5^2) + 4 & &\text{add } (b/2)^2 \\
y &= (x^2 + 10x + 25) + 4 - 25 & &\text{maintain balance} \\
y &= (x + 5)^2 - 21 & &\text{simplify}
\end{aligned}
$$

Linear Properties

properties

The Basics

Know the equation of a line. Everything revolves around this equation:

$$y = mx + b$$

Example 1

Which of the following is the graph of the equation $y = 3x - 1$ in the xy-plane?

A)
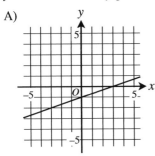

B)
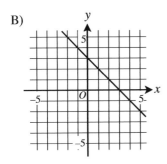

C)
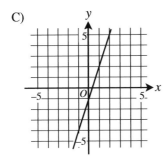

D)
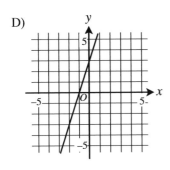

y-intercept

Given by b. Always has the coordinate $(0, b)$.

Example 2

If the line with equation $\frac{2}{3}x - \frac{3}{4}y = -2$ is graphed in the xy-plane, what is the y-coordinate of the y-intercept of the line?

slope

Given by m. Always constant—that's what makes it a line! You must memorize slope formula:

$$\text{slope} = \frac{\text{rise}}{\text{run}} = \frac{\Delta y}{\Delta x} = \frac{y_1 - y_2}{x_1 - x_2}$$

Example 3

The graph of a line in the xy-plane passes through the points $(1, 11)$ and $(-1, 9)$. The graph of a second line has slope -2 and includes the point $(1, 2)$. If the two lines intersect at point (a, b), what is the value of $b - a$?

The Twists

In addition to the basic line formula, there are a few other terms and properties that you need to be comfortable with:

origin
> the point (0, 0)

quadrant
> one of the 4 sectors of the xy-plane

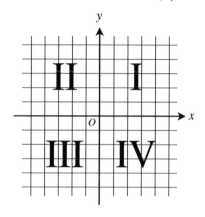

parallel
> lines that are parallel have the same slope:
>
> $y = 2x - 1$ and $y = 2x + 6$

perpendicular
> lines that are perpendicular have negative reciprocal slopes:
>
> $y = 2x - 1$ and $y = -\dfrac{1}{2}x + 6$

solution
> the point of intersection

no solutions
> Lines that do no intersect have no solutions. This only happens when lines are parallel.

infinitely many solutions
> This just means the two lines are the same, so they overlap/intersect at every point:
>
> $y = 2x - 1$ and $2y = 4x - 2$

Example 4

$$3x + 5y = 15$$
$$ax + by = 75$$

In the system of equations above, a and b are constants. If the system has infinitely many solutions, what is the value of $\dfrac{a}{b}$?

Inequalities

Don't panic. Remember that the essence of a linear inequality is still a line with a slope and a y-intercept. After you graph the line, you need to "shade" up or down, depending on whether y is greater than or less than the line. The solution is where the two shaded regions overlap.

Example 5

$$y < -2x + 5$$
$$y \le -\dfrac{1}{3}x - 5$$

If the system of inequalities above is graphed in the *xy*-plane, which quadrant will contain no solutions to the system?

A) Quadrant I

B) Quadrant II

C) Quadrant III

D) There are solutions in all four quadrants.

Exercise: Linear Properties

1

A line in the xy-plane passes through the origin. If the slope of the line is $-\frac{2}{5}$, which of the following points lies on the line?

A) $(-5, -2)$

B) $(-2, 5)$

C) $(5, 2)$

D) $(10, -4)$

2

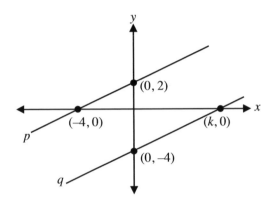

In the xy-plane above, line p is parallel to line q. What is the value of k ?

A) 2

B) 4

C) 6

D) 8

3

$$y \geq -6x + 360$$

$$y \geq 12x$$

In the xy-plane, if a point with coordinates (a, b) lies in the solution set of the system of inequalities above, what is the minimum possible value of b ?

4

The line $y = kx + c$, where k and c are constants, is graphed in the xy-plane. If the line contains the point (a, b), where $a \neq 0$ and $b \neq 0$, what is the slope of the line in terms of a, b, and c ?

A) $\dfrac{a - c}{b}$

B) $\dfrac{b + c}{a}$

C) $\dfrac{b - c}{a}$

D) $\dfrac{a}{c - b}$

5

$$5x + ay = 2$$

$$4x + 3y = 6$$

In the system of equations above, a is a constant. For what value of a will the system of equations have no solution?

A) $-\dfrac{15}{4}$

B) -1

C) 1

D) $\dfrac{15}{4}$

6

The graph of line *l* in the *xy*-plane has intercepts at $(a, 0)$ and $(0, a)$. If $a \neq 0$, which of the following is true about the slope of the graph of line *l*?

A) It is positive.

B) It is negative.

C) It equals 0.

D) It is undefined.

7

$$4x - 5y = 20$$

Which of the following equations, when graphed in the *xy*-plane, is perpendicular to the graph of the equation above?

A) $4x + 5y = 20$

B) $5x - 4y = 20$

C) $5x + 4y = 20$

D) $5x + 8y = 10$

8

When graphed in the *xy*-plane, linear function *f* contains the points $(c, 4)$ and $(36, c)$, where *c* is a constant. If *f* passes through the origin, which of the following could be the value of *c* ?

A) 0

B) 3

C) 6

D) 12

9

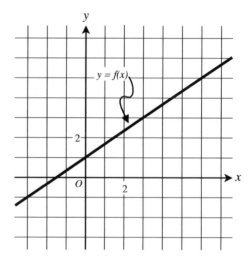

The linear function *f* is graphed in the *xy*-plane above. The slope of the graph of the linear function *g* is 3 times the slope of the graph of *f*. If the graph of *g* has an *x*-intercept at $(-1, 0)$, what is value of $g(6)$?

Quadratic Properties

properties

The Basics

Quadratic equations contain an x^2 term, and they form parabolas in the xy-plane. There are three main ways to express a quadratic equation, and each provides information about the graph. You need to be comfortable with all three!

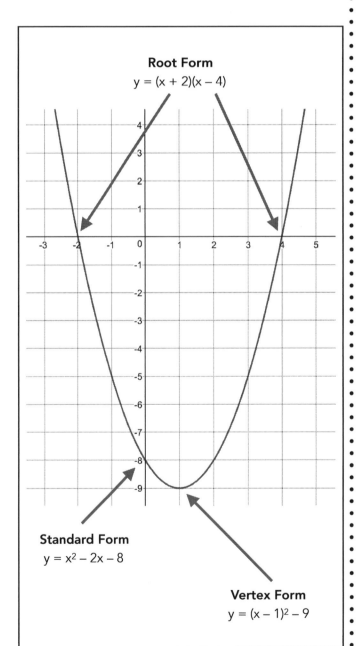

Root Form
$y = (x + 2)(x - 4)$

Standard Form
$y = x^2 - 2x - 8$

Vertex Form
$y = (x - 1)^2 - 9$

Root Form

Gives the points where the parabola crosses the x-axis, which are also known as:

- roots
- zeros
- solutions
- x-intercepts
- factors

$$y = (x - r)(x - s)$$

The roots are (r, 0) and (s, 0).

Standard Form

The most common way quadratics are expressed.

$$y = ax^2 + bx + c$$

The y-intercept is (0, c).
When **a > 0**, the parabola **opens upward** (smiles).
When **a < 0**, the parabola **opens downward** (frowns).

Vertex Form

Gives the vertex of the parabola, which is also known as the:

- turning point
- axis of symmetry
- maximum or minimum

$$y = a(x - h)^2 + k$$

The vertex is (h, k).

Example 1

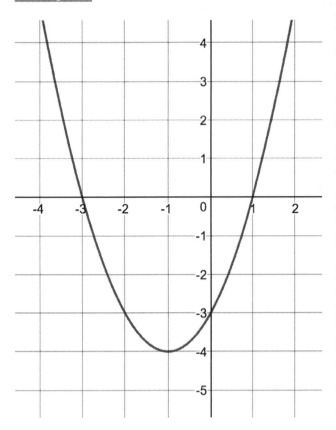

Root Form: _____

Standard Form: _____

Vertex Form: _____

Range: _____

Converting

Without a graph, you need to use algebra to move from one form to another. Use the Factor & FOIL packet for practice with those ideas. The one you might not remember is **completing the square**:

$y = x^2 + 10x + 4$	standard form
$y = (x^2 + 10x) + 4$	group a and b terms
$y = (x^2 + 10x + 5^2) + 4$	add $(b/2)^2$
$y = (x^2 + 10x + 25) + 4 - 25$	maintain balance
$y = (x + 5)^2 - 21$	simplify

Exercise: Convert Quadratics

Root → Standard
FOIL

1. $(x - 5)(x + 2)$

2. $(x - 3)(x + 3)$

3. $(2x - 1)(x + 4)$

Standard → Root
factor

4. $x^2 - 8x + 7$

5. $x^2 - 11x + 24$

6. $2x^2 - 16x - 18$

Standard → Vertex
complete the square

7. $x^2 - 8x + 21$

8. $x^2 + 2x + 5$

9. $x^2 - 6x - 20$

10. $x^2 + 2x - 9$

11. $x^2 - 10x + 24$

Exercise: Graphs of Quadratics

$$y = x^2 - 6x + 5$$

The equation above represents a parabola in the xy-plane. Which of the following equivalent forms of the equation displays the x-intercepts of the parabola as constants or coefficients?

A) $y = x(x - 6) + 5$

B) $y = (x - 3)^2 - 4$

C) $y = (x - 1)(x - 5)$

D) $y - 5 = x^2 - 6x$

$$y = (x + 1)(x - 3)$$

The equation above represents a parabola in the xy-plane. Which of the following equivalent forms of the equation displays the vertex of the parabola as constants or coefficients?

A) $y = x^2 - 2x - 3$

B) $y + 3 = x^2 - 2x$

C) $y = x(x - 2) - 3$

D) $y = (x - 1)^2 - 4$

3

The function f is defined by $f(x) = (x - 7)(x - 3)$. The graph of f in the xy-plane is a parabola. Which of the following intervals contains the x-coordinate of the minimum value of f?

A) $7 < x < 10$

B) $3 < x < 7$

C) $-7 < x < -3$

D) $-10 < x < -7$

The zeros of the polynomial function g are 2 and -4. If the range of g is the set of real numbers less than or equal to 9, which of the following could be the graph of $y = g(x)$ in the xy-plane?

A)

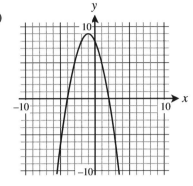

B)

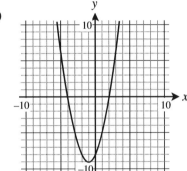

C)

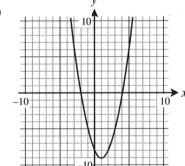

D)

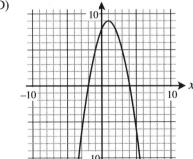

5

What is the sum of the solutions of
$(x + 4)(x - 9) = 0$?

A) 13

B) 5

C) −5

D) −13

6

$$x^2 - 5x - 6 = 0$$

If m is a solution of the equation above and $m > 0$,
what is the value of m ?

7

$$x^2 - 4x + 11$$

Which of the following is equivalent to the expression
above?

A) $(x + 2)^2 + 7$

B) $(x + 2)^2 - 7$

C) $(x - 2)^2 + 7$

D) $(x - 2)^2 - 7$

8

What are the solutions of the quadratic equation
$7x^2 - 21x - 70 = 0$?

A) $x = -2$ and $x = -5$

B) $x = -2$ and $x = 5$

C) $x = 2$ and $x = -5$

D) $x = 2$ and $x = 5$

9

The scatterplot below shows the number of bacteria in
a petri dish over a 12-hour period.

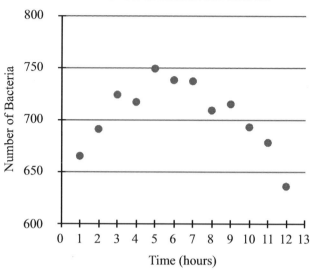

Number of Bacteria in Petri Dish

Which of the following equations best models the data
in the scatterplot?

A) $y = 2.31x^2 - 27.381x + 651.32$

B) $y = 2.31x^2 + 27.381x - 651.32$

C) $y = -2.31x^2 + 27.381x + 651.32$

D) $y = -2.31x^2 - 27.381x - 651.32$

10

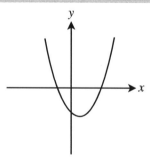

The parabola above has equation $y = ax^2 + bx + c$.
Which of the following is true about the parabola with
the equation $y = -ax^2 + bx - c$?

A) It has a positive y-intercept and opens upward.

B) It has a positive y-intercept and opens downward.

C) It has a negative y-intercept and opens upward.

D) It has a negative y-intercept and opens downward.

The Twists

Sometimes, the numbers won't work out in an easy way, and you'll need to rely on the **quadratic formula** to understand the parabola. Memorize it!

When y = ax² + bx + c, the roots are:

$$x = \frac{-b \pm \sqrt{b^2 - 4ac}}{2a}$$

Example 2

What are the solutions to $x^2 + 4x + 1 = 0$?

A) $x = -2 \pm \sqrt{3}$

B) $x = -2 \pm 2\sqrt{3}$

C) $x = -2 \pm \sqrt{5}$

D) $x = -2 \pm 2\sqrt{5}$

How to Memorize

Quadratic Formula can be intimidating, but it's something you need to know. If it helps, try to remember the two key pieces, both of which also reveal important information about the parabola.

axis of symmetry

$$x = \frac{-b}{2a}$$

gives the x-coordinate of the vertex

discriminant

$$b^2 - 4ac$$

gives the number and type of solutions:

- if discriminant > 0, then 2 real solutions
- if discriminant = 0, then 1 real solution
- if discriminant < 0, then 0 real solutions

Example 3

$$4x^2 = 8x + c$$

For what value of c does the quadratic equation above have no real solutions?

A) 5

B) 3

C) –3

D) –5

Exercise: Advanced Quadratics

1

$$y = 5x^2 + 1$$
$$y = k$$

In the system of equations above, k is a constant. For which value of k does the system of equations have exactly one real solution?

A) –2

B) –1

C) 1

D) 2

2

What is the sum of the solutions of $2x^2 + 6x - 10 = 0$?

A) –3

B) $-\dfrac{\sqrt{29}}{2}$

C) $\dfrac{\sqrt{29}}{2}$

D) 3

3

$$h(t) = -4.9t^2 + 30t + 5$$

The equation above expresses the approximate height h, in meters, of a projectile t seconds after it is launched vertically upward with an initial velocity of 30 meters per second from a platform that is 5 meters off the ground. After approximately how many seconds will the projectile hit the ground?

A) 5.8

B) 6.3

C) 6.8

D) 7.3

4

If $(3x + a)(2x + b) = 6x^2 + cx + 28$ for all values of x, and $a = 11 - b$, what are the two possible values for c ?

A) 4 and 7

B) 8 and 21

C) 12 and 14

D) 26 and 29

5

$$x^2 + \frac{m}{2} = \frac{n}{4}x$$

In the quadratic equation above, m and n are constants. Which of the following expressions represents the solutions of the equation?

A) $\dfrac{n \pm \sqrt{n^2 - 32m}}{2}$

B) $\dfrac{n \pm \sqrt{n^2 - 2m}}{2}$

C) $\dfrac{n \pm \sqrt{n^2 - 32m}}{8}$

D) $\dfrac{n \pm \sqrt{n^2 - 2m}}{8}$

Function Properties

properties

The Basics

Almost all of the SAT deals with functions and their properties. When you're working with lines and parabolas, the rules are fairly simple and easy to visualize, even without a graph. But when the SAT asks about "higher order" functions, things can get confusing. **Think back to parabolas and quadratics,** and you should be fine.

Example 1

$$y = ax^3 + bx^2 + cx + d$$

In the equation above, a, b, c, and d are constants. If the equation has x-intercepts at -2, 1, and 4, which of the following is a factor of $ax^3 + bx^2 + cx + d$?

A) $x - 2$

B) $x + 1$

C) $x + 2$

D) $x + 4$

Don't let the vocabulary confuse you. They tend to ask the same question lots of different ways:

Example 2

In the xy-plane, the graph of function f has roots 0, -2, and 2. Which of the following could define f?

A) $f(x) = x(x - 2)(x + 2)$

B) $f(x) = x(x + 2)^2$

C) $f(x) = x(x - 2)^2$

D) $f(x) = x^2(x - 2)^2$

The Twists

When functions are graphed, you need to keep one more thing in mind. Sometimes the graph **"bounces"** on the x-axis.

Example 3

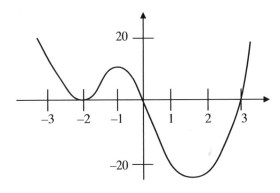

Which of the following could be the equation of the graph above?

A) $y = x(x - 2)(x + 3)$

B) $y = x(x + 2)(x - 3)$

C) $y = x(x - 2)^2(x + 3)$

D) $y = x(x + 2)^2(x - 3)$

There's also something called **remainder theorem**, which is a very confusing way of talking about factors and division:

If f(a) = b, then b is the remainder when f(x) is divided by (x – a).

If f(3) = 5, then 5 is the remainder when f(x) is divided by (x – 3).

Example 4

For polynomial function $g(x)$, the value of $g(-2)$ is 7. Which of the following must be true of $g(x)$?

A) $x + 2$ is a factor of $g(x)$.

B) $x - 2$ is a factor of $g(x)$.

C) The remainder when $g(x)$ is divided by $x + 2$ is 7.

D) The remainder when $g(x)$ is divided by $x - 2$ is 7.

Exercise: Functions and Factors

1

x	$f(x)$
2	5
0	2
−1	0
−3	−4

The function f is defined by a polynomial. Some values of x and $f(x)$ are shown in the table above. Which of the following must be a factor of $f(x)$?

A) $x - 2$

B) $x - 1$

C) $x + 1$

D) $x + 2$

2

In the xy-plane, the graph of function g has zeros at −5, 1, and 5. Which of the following could define g ?

A) $g(x) = (x + 5)(x - 1)(x - 5)$

B) $g(x) = (x + 5)(x + 1)(x - 5)$

C) $g(x) = (x + 5)^2(x - 1)$

D) $g(x) = (x - 5)^2(x + 1)$

3

If the function f has 4 distinct zeros, which of the following could represent the complete graph of f in the xy-plane?

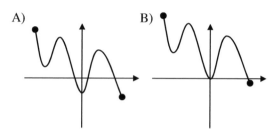

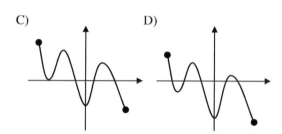

4

The polynomial $p^4 + 2p^3 - 3p^2 - 8p - 4$ can be written as $(p + 1)^2(p^2 - 4)$. What are all of the x-intercepts of the polynomial?

A) −1 and 4

B) −2, −1, and 2

C) −4, −1, and 4

D) −4, 1, and 4

Function Values

These get confusing because it's easy to mix up what they're asking for. Just remember that functions are collections of points, so you're either looking for the *x* or the *y*.

Example 5

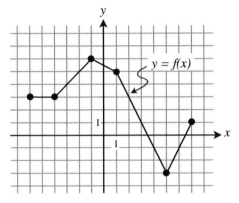

The complex function *f* is graphed on the *xy*-plane above. Which of the following are equal to 3 ?

    I. $f\left(-\dfrac{9}{2}\right)$

    II. $f(1)$

    III. $f(2)$

A) II only

B) III only

C) I and III only

D) I, II, and III

Example 6

For what value of *x* is the value of *f(x)* above at its minimum?

A) 5

B) 3

C) −3

D) −6

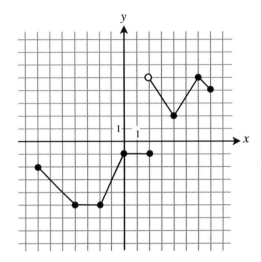

The complex function *f* is graphed on the *xy*-plane above for $-7 \le x \le 7$.

1

For what value of *x* does *f(x)* = 2 ?

A) −1

B) 2

C) 4

D) 5

2

If *k* is a constant such that the equation *f(x)* = *k* has exactly two real solutions, which of the following could be the value of *k* ?

A) −5

B) −3

C) 2

D) 4

3

$$g(x) = x + 4$$

The function *g* is defined by the equation above. For which of the following values of *x* does $f(x) + g(x) = 0$?

A) −6.5

B) −4

C) −3

D) −1

Undefined

Remember that the rules of math state that you can't divide by 0. When a question is asking for the value that makes a function undefined, they want you to **set the denominator of the fraction equal to 0**.

Example 7

Which of the following is a value of x for which the expression $\dfrac{5}{x^2 - 6x + 8}$ is undefined?

A) -2

B) 0

C) 4

D) 5

Translations

Functions can move and change, depending on what you do to them. Instead of thinking about the entire function, NARROW YOUR FOCUS to a point or two, and watch how that point changes. Or use your calculator!

Example 8

$$f(x) = (x - 2)^2 + 13$$

The function f is defined above and graphed in the xy-plane. The graph of f is translated k units to the left such that the image of f has equation $y = (x + 5)^2 + 13$. What is the value of k?

1

$$f(x) = \frac{x + 2}{(x + 2)^2 - 8(x + 2) + 16}$$

For what value of x is the function f above undefined?

A) -16

B) -2

C) 0

D) 2

2

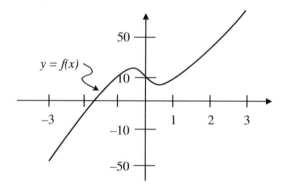

The function f is graphed in the xy-plane above. Which of the following could be the equation of $y = -f(x)$?

A) $y = -2x^3 + x - 10$

B) $y = 2x^3 - x + 10$

C) $y = -10x^3 + x - 2$

D) $y = 10x^3 - x + 2$

Circle Properties

properties

The Basics

Memorize the standard equation!

$$(x - h)^2 + (y - k)^2 = r^2$$

(h, k) is the center.

r is the radius.

Example 1

$$(x - 3)^2 + (y + 2)^2 = 4$$

center:

radius:

point on the circle:

graph it:

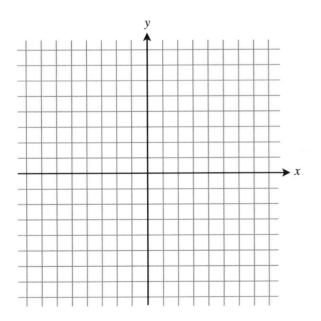

The Twists

Often, circle equations will not be in standard form, so you have to **complete the square** twice to get back to a usable equation:

$$x^2 + y^2 - 6x + 4y = -9$$

Group like terms:

$$(x^2 - 6x) + (y^2 + 4y) = -9$$

Complete the square:

add $\left(\dfrac{b}{2}\right)^2$

$$x^2 - 6x \underline{+9} = (x - 3)^2$$

$$y^2 + 4y \underline{+4} = (y + 2)^2$$

Maintain balance:

$$(x - 3)^2 + (y + 2)^2 = -9 \underline{+9+4}$$

$$(x - 3)^2 + (y + 2)^2 = 4$$

Example 2

What are the center and radius of the circle below?

$$x^2 + y^2 + 6x - 8y = 0$$

Exercise: Circle Properties

1

A circle in the xy-plane has center $(9, -4)$ and radius 5. Which of the following could be the equation of the circle?

A) $x^2 - 9x + y^2 + 4y + 25 = 0$

B) $x^2 + 9x + y^2 - 4y + 25 = 0$

C) $x^2 - 18x + y^2 + 8y + 72 = 0$

D) $x^2 + 18x + y^2 - 8y + 72 = 0$

2

Which of the following is an equation of a circle with center $(2, -4)$ and a circumference that includes the point $\left(1, -\dfrac{12}{5}\right)$?

A) $(x - 2)^2 + (y + 4)^2 = \dfrac{89}{25}$

B) $(x + 2)^2 + (y - 4)^2 = \dfrac{89}{25}$

C) $(x - 2)^2 + (y + 4)^2 = \dfrac{69}{5}$

D) $(x + 2)^2 + (y - 4)^2 = \dfrac{69}{5}$

3

A circle in the xy-plane has equation $(x - 4)^2 + (y - 5)^2 = 9$. Which of the following points lies in the interior of the circle?

A) $(-4, -5)$

B) $(1, 0)$

C) $(2, 3)$

D) $(3, 2)$

4

$$x^2 + y^2 - 2x - 12y = -12$$

The equation of a circle in the xy-plane is shown above. What is the radius of the circle?

A) 5

B) 6

C) 25

D) 36

Models

The Basics

If Properties questions test algebra theory, then Models questions test algebra in the real world. These are the story questions. Students absolutely hate them! I get it. Algebra is hard enough without weird situations that you need to decipher. The good news is that if you take the time to learn the rules, formulas, and properties for regular Algebra questions, you'll be able to apply that same knowledge to Models questions.

The Twists

The problem is that it's not always easy to figure out what type of Model you're dealing with. As you work through the packets, try to pay attention to the similarities between the questions. **Get Back to Basics!**

Linear Models will obviously look like lines, so you can "untwist" them by returning to the safety of y=mx+b. Think in terms of slopes and y-intercepts. Quantity & Value models are essentially Point of Intersection questions, except you'll be responsible for constructing the two equations. Luckily, they pretty much all follow the same format, so it should be relatively easy to learn the pattern and repeat it on the SAT. Rearrange Formula questions will involve a complicated story, but it almost never matters. Just solve for the variable they ask for, and don't make the common algebra mistakes they always try to trip you up on.

Some models won't have nice counterparts in the regular algebra world. Geometry Models are in this category because they don't actually involve much geometry. You can use area and perimeter equations to create an algebraic expression, and then it's all about solving for x. Exponential Models seem really complicated, but they also have a pattern that you can learn and repeat. WTF Models are the worst. They're just weird. There won't be much of a pattern, so you'll have to follow instructions and generate a model that works for the unique situation in the question. Just try your best!

Packets

- linear models
- quantity & value
- geometry models
- exponential models
- rearrange formulas
- WTF models

approximately 16 questions per test

worth approximately 160 points total

Math	grph	grph	grph	chrt
arith	arith	ratio	ratio	ratio	COP
perc	perc	stat	stat	stat	imag
CAM	CAM	CAM	CAM	CAM	rad/abs
exp	POI	POI	POI	alg+	MBT/div
LP	LP	LP	QP	QP	QP
FP	FP	CP	RF	XM	XM
LM	LM	LM	WTF	WTF	WTF
LM	LM	QV	WTF	WTF	WTF
GM	POW	ang	ST/cyl	trig	geo+

Important Ideas

Linear Models

If it looks like a line, it probably is a line. Get back to the safety of y=mx+b. In the real world, the letters take on new meaning:

- m = slope = rate, cost per item, speed
- b = y-intercept = starting value, flat fee
- (x, y) = points on the line = same thing!

Don't forget that you can **Plug Points Into Equations** to test them out. The variable might be different, but you can still plug in given points or make up your own (**Arithmetize**) to better understand what a model means.

Quantity & Value

Sometimes, the answer choices will give you possible sets of equations. Other times, you'll need to come up with them yourself. Either way, the two equations tell you the same two things:

- quantity (or number) of items
- value (or cost) of those items

These questions often test the difference between greater than and less than signs, so remember:

- **at least 5** means that 5 is the minimum, so the sign should open away from the 5, so **x ≥ 5**
- **at most 5** means that 5 is the maximum, so the sign should open toward the 5, so **x ≤ 5**

Geometry Models

These do not usually involve complicated Geometry. The area and volume formulas are in the Reference Chart. Remember that the **perimeter is the sum of the lengths of all the sides**.

If it seems like you don't have to solve for the length or width, you can usually make them up. Arithmetizing will help you visualize what's going on. So will drawing pictures!

Exponential Models

It's important to know the difference between linear and exponential growth. Lines are straight, which means that they increase by the exact same amount every year/month/day/whatever. Exponential growth is not constant. It gets bigger faster. Think of what happens when you keep multiplying something by 2. First, 2 becomes 4, then 8, then 16, then 32, then 64, then 128, then 256, then 512… See how it's increasing by more and more each time? The rate of growth is not constant.

Exponential Models can be understood using a version of the OPEN formula:

$$(O)(1 \pm P)^t = N$$

The packet explains what this means, and seeing several examples will help you recognize the pattern. But percentages play a big role in Exponential Models, so you might want to refer to that packet as well. In fact, most mistakes on Exponential Models come from incorrectly converting percentages into decimals.

Rearrange Formulas

These are often included in multi-part questions, but they don't usually require an understanding of the story. Just rearrange the equation to solve for the variable they want. Arithmetizing helps a lot, especially if they ask you to compare two hypothetical situations.

WTF Models

The name says it all. Some are actually pretty straightforward and look a lot like the "value" part of Quantity & Value models. But most are unique. You might never see a similar question ever again. That makes it difficult to find a pattern, but comfort with algebra will help you navigate the weird stories. Arithmetizing also helps because it lets you visualize what's going on.

Linear Models

models

The Basics

Most models are just lines in disguise. Don't let the story distract you. Think in terms of slopes and intercepts:

$$y = mx + b$$

Example 1

$$L = 2.1m + 0.6$$

An entomologist uses the equation above to model the length L of a certain insect, in centimeters, in terms of the number of months m since it hatched. Based on the equation, what is the estimated increase, in centimeters, of the insect's length each month?

A) 0.6

B) 1.5

C) 2.1

D) 2.7

If things are a little jumbled, **Get Back to Basics.** Make the equation look like y=mx+b and you'll understand what they're asking for:

Example 2

Mark is painting the outside of a house over the course of several days. Each day, he applies paint to a certain number of square feet of the house's exterior. The number of square feet he has left to paint at the end of each day can be estimated with the equation $n = 1{,}562 - 225d$, where n is the number of square feet left to paint and d is the number of days he has painted. What is the meaning of the number 1,562 in this equation?

A) Mark will paint the entire house in 1,562 days.

B) Mark has a total of 1,562 square feet to paint.

C) Mark paints at a rate of 1,562 square feet per hour.

D) Mark paints at a rate of 1,562 square feet per day.

The Twists

Don't get complacent. Linear models are designed to twist the normal stuff you know about lines. Stay on your toes, and you should be fine.

Example 3

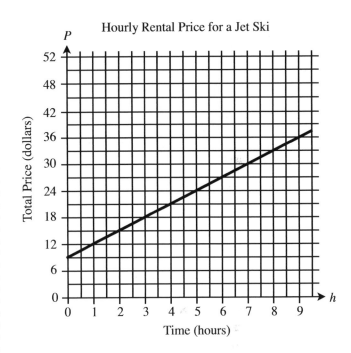

Hourly Rental Price for a Jet Ski

The graph above shows the price P, in dollars, to rent a jet ski for h hours. Which of the following expresses the relationship between h and P ?

A) $P = 9h$

B) $P = 3h + 9$

C) $P = h + 3$

D) $P = \dfrac{1}{2}h + 9$

Exercise: Linear Models

1

At a bakery, c cupcakes are made using f bags of flour. If $c = 3 + f$, how many additional bags of flour are needed to make each additional cupcake?

A) One

B) Two

C) Three

D) Four

Questions 2-4 refer to the following information.

Fish species	Growth Constant
Blue snapper	3.4
Pike fin	4.1
Toothless guppy	2.4
Yellowback stickler	3.7
Striped grouper	3.4
Speckled guppy	4.4
Redfin velchfish	3.9
Spotted fluke	3.3

One method of estimating the length, in centimeters, of certain species of fish is to multiply the age of the fish, in years, by a growth constant that is unique to each species. The table above gives the growth constants for eight species of fish.

2

According to the information in the table, what is the approximate length of a 3-year-old speckled guppy?

A) 4.4 centimeters

B) 7.4 centimeters

C) 8.7 centimeters

D) 13.2 centimeters

3

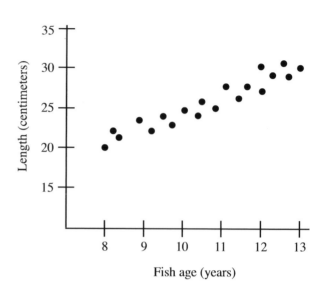

The scatterplot above gives the lengths of 20 fish of the same species based on their ages. Based on the graph and the table, the species on the scatterplot is most likely

A) Speckled guppy.

B) Yellowback stickler.

C) Toothless guppy.

D) Pike fin.

4

If a blue snapper and a yellowback stickler are each 8 centimeters long, which of the following is closest to the difference in their lengths 18 <u>months</u> from now?

A) 0.15

B) 0.30

C) 0.45

D) 0.60

Models

5

$$a = 9y + 13$$

The model above can be used to estimate the number of apples, a, produced by an apple tree, in terms of the tree's age y, in years, between 5 and 40 years after it is planted. Based on the model, what is the estimated increase in the number of apples produced by a tree each year?

A) 2.7

B) 3.9

C) 9

D) 13

6

A cargo ship weighing 255,000 tons can be loaded with crates that weigh 120 tons each. The total weight of the cargo ship and the crates cannot exceed 340,000 tons. If n represents the number of crates loaded onto the cargo ship, which of the following inequalities models the situation described above?

A) $120 \leq 340,000 - n$

B) $120n \geq 85,000$

C) $120n \leq 340,000$

D) $340,000 \geq 255,000 + 120n$

Questions 7 and 8 refer to the following information.

$$w = 80 + 8t$$

Devin uses the equation above to plan a workout routine, where w represents the total weight he wants to bench, in pounds, t weeks from now.

7

Devin's goal is to increase the total weight he can bench by at least 100 pounds. According to the equation, how many weeks will it take for Devin to achieve his goal?

A) 3

B) 13

C) 23

D) 33

8

Which of the following represents the number of weeks in terms of the total weight Devin wants to bench?

A) $t = w - 10$

B) $t = w + 10$

C) $t = \dfrac{w - 80}{8}$

D) $t = \dfrac{w + 80}{8}$

Weather in Desert Springs in April

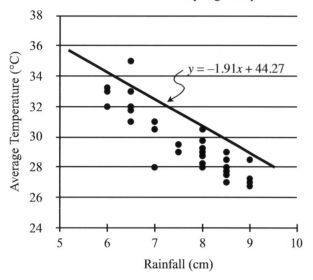

$y = -1.91x + 44.27$

The scatterplot above shows data collected about the weather in Desert Springs during the month of April. A line of best fit for the data is also shown. According to the line of best fit, what is the predicted average temperature, in degrees Celsius, on a day with 3 cm of rainfall?

A) 35.73

B) 38.54

C) 47.27

D) 50.00

10

Height of a Tree

Year	Height (feet)
2010	46
2015	52

The height of a certain tree was measured in 2010 and 2015. If the tree grows at a constant rate, which of the following functions h models the height, in feet, of the tree t years after 2010 ?

A) $h(t) = 1.2t + 46$

B) $h(t) = 1.2(t - 2010) + 46$

C) $h(t) = 46t + 6$

D) $h(t) = 46(t - 2010) + 6$

A storage company calculates the price for a customer to rent a storage unit, in dollars, using the expression $35 + 2am$, where a is the area of the storage unit, in square feet, and m is the number of months the customer rents the storage unit. Which of the following is an accurate interpretation of the expression?

A) The company charges $2 per month for each square foot of storage space.

B) The company charges $35 per month for each square foot of storage space.

C) The minimum area of a storage unit is 2 square feet.

D) A customer must rent a storage unit for at least 2 months.

Quantity & Value
models

The Basics

The SAT consistently tests this type of model, so understanding its format is essential. It's best illustrated through an example:

> **Example 1**
>
> Mike has 15 coins worth a total of $2.70. If Mike only has dimes and quarters, how many dimes does Mike have?
>
> A) 6
>
> B) 7
>
> C) 8
>
> D) 9

You could **Guess & Check**, but sometimes you won't have answer choices, so you also need to know how to construct Quantity & Value models:

Set your variables:

Quantity of coins:

Value of coins:

Find the point of intersection:

The Twists

Mathematically, there isn't one. Sometimes, the story disguises the fact that it's a QV model, but you'll start to recognize the pattern.

> **Example 2**
>
> Brad is organizing a wedding reception for 152 people. He has 18 tables where they can sit. Some of the tables can seat up to 6 people each, and the rest can seat up to 10 people each. Assuming that all of the tables are filled to capacity and every person has a seat, how many of the tables are 10-person tables?

Other times, you just need to choose the correct set of equations:

> **Example 3**
>
> Mona needs to order pizzas for a party. To make sure everyone has enough food, she needs to order at least 12 pizzas. Regular pizzas cost $14 each, and pepperoni pizzas cost $16 each. Her budget for the party is no more than $180, and she has to order at least one pizza of each type. Which of the following systems of inequalities represents the conditions described if x is the number of regular pizzas and y is the number of pepperoni pizzas that Mona orders?
>
> A) $14x + 16y \geq 180$
> $x + y \leq 12$
> $x \geq 1$
> $y \geq 1$
>
> B) $14x + 16y \geq 180$
> $x + y \leq 12$
> $x \leq 1$
> $y \leq 1$
>
> C) $14x + 16y \leq 180$
> $x + y \geq 12$
> $x \geq 1$
> $y \geq 1$
>
> D) $14x + 16y \leq 180$
> $x + y \geq 12$
> $x \leq 1$
> $y \leq 1$

Exercise: Quantity & Value

1

A hardware store sells hammers and screwdrivers. Each hammer costs $5, and each screwdriver costs $3. If Dolores purchased a total of 11 hammers and screwdrivers for a combined price of $39, how many screwdrivers did she purchase?

2

A cargo plane is loaded with boxes weighing 50 pounds and crates weighing 125 pounds. The cargo plane can carry a maximum weight of 10,000 pounds. If there is a combined total of 90 boxes and crates to be loaded onto the cargo plane, which of the following systems of inequalities represents this situation in terms of x and y, where x is the number of boxes and y is the number of crates?

A) $125x + 50y \leq 10,000$
   $x + y = 90$

B) $125x + 50y \geq 10,000$
   $x + y = 90$

C) $50x + 125y \leq 10,000$
   $x + y = 90$

D) $50x + 125y \geq 10,000$
   $x + y = 90$

3

In a certain card game, red cards are worth 2 points and black cards are worth 5 points. If Kristen has 19 cards worth a total of 77 points, how many black cards does she have?

4

A golf club offers standard and premier memberships. The monthly cost of a standard membership is $3,500, and the monthly cost of a premier membership is $6,725. Last year, the golf club made $577,550 off of 130 total memberships. Which of the following systems of equations could be used to find the number of standard memberships, S, and the number of premier memberships, P, that the golf club had last year?

A) $\dfrac{S}{6,725} + \dfrac{P}{3,500} = \dfrac{1}{577,550}$
   $S + P = 130$

B) $6,725S + 3,500P = 577,550$
   $S + P = 130$

C) $3,500S + 6,725P = 130$
   $S + P = 577,550$

D) $3,500S + 6,725P = 577,550$
   $S + P = 130$

5

A certain type of flower can have either 12 petals or 14 petals. Layla frolics through a field containing this type of flower, and she picks 16 of them. Later, she counts the petals as she pulls them off of each flower. If Layla counts a total of 196 petals, how many of the flowers that she picked had 14 petals?

Geometry Models

models

The Basics

Geometry with a cute story is more about algebra than it is geometry. Most of these questions involve lengths and widths, so either make equations or **Arithmetize**.

Example 1

The length of a rectangular carpet is 5 feet shorter than twice its width. If the width of the carpet is w feet, which of the following expressions represents the perimeter, in feet, of the carpet in terms of w ?

A) $5 - 2w$

B) $4w - 10$

C) $6w - 10$

D) $2w^2 - 5w$

Example 2

An artist modified a rectangle by increasing its length by 20 percent and decreasing its width by n percent. These modifications decreased the area of the rectangle by 16 percent. Based on the artist's changes, what is the value of n ?

A) 16

B) 25

C) 30

D) 36

The Twists

A lot of Geometry Models are similar to other question types, so be flexible. What does this equation remind you of? Just make sure it's set up the way the question wants. **Arithmetize** to play it safe.

Example 3

A gardener is planting a rectangular flowerbed with a 5-foot-wide path surrounding it. The equation $A = 5p + 100$ will relate the area A, in square feet, of the path to the perimeter p, in feet, of the flowerbed. Based on this design, how many feet will the perimeter of the flowerbed increase for each additional square foot of the path's area?

A) $\dfrac{1}{100}$

B) $\dfrac{1}{5}$

C) 5

D) 100

Exercise: Geometry Models

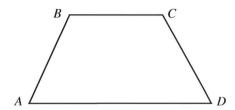

In quadrilateral *ABCD* above, *AD* is parallel to *BC*, and *A B* = *CD*. If *AD* and *BC* were each reduced by 25 percent, then by what percent would the area of *ABCD* decrease?

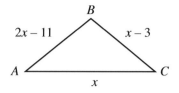

Note: Figure not drawn to scale.

In isosceles triangle *ABC* above, *AB* = *BC*. What is the perimeter of triangle *ABC* ?

A fish tank in the shape of a rectangular prism has a length of 30 centimeters, a width of 20 centimeters, and a height of 20 centimeters. The tank is filled halfway with water. If an additional 1,800 cubic centimeters of water are poured into the tank, what is the total height of water in the tank, in centimeters?

A) 10

B) 13

C) 16

D) 17

A room has an area of 153 square feet. If the width is 8 feet shorter than the length, what is the width of the room, in feet?

Models

Exponential Models

models

The Basics

What makes exponential models different from everything else?

Linear growth
(the increase is constant)

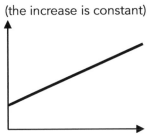

Exponential growth
(the increase increases)

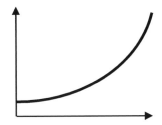

Example 1

Grover has four job offers, each with different salary options. If he wants to accept the job that yields exponential salary growth, which of the four options should he choose?

A) At the end of each year that he works for the company, Grover's salary will increase by 1% of his initial salary.

B) At the end of each year that he works for the company, Grover's salary will increase by 2% of his initial salary and he'll receive a $500 annual bonus.

C) At the end of each year that he works for the company, Grover's salary will increase by 1.2% of his previous year's salary.

D) At the end of each year that he works for the company, Grover's salary will increase by $1000.

The Twists

Exponential equations make more sense in the context of a story, but the standard form of the equation can mirror the **OPEN** formula you used for Percentages questions.

$$(O)(1 \pm P)^t = N$$

O = original amount

t = time (in days, months, years, etc.)

P = percent change per unit of time

  1 + P = rate of growth

  1 − P = rate of decay

N = new amount after t time has passed

Example 2

A population of bacteria in a petri dish grows at a rate of 2 percent per hour. If there were 120 bacteria in the petri dish to start, which equation best models the number of bacteria B in the petri dish after h hours?

A) $B = 120(0.02)^h$

B) $B = 120(1.02)^h$

C) $B = 120(1.2)^h$

D) $B = 120(2)^h$

Example 3

An antibiotic is introduced into a different petri dish when there are 800 bacteria present. The antibiotic kills the bacteria, and the population decreases by 12 percent every hour. To the nearest whole number, how many bacteria will remain in the petri dish after 3 hours?

Exercise: Exponential Models

1

Richard invests $100 in a stock that increases in value by 3% each year. How much money does Richard have after 5 years? (Round your answer to the nearest whole dollar.)

2

The population of wolves on a preserve has increased by approximately 80 percent every year since 2005. If there were 408 wolves on the preserve in 2011, how many wolves were there in 2005?

3

$$C(x) = 150(1.04)^x$$

The equation above models the number of customers, $C(x)$, at a certain grocery store x years after it moves to a new location. Which of the following best models the number of customers at the grocery store m months after it moves to a new location?

A) $C(m) = 150(1.04)^{\frac{m}{12}}$

B) $C(m) = 150(1.04)^{12m}$

C) $C(m) = 150(1.003)^{12m}$

D) $C(m) = 150(1.60)^m$

4

A cable company wants to increase the cost of a yearly contract by d dollars per year. This same yearly contract currently costs c dollars per year. Which of the following best models the cost y, in dollars, of a yearly contract for the cable company x years from now?

A) $y = c(d)^x$

B) $y = d(c)^x$

C) $y = cx + d$

D) $y = dx + c$

5

A pool of water evaporates by the same percentage every hour. If only 5% of the pool remains after 6 hours, by approximately what percent does the pool evaporate every hour?

A) 5%

B) 16%

C) 39%

D) 61%

6

A botanist calculates that a certain fungus has killed 4 percent of the trees in a forest every 10 years since 1940. If there were approximately 3,075 trees in the forest in 2010, approximately how many trees died between 1960 and 1980?

A) 206

B) 296

C) 2337

D) 4092

Rearrange Formulas

models

The Basics

It's Algebra. And they add in a boring story. So it's Algebra, but worse.

Example 1

The speed s of an object is found by dividing the distance d the object travels by the time t that it takes the object to travel that distance. Which of the following equations give the distance d in terms of s and t ?

A) $d = st$

B) $d = \dfrac{s}{t}$

C) $d = \dfrac{t}{s}$

D) $d = t + s$

Example 2

$$E_k = \frac{1}{2}mv^2$$

An object's kinetic energy E_k is related to the mass of the object m and the velocity of the object v by the formula above. Which of the following expresses the square of the velocity of the object in terms of the kinetic energy of the object and the mass of the object?

A) $v^2 = 2mE_k$

B) $v^2 = \dfrac{E_k}{2m}$

C) $v^2 = \dfrac{2E_k}{m}$

D) $v^2 = \dfrac{2m}{E_k}$

The Twists

Sometimes they ask you to strip away the algebra and understand the relationship in terms of numbers. What's that called again? **Arithmetize!**

Example 3

A city planner lays out two rectangular plots of land with the same width. If the area of Plot A is three times the area of Plot B, the length of Plot B is what fraction of the length of Plot A?

A) $\dfrac{1}{2}$

B) $\dfrac{1}{3}$

C) $\dfrac{1}{6}$

D) $\dfrac{1}{9}$

Example 4

Containers A and B are in the shape of a right circular cylinder and have the same volume. If the radius of the base of Container A is 4 times the length of the radius of the base of Container B, what is the ratio of the height of Container A to the height of Container B?

A) $1 : 2$

B) $1 : 4$

C) $1 : 8$

D) $1 : 16$

Exercise: Rearrange Formulas

1

A dog walker uses the formula $p = 5dwm$ to estimate his weekly profit p, in dollars, based on the number of dogs he walks d for m minutes per walk for w walks per week. Which of the following correctly expresses w in terms of p, d, and m ?

A) $w = \dfrac{5p}{dm}$

B) $w = \dfrac{dm}{5p}$

C) $w = \dfrac{p}{5dm}$

D) $w = \dfrac{5dm}{p}$

2

If the height of a rectangular pyramid is multiplied by 6, its volume will be how many times greater?

(Note: The volume of a rectangular pyramid is found using the formula $V = \dfrac{1}{3}lwh$.)

A) 2

B) 6

C) 18

D) 216

Questions 3 and 4 refer to the following information.

Cadmium's formula: $L = \dfrac{(c + s)^2}{v}$

Cadmium's formula estimates the length of a wire L, in centimeters based on the current passing through the wire c, in amperes, the size of the wire s, in square centimeters, and the velocity v, in meters per second, of the wire in a vacuum.

3

Which of the following expressions is equivalent to $c + s$?

A) $\sqrt{\dfrac{L}{v}}$

B) $\sqrt{Lv}$

C) $(Lv)^2$

D) Lv^2

4

If the velocity of a wire is doubled, what happens to its length?

A) It is increased by 200 percent.

B) It is increased by 50 percent.

C) It is decreased by 50 percent.

D) It is decreased by 200 percent.

WTF Models

models

The Basics

These are models that don't fit one of the standard categories or formats. They don't necessarily have easily recognizable counterparts in the Algebra world. They can be difficult precisely because each one is unique. Or so it would seem...

1

During a typical week, Bill drinks w bottles of water and s bottles of soda. If each bottle of water is 16 ounces and each bottle of soda is 20 ounces, which of the following could represent the total number of ounces that Bill drinks in a week if he only drinks water and soda?

A) $20w + 16s$

B) $16w + 20s$

C) $36ws$

D) $320ws$

2

Stephanie bought a pair of pants and a blouse on sale. The pair of pants was 20% off the original price and the blouse was 15% off the original price. In total, Stephanie saved \$36 because of the sale. Which equation models Stephanie's savings, where x is the original cost of the pair of pants and y is the original cost of the blouse?

A) $20x + 15y = 36$

B) $15x + 20y = 36$

C) $0.2x + 0.15y = 36$

D) $0.15x + 0.2y = 36$

The Twists

When they get weird, you can almost always solve easily, as long as you STAY CALM!

Arithmetize to visualize:

3

Luis rents a truck at a rate of \$50 per day. Which of the following equations represents the total cost c, in dollars, to rent the truck for w weeks?

A) $c = \dfrac{50w}{7}$

B) $c = \dfrac{7w}{50}$

C) $c = 50w + 7$

D) $c = 50(7w)$

4

A population of Arctic hares increased by 10 percent from January to December of 2010. In 2011, the population decreased by 6 percent. If there were h Arctic hares at the end of 2011, which of the following represents the number of Arctic hares at the beginning of 2010?

A) $\dfrac{h}{(1.1)(0.94)}$

B) $\dfrac{h}{1.04}$

C) $(1.1)(0.94)h$

D) $1.04h$

5

Jody and Larry spent a combined $300 on furniture. If Larry spent $60 more than Jody, how much did Jody spend on furniture?

6

In a certain game, a *blerg* is worth 3 points less than a *snark*. If 5 *blergs* and 3 *snarks* are worth a total of 49 points, how many points is a *blerg* worth?

7

The sum of three numbers is 138. If one of the numbers, n, is half of the sum of the other two numbers, what is the value of n?

8

Ivy goes apple picking because she has nothing better to do. In the morning, she picks 19 red apples and 6 green apples. In the afternoon, she picks 5 more green apples. How many more red apples does Ivy need to pick so that 80% of all of her apples are red?

9

A baseball season consists of 162 games. A certain team wins 55 percent of its first 120 games. The coach of this team estimates that the team will make the playoffs if it wins at least 58 percent of its games over the entire season. In order to accomplish this, the team needs to win x games during the remainder of the season. Which of the following inequalities best describes the possible values of x such that the team makes the playoffs?

A) $(0.55)(120) - x \geq (0.58)(162)$, where $x \leq 42$

B) $(0.55)(120) + x \geq (0.58)(162)$, where $x \leq 42$

C) $(0.55)(120 + x) \geq (0.58)(162)$, where $x \leq 42$

D) $(0.55)(120 - x) \geq (0.58)(162)$, where $x \leq 42$

Multi-Part Models

Multi-part questions are still fairly independent of each other. In other words, if you don't know how to do the first question, it doesn't mean that you won't be able to answer any of them. Treat them as separate questions that just happen to refer back to the same information.

───────── ▼ ─────────

Questions 10 through 15 refer to the following information.

Lauren is getting married and needs to decide on a venue for the reception. The table below shows the quoted prices for four different venues.

Venue	Hosting Fee, H (dollars)	Cost to hire a band, B (dollars)	Cost per plate of food, F (dollars per guest)
A	3000	800	75
B	5500	650	85
C	4250	900	80
D	3500	875	60

The total cost, c, for the reception is given by the formula $c = (H + B) + Fn$, where n is the number of guests.

10

Which of the following expresses the cost per plate of food in terms of $c, H, B,$ and n ?

A) $F = c - H + B - n$

B) $F = c - H - B - n$

C) $F = \dfrac{c - H + B}{n}$

D) $F = \dfrac{c - H - B}{n}$

11

For what number of guests, n, will the cost of having the wedding reception at Venue A exceed the cost of having the wedding reception at Venue D?

12

Lauren's friend Tabitha had her wedding reception at Venue B, but she received a 30 percent discount on the band because her uncle was the keyboard player. If Tabitha spent a total of $16,325, how many guests attended her wedding reception?

If Lauren wants to spend no more than $10,000 on her wedding reception, at which venue could she have the most guests without exceeding her budget?

A) Venue A

B) Venue B

C) Venue C

D) Venue D

If the cost of having a wedding reception at Venue C were plotted in the xy-plane with the number of guests, n, on the x-axis and the cost of the wedding reception, c, on the y-axis, which of the following best describes the y-intercept of the resulting graph?

A) The total cost of a wedding reception at Venue C

B) The minimum number of guests needed for a wedding reception at Venue C

C) The total cost of the hosting fee and the band at Venue C

D) The cost of one plate of food at Venue C

15

Lauren chooses Venue A and invites g guests to her wedding reception. However, Lauren knows that a guests will be invited but will not be able to attend her wedding reception. Which of the following inequalities could Lauren use to determine whether the number of guests who attend her wedding reception will keep the cost within her $10,000 budget limit?

A) $3,800 + 75(g - a) \geq 10,000$

B) $3,800 + 75(g - a) \leq 10,000$

C) $3,800 + 75g - a \geq 10,000$

D) $3,800 + 75g - a \leq 10,000$

Models

Geometry

The Basics

Reference Chart! Reference Chart! Reference Chart! If you get a Geometry question wrong because you're too lazy to look back and double check a formula, you have no one to blame but yourself. REFERENCE CHART!!!

The Twists

Okay, so not everything you need is in the Reference Chart. There are a few constants and formulas that you need to memorize, but it's not nearly as many as you had to learn for Geometry class in school. If you hated Geometry (everybody seems to, for some reason) you can rest easy knowing that SAT Geometry is relatively simple.

There are a few question types that the SAT loves to repeat. Part Over Whole questions are all about circle sectors, and Similar Triangles questions are really just ratios. The process is so consistent that you should have no problem recognizing the pattern.

Cylinders also tend to come up a lot, but you usually just need the formula (reference chart!). Hexagons also appear from time to time, but that formula isn't given. (It's included on the next page, though.) They usually want you to solve hexagon questions by turning them into equilateral and/or 30-60-90 right triangles.

The Advanced Geometry packet has some of the most twisted questions. They usually take the familiar shapes and hide them by adding or subtracting pieces. As always, "untwist" the questions by **Getting Back to Basics**—rectangles, triangles, and circles. Even questions with three-dimensional shapes can often be solved by thinking in terms of the two-dimensional shapes you're used to.

Packets

- part over whole
- angle rules
- similar triangles
- cylinders
- trigonometry
- advanced geometry

approximately 5 questions per test

worth approximately 50 points total

Math	grph	grph	grph	chrt
arith	arith	ratio	ratio	ratio	COP
perc	perc	stat	stat	stat	imag
CAM	CAM	CAM	CAM	CAM	rad/abs
exp	POI	POI	POI	alg+	MBT/div
LP	LP	LP	QP	QP	QP
FP	FP	CP	RF	XM	XM
LM	LM	LM	WTF	WTF	WTF
LM	LM	QV	WTF	WTF	WTF
GM	POW	ang	ST/cyl	trig	geo+

Important Ideas

Reference Chart

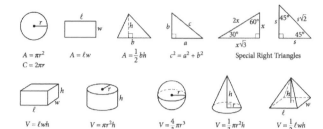

$A = \pi r^2$ $A = \ell w$ $A = \frac{1}{2}bh$ $c^2 = a^2 + b^2$ Special Right Triangles
$C = 2\pi r$

$V = \ell wh$ $V = \pi r^2 h$ $V = \frac{4}{3}\pi r^3$ $V = \frac{1}{3}\pi r^2 h$ $V = \frac{1}{3}\ell wh$

The number of degrees of arc in a circle is 360.
The number of radians of arc in a circle is 2π.
The sum of the measures in degrees of the angles of a triangle is 180.

Angles

A right angle is 90°. Complementary angles add up to 90°.

A straight line is 180°. Supplementary angles add up to 180°.

The interior angles of a quadrilateral (4-sided figure) add up to 360°. Squares, rectangles, trapezoids, and parallelograms are all quadrilaterals.

The sum of the interior angles of any figure can be found using the formula below, where *n* is the number of sides the figure has:

sum of interior angles = 180(n – 2)

Vertical angles are congruent (equal). The angles *b* and *c* below are vertical angles.

Parallel lines create lots of congruent angles. If the lines below are parallel, then:
- $a = d = e = h$
- $b = c = f = g$

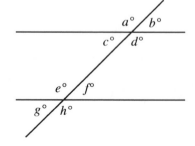

Circles

A fraction (or sector) of a circle contains the same fraction of the degrees, radians, circumference, and area. Whenever a question discusses a fraction of a circle, write down:

$$\frac{\text{part}}{\text{whole}}$$

A line that is tangent to a circle forms a right angle with the radius:

Triangles

Isosceles triangles have two congruent angles opposite two congruent sides.

Equilateral triangles have three equal sides, and all three angles are 60°.

The largest side of a triangle will be opposite the largest angle, and the smallest side will be opposite the smallest angle.

Triangles that have the same angle measures are similar. Their sides will be in proportion.

Area of a hexagon with sides of length x $= \frac{3\sqrt{3}}{2}x^2$

Trigonometry

The most important rule is soh-cah-toa, which helps you remember the meanings of the functions:

$$\sin = \frac{\text{opposite}}{\text{hypotenuse}} \qquad \cos = \frac{\text{adjacent}}{\text{hypotenuse}}$$

$$\tan = \frac{\text{opposite}}{\text{adjacent}}$$

Also:

$$\sin(x°) = \cos(90 - x°)$$

$$\cos(x°) = \sin(90 - x°)$$

Part Over Whole

geometry

The Basics

A quarter of a circle contains a quarter of the degrees, a quarter of the area, and a quarter of the circumference. Use ratios to compare these attributes, no matter what the fraction.

Example 1

Point O is the center of the circle above. If the area of the entire circle is 64π, what is the area of the shaded region?

A) 11π

B) 12π

C) 13π

D) 14π

Reference Chart

Don't forget that the SAT gives you many of the formulas you need. Those relevant to Part Over Whole are highlighted:

REFERENCE

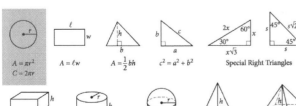

$A = \pi r^2$ $A = \ell w$ $A = \frac{1}{2}bh$ $c^2 = a^2 + b^2$ Special Right Triangles
$C = 2\pi r$

$V = \ell wh$ $V = \pi r^2 h$ $V = \frac{4}{3}\pi r^3$ $V = \frac{1}{3}\pi r^2 h$ $V = \frac{1}{3}\ell wh$

The number of degrees of arc in a circle is 360.
The number of radians of arc in a circle is 2π.
The sum of the measures in degrees of the angles of a triangle is 180.

The Twists

Like all Geometry questions, the SAT likes to disguise familiar questions so that they appear new and confusing. Chances are, if a question involves part of a circle, it's a Part Over Whole question.

Example 2

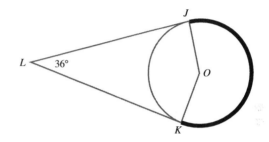

In the figure above, point O is the center of the circle and segments JL and KL are tangent to the circle at points J and K, respectively. If the radius of the circle is 10, what is the length of arc $\overset{\frown}{JK}$ (shown in bold)?

A) 8π

B) 12π

C) 20π

D) 60π

Exercise: Part Over Whole

1

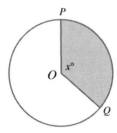

In the figure above, the circle has center O and radius 4. If the length of minor arc PQ is 3π, what is the value of x?

2

In a circle with center O, the central angle COD has a measure of $\dfrac{7\pi}{8}$ radians. The length of minor arc COD is what fraction of the circumference of the circle?

3

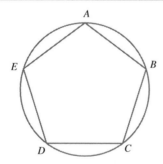

A regular pentagon is inscribed in the circle above. If the circumference of the circle is 100, what is the length of minor arc BD?

4

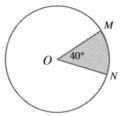

The area of the shaded region is π. What is the radius of circle O?

5

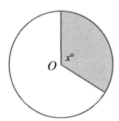

Note: Figure not drawn to scale.

In the figure above, the circle has center O and has radius 5. If the area of the shaded region is between 10 and 11, what is one possible <u>integer</u> value of x?

Angle Rules

geometry

The Basics

Most Angle questions will involve filling in all or most of the angles based on a few that are given. The Reference Chart includes a few of the constants, but others need to be memorized.

REFERENCE

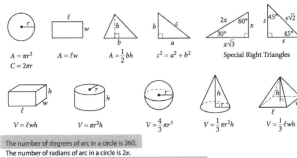

The number of degrees of arc in a circle is 360.
The number of radians of arc in a circle is 2π.
The sum of the measures in degrees of the angles of a triangle is 180.

Example 1

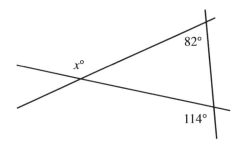

In the figure above, what is the value of x?

The Twists

It's easy to get stuck on Angle questions if you don't know the rules, but knowing them might not be enough if you don't know when to apply them. These two rules, in particular, can be difficult to see:

Parallel Lines

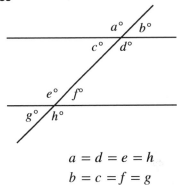

$$a = d = e = h$$
$$b = c = f = g$$

Isosceles Triangles

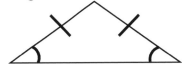

A pair of congruent sides opposite a pair of congruent angles.

Example 2

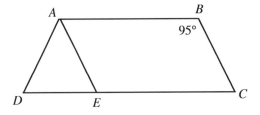

Note: Figure not drawn to scale.

In the figure above, $\overline{AB}$ and $\overline{CD}$ are parallel, $\overline{AE}$ and $\overline{BC}$ are parallel, and $AD = AE$. If the measure of $\angle ABC$ is 95°, what is the measure of $\angle ADE$?

Exercise: Angle Rules

1

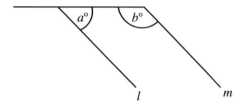

If line *l* is parallel to line *m*, which of the following describes the relationship between *a* and *b*?

A) $a = 360 - b$

B) $a = 360 + b$

C) $a = 180 - b$

D) $a = 180 + b$

2

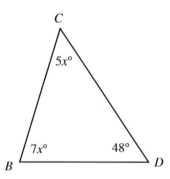

What is the measure of $\angle B$ in degrees?

A) 11

B) 33

C) 55

D) 77

3

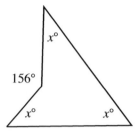

In the figure above, what is the value of *x*?

4

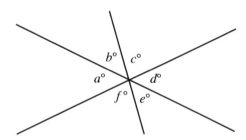

Note: Figure not drawn to scale.

In the figure above, if $b + c = d + e$, which of the following must be true?

A) $a = b$

B) $b = c$

C) $a = f$

D) $e = f$

Geometry

Similar Triangles

geometry

The Basics

Similar Triangles have the same angle measures, which means that the side lengths are in proportion. In school, Similar Triangles involve tons of rules and long geometry proofs. On the SAT, you can skip the proof and go straight to the ratio. Just make sure you know what the question wants.

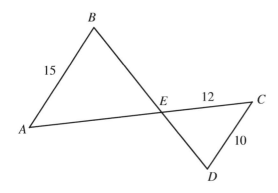

In the figure above, $\overline{AB} \parallel \overline{CD}$ and segment BD intersects segment AC at E. What is the length of AC ?

A) 18

B) 24

C) 29

D) 30

The Twists

They will try to disguise Similar Triangles questions, but don't be fooled. If a question involves triangles with non-specific angles, there's a good chance the triangles are similar.

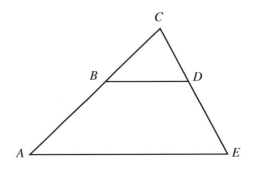

Note: Figure not drawn to scale.

In the figure above, $\overline{BD} \parallel \overline{AE}$ and $AC = 40$. The ratio of BD to AE is 2:5. What is the length of AB ?

A) 8

B) 16

C) 24

D) 30

Exercise: Similar Triangles

1

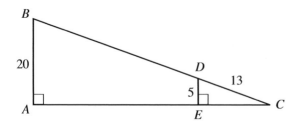

In the figure above, what is the length of *AC* ?

A) 12

B) 39

C) 48

D) 52

2

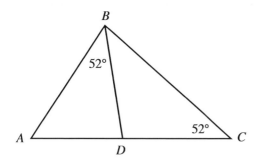

In the figure above, which of the following ratios has the same value as $\dfrac{AB}{BC}$?

A) $\dfrac{AB}{BD}$

B) $\dfrac{AC}{BC}$

C) $\dfrac{AD}{BD}$

D) $\dfrac{BD}{CD}$

3

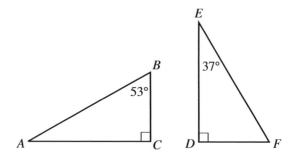

Triangles *ABC* and *DEF* are shown above. Which of the following is equal to the ratio $\dfrac{AC}{AB}$?

A) $\dfrac{DE}{DF}$

B) $\dfrac{DE}{EF}$

C) $\dfrac{DF}{EF}$

D) $\dfrac{EF}{DE}$

4

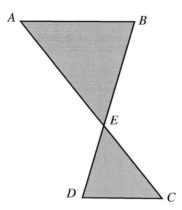

A gardener designed a flowerbed which is represented in the sketch above. The lengths represented by *AB*, *BE*, *AE*, and *CD* on the sketch represent lengths of 540 inches, 270 inches, 330 inches, and 180 inches, respectively. Segments *AC* and *BD* intersect at *E*, and $\angle BAE$ and $\angle ECD$ have the same measure. What is the value of *CE* ?

Cylinders

geometry

The Basics

For some reason, the SAT really loves cylinders. They give you the formula.

REFERENCE

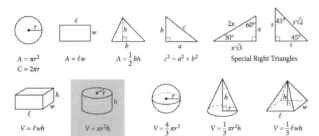

$A = \pi r^2$
$C = 2\pi r$

$A = \ell w$

$A = \frac{1}{2}bh$

$c^2 = a^2 + b^2$

Special Right Triangles

$V = \ell wh$

$V = \pi r^2 h$

$V = \frac{4}{3}\pi r^3$

$V = \frac{1}{3}\pi r^2 h$

$V = \frac{1}{3}\ell wh$

The number of degrees of arc in a circle is 360.
The number of radians of arc in a circle is 2π.
The sum of the measures in degrees of the angles of a triangle is 180.

Example 1

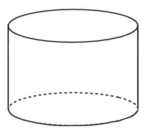

A company is designing packaging for a food product. The packaging is in the shape of a right circular cylinder, as shown above. The height of the packaging is 9 centimeters, and the volume must be exactly 144π cubic centimeters. What is the <u>diameter</u> of the packaging, in centimeters?

The Twists

Sometimes there are two cylinders. This one is similar to a Rearrange Formulas question.

Example 2

A grain silo in the shape of a right circular cylinder has a volume of 256 cubic yards. What is the volume of a second grain silo that is three times as tall and one half as wide?

Exercise: Cylinders

1

A packaging company is designing a jar in the shape of a right circular cylinder. The height of the jar will be 8 inches. If the internal radius will be between 2.45 and 2.50 inches, what is one possible integer value of the volume of the jar in cubic inches?

3

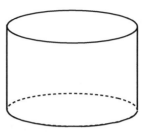

A container in the shape of a right circular cylinder is shown above. The radius of the base is equal to the height. If the volume of the container is 125π cubic centimeters, what is the <u>diameter</u> of the base of the container, in centimeters?

2

A container in the shape of a right circular cylinder is filled with water to a height of 20 inches. The base of the container has an area of 80 square inches. When a rock is dropped into the container, the height of the water rises to 22 inches total. What is the volume of the rock to the nearest cubic inch?

4

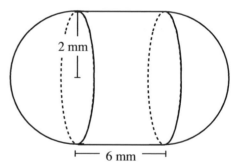

A pharmaceutical company designed a pill in the shape of a right circular cylinder with half of a sphere on both ends. What is the volume of the pill to the nearest cubic millimeter?

Trigonometry

geometry

The Basics

Trigonometry is complex, but the SAT mostly tests the simplest concepts. In fact, you will almost never need to use the SIN, COS, and TAN buttons on your calculator. If you think you need to, you probably did something wrong. Instead, start each Trigonometry problem by writing this on the page:

soh cah toa

This helps you remember that:

$$\sin = \frac{\text{opposite}}{\text{hypotenuse}}$$

$$\cos = \frac{\text{adjacent}}{\text{hypotenuse}}$$

$$\tan = \frac{\text{opposite}}{\text{adjacent}}$$

If there's no picture, draw a right triangle so it's easier to visualize the trigonometric ratios.

Example 1

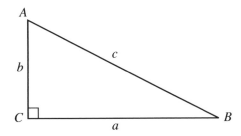

Given the right triangle *ABC* above, which of the following is equal to $\frac{a}{c}$?

A) $\sin B$

B) $\cos B$

C) $\tan B$

D) $\tan A$

The Twists

They'll complicate the triangles or give you side lengths that don't match with the trig fraction. Just remember that these are ratios!

Example 2

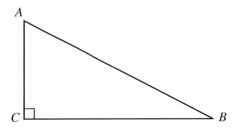

In the figure above, $\sin B = \frac{3}{5}$ and *AC* = 12. What is the length of *BC* ?

Formulas

The SAT doesn't give any Trigonometry formulas besides the fact that 2π radians equals 360 degrees. You need to know soh-cah-toa, and this:

Example 3

Why are the following two <u>essential</u> formulas true?

$\sin (x°) = \cos (90 - x°)$

$\cos (x°) = \sin (90 - x°)$

Exercise: Trigonometry

1

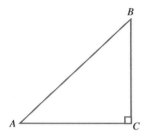
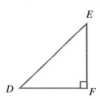

Note: Figure not drawn to scale.

Similar triangles *ABC* and *DEF* are shown above, where vertices *A, B,* and *C* correspond to vertices *D, E,* and *F*, respectively. If *EF* = 5 and *DE* = 13, what is the value of sin *A* ?

2

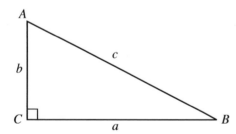

In right triangle *ABC* above, cos *B* = 0.8. What is the value of tan *A*?

3

One angle in a right triangle measures $a°$, where $\cos a° = \dfrac{3}{5}$. What is the value of $\sin(90° - a°)$?

4

Angle x has a measure of 900 degrees. What is the measure of angle x in radians?

A) 5π

B) 6π

C) 8π

D) 9π

5

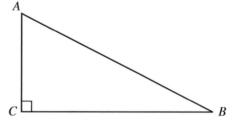

In triangle *ABC* above, $\overline{AC} = 3$ and $\overline{BC} = 4$. If point *D* (not shown) lies on $\overline{AB}$, what is the value of $\sin(\angle ACD) - \cos(\angle DCB)$?

Advanced Geometry

geometry

The Basics

Know the geometry rules. You'll need to solve a complicated puzzle, and it's not always clear which rules you're going to need. Be on the lookout for clues, and use the Reference Chart. Many Advanced Geometry questions involve the often-forgotten special right triangle ratios:

REFERENCE

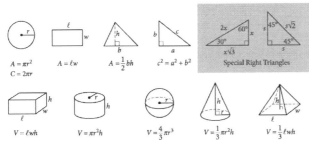

The number of degrees of arc in a circle is 360.
The number of radians of arc in a circle is 2π.
The sum of the measures in degrees of the angles of a triangle is 180.

Example 1

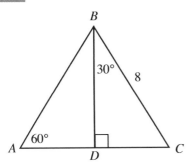

In △ABC above, what is the value of $\overline{BD}$?

A) 4

B) $4\sqrt{2}$

C) $4\sqrt{3}$

D) 6

The Twists

You have to be clever. Add and subtract shapes and pieces. Look for known angles and constants. Make triangles and draw radii. If the shape is three-dimensional, you can usually use two-dimensional shapes to solve.

Example 2

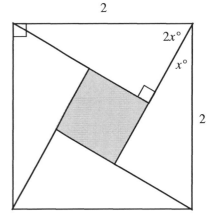

The large square above has sides of length 2. Which of the following represents the area of the small shaded square?

A) 2

B) 3

C) $\sqrt{3} - 1$

D) $4 - 2\sqrt{3}$

Exercise: Advanced Geometry

1

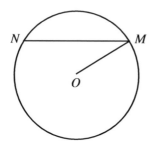

In the figure above, O is the center of the circle and OM is a radius. If the measure of angle OMN is $30°$, then the length of minor arc MN is what fraction of the circumference of circle O ?

2

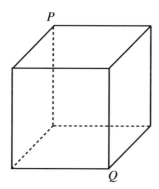

The cube above has edges of length 2. What is the length of line segment PQ (not shown)?

A) 2

B) $2\sqrt{2}$

C) $2\sqrt{3}$

D) $3\sqrt{2}$

3

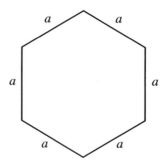

In the figure above, a regular hexagon has sides of length a. Which of the following represents the area of the hexagon in terms of a ?

A) $3a^2$

B) $6a^2$

C) $\dfrac{\sqrt{3}}{4}a^2$

D) $\dfrac{3\sqrt{3}}{2}a^2$

4

It is given that $\cos x = a$, where x is the radian measure of an angle and $0 < x < \dfrac{\pi}{2}$. Which of the following is equal to $-a$?

A) $\cos(-x)$

B) $\cos(\pi - x)$

C) $\cos(x + 2\pi)$

D) $\cos(2\pi - x)$

Lessons and Answers

Remember to try the Examples on your own first. It's okay if you feel lost and confused. You need to learn how to get past that feeling!

Guess & Check lesson

The Basics

Work backwards from the answer choices.

Example 1

Let's plug –2 in for x to test the value. We'll use parentheses to stay organized. It's easy to lose negatives:

$$\sqrt{10 - 3(-2)} - 7 = (-2) - 9$$

Show your work as you simplify the equation:

$$\sqrt{10 + 6} - 7 = -11$$

$$\sqrt{16} - 7 = -11$$

$$4 - 7 = -11$$

$$-3 = -11 \; X$$

This result doesn't make sense, which means that –2 is not a valid solution. Eliminate Choices A, C, and D because they all contain –2. We could be done with the question if we want. One of the best things about Guess & Check is that once you've found the answer that works, you don't need to check the others. But since we only got to Choice B through elimination, it's a little safer to actually check 3 in the equation to make sure we didn't make a careless mistake:

$$\sqrt{10 - 3(3)} - 7 = (3) - 9$$

$$\sqrt{10 - 9} - 7 = -6$$

$$\sqrt{1} - 7 = -6$$

$$1 - 7 = -6$$

$$-6 = -6 \; \checkmark$$

Now we're confident that Choice B is the answer.

Example 2

Lots of people look at a question like this and give up before they start. Or they get careless and ignore the twist—that fraction is going to cause problems if you try to factor. Instead, use the answer choices to Guess & Check different values for k in the second expression. Factoring is hard because you have to think about division and subtraction at the same time, which is more difficult with fractions. But FOILing is just multiplication. Try Choice A:

$$\frac{1}{2}(x + 2)(x - 2)$$

FOIL the two binomials first:

$$\frac{1}{2}\left(x^2 - 2x + 2x - 4\right)$$

$$\frac{1}{2}\left(x^2 - 4\right)$$

Now distribute the fraction:

$$\frac{1}{2}x^2 - 2$$

This isn't what we want. The last number should be 8. Try Choice B:

$$\frac{1}{2}(x + 4)(x - 4)$$

Another great thing about Guess & Check is that the process is repetitive. Once you figure out what to do for the first choice, you can repeat the process until you find the right answer. So again, FOIL the binomials:

$$\frac{1}{2}\left(x^2 - 4x + 4x - 16\right)$$

$$\frac{1}{2}\left(x^2 - 16\right)$$

And distribute the fraction:

$$\frac{1}{2}x^2 - 8$$

That's it. We're done. No need to check the other choices. **The correct answer is Choice B.**

Guess & Check — The Basics

Work backwards by testing the answer choices.

Guess & Check to avoid solving complicated equations.

It can also help you make algebra easier by reversing the process. Multiplication is usually easier than division, for example.

Once you've found an answer that "works", you're done. You do not have to check all the choices.

The Twists

Example 3

This question has a lot of information. In fact, sorting through it all is what makes this question difficult. Guessing an answer choice gives you a place to start. You'll be surprised how often you can stumble your way to the right answer by using Guess & Check.

Start with Choice B. It's a middle number so you'll be able to move up or down if it doesn't work, depending on why it doesn't work. It helps to focus on the last part of the question. What does the answer choice represent?

4 cars that seat 7 people each

Turn that into math:

$$4 \times 7 = 28$$

What else do you know? Stay focused on the answer choice. If there are 4 cars that seat 7 people, then how many cars seat 5 people?

$$\begin{array}{r} 4 \times 7 = 28 \\ +5 \\ \hline 9 \end{array}$$

The question tells us there are 9 cars total, so there must be 5 cars left. How many people are in those 5 cars?

$$\begin{array}{r} 4 \times 7 = 28 \\ +5 \times 5 = 25 \\ \hline 9 \end{array}$$

Is that the right number of people?

$$\begin{array}{r} 4 \times 7 = 28 \\ +5 \times 5 = \underline{25} \\ \hline 9 53 \; X \end{array}$$

The question says we're supposed to have 55 people total. Our guess gave us only 53. We should try a larger number so that there are more 7-person cars. Guess Choice C, which means 5 cars that seat 7 people. The process is the same:

$$\begin{array}{r} 5 \times 7 = 35 \\ +4 \times 5 = \underline{20} \\ \hline 9 55 \; \checkmark \end{array}$$

Choice C is the correct answer. There's no need to check any of the other choices.

Guess & Check — The Twists

Use Guess & Check as a starting point when questions give you a lot of information.

Focus on what the answer choices mean.

Start with Choice B so that you can move up or down if B doesn't work.

If a question asks for the "least" or "greatest" possible value, then start with the least or greatest answer choice.

Stay organized and show your work!

Arithmetize lesson

The Basics

Arithmetizing takes time to get used to. It's not something you typically use in school. But it definitely works, so keep practicing it!

Example 1

The SAT is really hoping that you get confused by all the exponents. We can't use 0, so let's pick the next easiest number to Arithmetize with:

$$\text{Let } x = 1$$

Substitute for all the x's in the equation. Use parentheses to stay organized, especially since distribution seems like a big part of the question:

$$y = \frac{2(1)^2\big(3(1)\big)^2}{6(1)^4}$$

Carefully work through all the exponents and multiplication:

$$y = \frac{2(1)(3)^2}{6(1)}$$

$$y = \frac{2(9)}{6}$$

$$y = \frac{18}{6}$$

$$y = 3$$

That's it. **Choice D is the correct answer.** Instead of worrying about how the exponents would affect the variables, we were able to focus on how they would affect the numbers.

Arithmetize — The Basics

Pick your own numbers for the variables.

Pick easy numbers. Most of time 0 and 1 will be fine, but use your judgment. If the question doesn't let you pick 0 or 1, then don't pick them. If you have to divide by 2, then pick a number that is divisible by 2. Just make sure you write down a "Let" statement so that you remember the number that you picked.

When you substitute, use parentheses to stay organized.

The Twists

Example 2

If you remember how to complete the square, the algebra is easy. If you don't, you can still get the answer. Pick an easy number:

$$\text{Let } x = 0$$

What's the value of the original expression?

$$(0)^2 - 2(0) + 5$$

$$0 - 0 + 5 = \underline{5}$$

Underline or box the 5. That's the value that we want the answer choices to equal, so we don't want to forget it. In fact, that's the most confusing thing about Arithmetizing. You have a number that you picked that gets substituted and a number that you need the answer choices to equal after you substitute. Stay organized and you'll be fine.

Let's put 0 in for x in the answer choices. We need the choice to equal 5.

Choice A

$$(0 + 1)^2 + 4$$

$$(1)^2 + 4$$

$$1 + 4 = 5 \checkmark$$

Choice A works! But unlike Guess & Check, we <u>must</u> check every answer choice. Sometimes we pick a number that works for more than one choice. Checking everything is our way of being sure we have the right answer:

Choice B

$$(0 + 1)^2 - 4$$

$$(1)^2 - 4$$

$$1 - 4 = 5 \ \text{X}$$

Eliminate Choice B. Keep going:

Choice C

$$(0 - 1)^2 + 4$$

$$(-1)^2 + 4$$

$$1 + 4 = 5 \checkmark$$

Choice C also works. We'll have to try a different number, but let's finish checking with the numbers we have:

Choice D

$$(0 - 1)^2 - 4$$

$$(-1)^2 - 4$$

$$1 - 4 = 5 \ \text{X}$$

Choice D can also be eliminated. We need to pick a new number for x and try again, but we don't need to check Choices B and D since we already know they don't work. Stick with easy numbers:

$$\text{Let } x = 1$$

$$(1)^2 - 2(1) + 5$$

$$1 - 2 + 5 = \underline{4}$$

Now we're substituting 1 in for x and looking for the choices to equal 4.

Choice A

$$(1 + 1)^2 + 4$$

$$(2)^2 + 4$$

$$4 + 4 = 4 \ \text{X}$$

This time, Choice A didn't work. Choice C is probably the answer, but it's safer to check and know for sure:

Choice C

$$(1 - 1)^2 + 4$$

$$(0)^2 + 4$$

$$0 + 4 = 4 \checkmark$$

Choice C is the correct answer. To be honest, solving this question is faster with algebra, so it's better to know how to complete the square. But Arithmetize is a great tool to help you pick up a few extra points. You won't always know how to solve using algebra, so Arithmetizing is a useful backup.

Example 3

When the algebra is really hard, Arithmetizing may be the only way to get an answer.

$$\text{Let } x = 1 \text{ and } y = 2$$

In this case, we won't Arithmetize for a and b because those variables are dependent on our values for x and y. Usually you can pick whatever numbers you want. However, if the question gives you rules to follow, make sure you follow them.

Use x and y to find a and b:

$$(1)^2 + (2)^2 = a$$

$$1 + 4 = a$$

$$\underline{5 = a}$$

$$(1)(2) = b$$

$$\underline{2 = b}$$

Use the values of a and b to find the value of the expression in the question:

$$2a + 4b = 2(5) + 4(2)$$

$$2a + 4b = 10 + 8$$

$$2a + 4b = \underline{18}$$

There are a lot of numbers to keep track of. We should substitute the values we picked for x and y into each of the answer choices, and the right answer will equal 18.

Choice A

$$(1 + 2)^2$$

$$(3)^2 = 9 \text{ X}$$

Choice B

$$2(1 + 2)^2$$

$$2(3)^2$$

$$2(9) = 18 \checkmark$$

Choice C

$$\left(1 + 2(2)\right)^2$$

$$(1 + 4)^2$$

$$(5)^2 = 25 \text{ X}$$

Choice D

$$2\left(1 + 2(2)\right)^2$$

$$2(1 + 4)^2$$

$$2(5)^2$$

$$2(25) = 50 \text{ X}$$

Choice B was the only answer that equalled 18, so it must be the correct answer. If we had picked 0 for x or y, we might have ended up having to try new numbers. It really depends on the situation whether Arithmetizing with 0 is a good choice. Most of the time it works out, but you'll get better at knowing when to pick which numbers.

Arithmetize — The Twists

Sometimes you need to pick numbers so you can get the value of an expression, and then look for that same value by plugging your numbers into the choices.

Always Arithmetize with all of the answer choices.

If two answer choices work, pick new numbers and try again with the choices you did not eliminate.

When there are a lot of variables, stay organized.

Plug Points Into Equations lesson

The Basics
Equations are just collections of points.

Example 1

Both the points and the equations are annoying. Start with the easiest point to work with. Points with 0's and 1's are usually the easiest:

$$\left(1, \frac{7}{2}\right)$$

Test the point in all the choices and eliminate any that don't work:

Choice A

$$\frac{7}{2} = \left(\frac{7}{2}\right)^1$$

$$\frac{7}{2} = \frac{7}{2} \checkmark$$

Choice B

$$\frac{7}{2} = 4^1 + \frac{5}{4}$$

$$\frac{7}{2} = \frac{16}{4} + \frac{5}{4}$$

$$\frac{7}{2} = \frac{21}{4} \ \text{X}$$

Choice C

$$\frac{7}{2} = \frac{5}{2}(1) + 2$$

$$\frac{7}{2} = \frac{5}{2} + \frac{4}{2}$$

$$\frac{7}{2} = \frac{9}{2} \ \text{X}$$

Choice D

$$\frac{7}{2} = \frac{1}{2}(1) + 3$$

$$\frac{7}{2} = \frac{1}{2} + \frac{6}{2}$$

$$\frac{7}{2} = \frac{7}{2} \checkmark$$

Choices A and D both work, so we'll have to check another point. Stick with the easy points. The second easiest to plug in is:

$$(2, 4)$$

Choice A

$$4 = \left(\frac{7}{2}\right)^2$$

$$4 = \frac{49}{4} \ \text{X}$$

Choice D

$$4 = \frac{1}{2}(2) + 3$$

$$4 = 1 + 3$$

$$4 = 4 \checkmark$$

Choice A gets eliminated, which means that **Choice D is the correct answer.** As it turns out, this second point was probably even easier than the first. Though, it doesn't really matter. Pick the point that you think is the easiest. Just make sure you test all the equations.

Plug Points Into Equations — The Basics

Plug points into equations. It's in the name!

This strategy lets you see what's happening at one point instead of trying to think about the entire equation. It makes things much easier to understand and visualize.

Usually the easiest points to plug in will include 0's and 1's, but pick the best point for the situation.

The Twists

Example 2

The SAT loves to twist graphs to mess with your expectations. As you can see, all of the choices have the exact same y-intercept, so this question really comes down to slopes.

You should be able to eliminate Choices B and D because they have positive slopes, but the graph is clearly negative.

You've probably been taught to look at the line and count the boxes. The line looks like it drops 1 box and runs 3 boxes, which would be a slope of $\frac{-1}{3}$.

To be sure, test an actual point in the equations. The line looks like it includes the point (3.0, 4.2). You can use your calculator to plug this point into the equations:

Choice A

$$4.2 = \frac{9}{2} - \frac{9}{80}(3.0)$$

$$4.2 = 4.5 - (0.1125)(3.0)$$

$$4.2 = 4.5 - 0.3375$$

$$4.2 = 4.1625$$

It's not exact, but that doesn't mean it's wrong. Remember that we got our point by looking at the graph. We were estimating, so it's possible that we were slightly off. Try Choice C and see if it's closer:

Choice C

$$4.2 = \frac{9}{2} - \frac{1}{3}(3.0)$$

$$4.2 = 4.5 - 1$$

$$4.2 = 3.5 \text{ X}$$

This is way off. The SAT twisted this graph by messing with the scale. You can't easily count the boxes to get the slope because the boxes don't mean the same thing. One box up and down is 0.1 units, but one box left and right is 0.3 units.

It's much safer to Plug Points Into Equations so that you can actually prove that the point lies on the equation. **Choice A is the correct answer because the point works in the equation, which is exactly what we'd expect from looking at the graph.**

Plug Points Into Equations — The Twists

The SAT changes the scales on graphs because they know you'll count the boxes to get the slopes. Don't let them trick you!

Lines and other graphs are just collections of points. Pick one and plug it into an equation to test it. This is essentially Guess & Check, but in this case you need to test all of the choices, or at least all of the choices that can't be easily eliminated.

Get Back to Basics lesson

The Basics

Untwist questions so that you have a better idea of what they're testing. When a question is confusing, ask yourself what aspect of the question confuses you the most. Solve that problem first.

Example 1

In this case, the fractions are scary. Many people give up on this question because they don't feel confident with fractions. Get rid of them to make this question much easier.

If you multiply the first equation by 4, both of the fractions will disappear:

$$4\left[\frac{1}{2}x + \frac{1}{4}y = 9\right]$$

$$\frac{4}{2}x + \frac{4}{4}y = 36$$

$$2x + y = 36$$

Now it's much easier to substitute the second equation in for y in the first equation. And there are no fractions to make the multiplication difficult:

$$2x + 6x = 36$$

$$8x = 36$$

$$x = \frac{36}{8}$$

$$x = \frac{9}{2}$$

The correct answer is 9/2. You still need to work with fractions, but it's pretty basic. And it's much less intimidating than dealing with common denominators. Even if eliminating the fractions just makes the equations easier to look at, it's still worthwhile because you're less likely to lose negatives or distribute incorrectly.

The Twists

Example 2

The Properties packets later in the book will help you a lot because most equations have a standard form. Try to get back to that safe place. You'll have a better sense of what's going on.

In this question, the equation looks a lot like a line. We could multiply by 2 to get rid of the fraction, but it's actually better to divide both parts by 2. We want our equation to look like the standard equation of a line:

$$y = mx + b$$

$$h = 2.5t + 25.5$$

See how the values in this model match up with the parts of a line? That helps you NARROW YOUR FOCUS to just the part that the question is asking for.

All of the choices are asking for a rate—increase in height every year. For lines, the rate of increase is the slope. Since m is the slope, we should pick the number that is in the m spot of our model.

Choice D is the correct answer. The story and the original equation make this seem like a really strange question that you've never encountered before. But Getting Back to Basics turns the weird

equation into a standard line. Once you're at y=mx+b, this question is really easy.

Read the Graph lesson

The Basics

Don't feel bad if these first two examples were hard. You'll get better at reading the graphs.

Example 1

Go through the choices, one at a time. It's really important that you read each one:

A) This is very tempting. It looks like the graph generally goes up. But the choice is trying to fool you. It says the graph increases "each year since 2002," but that's not exactly true. For the first 5 years, the graph decreases, so it's not increasing "each year". If this choice said, "Sales generally increased between 2002 and 2015," then it would be right. But that one word—each—makes all the difference.

B) Clearly wrong. It's only decreasing a little at the beginning.

C) This is also tempting, but be careful. The SAT loves to mess with the units on the axes. The graph definitely decreases up until Year 5, but Year 5 does not represent 2005. Year 0 is supposed to be 2002, so Year 5 is actually 2007.

D) **And that's why Choice D is correct.** The graph decreases until 2007, and then increases afterward. Notice that we didn't really need to do any math. We just needed to be careful of the wording of the choices and the units on the axes.

Example 2

If you had difficulty with this question, it's probably because you were confused about what they were asking. The "greatest change" means the steepest slope. A lot of Read the Graph questions are about slope. The slope is steepest from Years 6 to 10, which correspond with 2008 to 2012. **Choice B is correct because it's the only one that falls within that range.** An important note—when they say "greatest change," it doesn't necessarily need to be a positive change. In this case, the graph is increasing. But on another question, the greatest change might actually be a decrease. Usually they're asking for the magnitude of the change, so the direction doesn't matter. It can be steep up or steep down. But read carefully because they could ask specifically for the positive or negative change instead.

Also, be careful of Choice A. Once again, the SAT is trying to trick you by messing with the units on the graph. Years 6 through 8 are 2008 to 2010, not 2006 to 2008.

Read the Graph — The Basics

Read all of the choices carefully. Words that don't usually matter might make all the difference.

Check the units on both the x- and y-axes. They often mess with the units to trick you. Just training yourself to pause for a second before you circle an answer could save you 10 points.

If they're asking about the "change," they are probably asking about slopes. They're usually asking for the magnitude of the change, so the direction might not matter. The greatest change will have the steepest slope.

The Twists

Example 3

The main twist for this question is that scatterplots are confusing. But if you trust yourself, you'll do fine. The question wants to know the year when the area was 150 acres, so find 150 on the y-axis. Draw a line across the graph until you intersect the line of best fit. What's the x-value of that point? **It's just after 2000, so Choice B is correct because 2002 is a good estimate.**

Be careful of Choice C. They're hoping that you think 2005 would be the middle of the box. It's not. Each box is a 5 year period, so 2005 would be the unlabeled line between 2000 and 2010. Once again, they're hoping you answer too quickly to pay attention to the units.

Example 4

You can also trust your instincts on this question. They say 1990, so find that point on the x-axis. If you draw a line up, you'll see that there's a point on the line of best fit at approximately 250, and a data point at approximately 325 (halfway between the labeled lines of 300 and 350). The question sounds like they want a difference, so subtract those two values:

$$325 - 250 = 75$$

Choice A is close enough, so it's correct. For the future, it's important to know what they're actually asking. A scatterplot shows two things: 1) the actual data that was collected, which is represented by the black dots, and 2) an estimate of the data's trend, which is represented by the line of best fit. Many scatterplot questions ask you to compare the "actual" value and the "estimated" or "predicted" value. Just look at the data point and the line of best fit.

Scatterplots look scary because there's a lot going on. Just know that the black dots represent actual values that were found with an experiment, survey, or something else scientific. The line of best fit is an estimate that lets us fill in the gaps. We can see a general trend, or even use the line of best fit to predict what would happen at places where we don't have actual data. So the twist is really just that they're throwing a lot of information at you and hoping you get too confused to answer. Untwist the question by focusing on the coordinates of the points and the units on the axes.

Answers: Read the Graph

#1 — Answer = A
Start on the x-axis to find the player with the most games. It's the dot that is furthest to the right, specifically at around 37 games played. The y-coordinate of that point is 18.

#2 — Answer = C
This is similar to #1, but with a slight twist. Notice that the question is asking for "most goals scored per game played". That's a rate, so we'll need to compare two values as a ratio: goals scored divided by games played. Calculate the value for each point. Point A is approximately 14/27, which is 0.52. Point B is approximately 9/30, which is 0.3. Point C is 10/8, which is 1.25. Point D is 6/13, which is 0.46. The greatest number is at Point C.

#3 — Answer = C
Choice A is true because the slope of the line from (0, 0) to (1, 4) is constant. The line represents Rodrigo's drive from home to the dry cleaner, and the slope represents his speed. Choice B is true because you can draw a line where y = 2, and you'll intersect the graph twice. Choice D is true because the flat line at y = 4 (when Rodrigo is at the dry cleaner) is 0.5 hours long. Choice C is NOT true because the flat line at the top of the graph (when he's at dinner) is 1.5 hours long, not 3 hours long. The twist is that the

scale of the graph is not what you would expect. Always check the units!

#4 — Answer = C
The restaurant is 6 miles from Rodrigo's home, so he drove 6 miles to get there and 6 miles to get back home. That's a total of 12 miles. The twist is that you need to count the return trip home.

Read the Chart lesson

The Basics
For these questions, the wording of the question is more important than the chart. In fact, you probably won't use most of the information in the chart. Instead, you'll need to use the question to pick out the right values from the right rows and columns.

Example 1

As you can tell by the answer choices, we're going to construct a fraction. We'll focus on the denominator (bottom number) first because it represents the group that we care about. In this case, we care about the entire chart. The "of" statement usually tells us where to look, and this question is asking about the "proportion of the arrivals". The entire chart is arrivals, so the denominator is 300.

Now we need to figure out which of the arrivals they're talking about. The question is pretty clear: "trains that were late". That's the top left box, which means our numerator (top number) is 36. The whole fraction is:

$$\frac{36}{300}$$

Since that's not a choice, we need to simplify. I'd start by dividing both parts by 3, and then reduce in little steps:

$$\frac{36}{300} = \frac{12}{100} = \frac{6}{50} = \frac{3}{25}$$

So Choice A is the answer.

Example 2

As we solve this one, notice that we're following the same process as Example 1. Read the Chart questions follow a clear pattern.

This time, our "of" statement limits us to "the on-time arrivals". That means that our denominator will not be 300 because we don't actually care about the late arrivals. You might consider this a twist, but it happens often enough that I think it's just part of the basics. The total number of on-time arrivals is 166.

The numerator is the "buses" that were on-time. Again, the question does not care about late arrivals, so we're just looking at that middle row. The number of on-time buses is 52. So our full fraction is:

$$\frac{52}{166}$$

Sometimes we don't need to reduce, so Choice B is the answer.

Read the Chart — The Basics

Start with the denominator, which is the group that the question cares about. Sometimes it's the entire chart. But sometimes it's just a few rows or columns. Often you can use the "of" statement to figure it out.

The numerator will always be a little more specific or narrow. You should always have a fraction with a smaller number on top of a bigger number. Reduce the fraction if needed.

The Twists

Example 3

The question is worded a little differently, but the pattern is the same. Start with the "of" statement, which says that we care about all "of the movies". The chart doesn't have a box for the total, but the description underneath tells us that there were 75 movies, so our denominator is 75.

Now just go to the specific place they tell you. We need "a drama that received 1 star," which is 10. Our fraction is:

$$\frac{10}{75}$$

The twist here is that they're asking about probability, but that doesn't really mean anything on the SAT. Essentially, our fraction means that, if we chose a movie randomly, 10 out of every 75 movies would be a 1-star drama. But both probability and fractions can also be expressed as decimals. Just divide 10 by 75 in your calculator, and you should get 0.13333… **This is approximately 0.13, so Choice B is the correct answer.**

Example 4

This question has a lot of twists. For one, there's no "of" statement. We need to figure out for ourselves which columns and rows they care about. Again, we're choosing a movie randomly, but it's "a movie that received at least 2 stars." They only care about the last two columns. We need to add up all the values in those columns to get the total, but be careful of another twist—the 2 and 3 at the top are not going to be added in. Those are headers, meaning they just tell us the number of stars. Add everything else to get our denominator:

$$6 + 9 + 7 + 8 + 7 + 7 = 44$$

As always, the numerator will be a smaller group chosen from the larger group. They want the comedies, which also need to be added together:

$$6 + 8 = 14$$

So our completed fraction is:

$$\frac{14}{44}$$

Put that in your calculator, and you'll get 0.318… which rounds to 0.32. **So Choice C is the answer.**

Read the Chart — The Twists

Probability doesn't really matter on the SAT. You can think in terms of fractions. In fact, almost every chart question will involve fractions in some way, so that's a good place to start. If the question is twisted, try to get back to basics by building a fraction.

If there's no "of" statement, you'll need to figure out the denominator on your own. Read carefully. It's really just the group that you're choosing from. Which rows and columns do they care about? Which ones do they seem to be leaving out?

Answers: Read the Chart

#1 — Answer = B
The denominator is only the people who bought the product (left column). Add 52 and 32 to get that the denominator is 84. The numerator is only the people who bought the product AND saw the advertisement, which is 52. The fraction is $\frac{52}{84}$.

#2 — Answer = B
The denominator is people who saw the movie, which is the left column only. The total is given as 63. The numerator is women who saw the movie, which is 22. The fraction is $\frac{22}{63}$, which is 0.35 as a decimal.

#3 — Answer = B
The twist is that the wording is different than what you're used to. Follow instructions. Each answer choice refers to one box in the chart. They want the box that represents "one third of the money spent on all projects in the given year", which means one third of the total for that year. To test Choice A, take the total in 2006 ($10,899) and find one-third of it by dividing by 3, which should give you $3,633. That's way more than the box for Project A in 2006 ($1,345), so Choice A is incorrect. Repeat the process for Choice B. One third of the total for 2008 ($14,569) is $4,856, which is very very close to the box for Project B in 2008. Check the other choices to be sure, but none are closer than Choice B.

#4 — Answer = A
Find the total change for Project C from 2006 to 2008 by subtracting those boxes ($1,321 – $1,040 = $281). The twist is that they want the average rate of change, so Choice D is a trick. Divide $281 by 2 to find the change per year, which is approximately $140.

Chart of Points lesson

The Basics
These questions take advantage of one of our most important Math strategies—Plug Points Into Equations. In fact, that's pretty much all it is!

Example 1

Start with the easiest point, which is (1, –1). Be organized, and start with Choice A:

$$-1 = 1 - 2(1)$$

$$-1 = 1 - 2$$

$$-1 = -1 \checkmark$$

But don't stop here! The SAT designs Chart of Points questions so that the first equation works for the first point. You should continue to test the same point in the other equations. Let's try Choice B:

$$-1 = 2 - 3(1)$$

$$-1 = 2 - 3$$

$$-1 = -1 \checkmark$$

Looks like we'll need to revisit both Choices A and B, but let's keep going with the point (1, –1). Sticking with the same point makes it less likely that you'll plug in the wrong value accidentally. Here's Choice C:

$$-1 = 3 - 2(1)$$

$$-1 = 3 - 2$$

$$-1 = 1 \text{ X}$$

And Choice D:

$$-1 = 7 - 4(1)$$

$$-1 = 7 - 4$$

$$-1 = 3 \text{ X}$$

Now let's retry Choices A and B using the next point, which is (3, –7). First, Choice A:

$$-7 = 1 - 2(3)$$

$$-7 = 1 - 6$$

$$-7 = -5 \text{ X}$$

Since that doesn't work, we now know that Choice B has to be the correct answer.

Example 2

Once again, we're just reading a chart, even if the chart is a little more complicated than the last one. You don't really need to know function notation in order to get this right. Just follow instructions. For Choice A, put the values from the 0 row into the right places:

$$g(x) - h(x) = x$$

$$5 - 6 = 0$$

$$-1 = 0 \text{ X}$$

Cross out Choice A, and try Choice B:

$$3 - 2 = 1$$

$$1 = 1 \checkmark$$

Choice B is the correct answer. On this question, we don't need to check the other choices. It's almost the reverse of Example 1, where they gave us lots of points and we needed to choose the equation. Here,

they're giving us the equation, and we need to choose the one point that fits. If you're feeling nervous, take another few seconds to check the other answers. Nothing wrong with being sure.

Chart of Points — The Basics

Chart of Points questions are a really great opportunity to use our Plug Points Into Equations strategy. Be organized, and show your work.

When you have multiple points and multiple equations, do not pick the first choice that checks out. The SAT almost always puts a decoy answer near the top to trick the people who are too lazy to check all the answers.

The Twists

Example 3

The twist is that this is a graph, not a chart. But as the text says, a line is made up of points, so it's still a list of points like the other two examples. Pick a spot where the line of best fit intersects the boxes. In the bottom left, it looks like the point (5, 50) lies on the line. The story doesn't really matter. As always, Plug Points Into Equations. Let's start with Choice A:

$$50 = 2(5) + 31$$

$$50 = 10 + 31$$

$$50 = 41 \text{ X}$$

This isn't close enough, so we can eliminate Choice A. Let's try the same point in Choice B:

$$50 = 3.45(5) + 32$$

$$50 = 17.25 + 32$$

$$50 = 49.25 \checkmark$$

It's not exact, but that's really close. If another choice works, we might need to try another point, but Choice B should definitely be kept. Let's try Choice C:

$$50 = 4.24(5) + 38$$

$$50 = 21.2 + 38$$

$$50 = 59.2 \text{ X}$$

This also isn't close enough. Let's try Choice D:

$$50 = 5(5) - 40$$

$$50 = 25 - 40$$

$$50 = -15 \text{ X}$$

Not even close. **Choice B is the correct answer because it's the only one that was close.**

Chart of Points — The Twists

Graphs are still lists of points. Plug Points Into Equations.

Answers: Chart of Points

#1 — Answer = C
Plug Points Into Equations. Start with the easiest point, which is (1, −4). Unfortunately, the point works in all four equations. Try the second point, which is (2, 1). The point only works in Choice C.

#2 — Answer = D
Plug Points Into Equations. Remember that anything raised to the 0 power is equal to 1. Testing the first point eliminates Choice A. Testing the second point eliminates Choice C. Testing the third point eliminates Choice B, leaving Choice D as the answer.

#3 — Answer = B
Plug Points Into Equations. According to the question, the Ounces column should be plugged in for x, and the Grams column should be plugged in for g. Test the point (0.28, 8.0) in each of the choices. It only fits in Choice B.

#4 — Answer = B
Plug Points Into Equations. Make sure you plug in correctly, though. The twist is that y is the first variable in the equation, so it's easy to accidentally plug the point in backwards because you're used to x being first. Messing with your expectations is a common twist. Numerals I and II work, but III does not.

Basic Arithmetic lesson

The Basics
As the packet says, these questions are usually much easier than they look. Try to turn the story into math by reading carefully and staying organized.

Example 1

It's best to look for a starting point or total. In this case, we know that the store sold "a total of 50 cupcakes". Write that number down. We're going to use it.

The question also says that the store sold "at least one large package of 6 cupcakes". Let's remove those 6 from our total by subtracting:

$$50 - 6 = 44$$

The end of the question tells us to find a possible number of "small packages of 4 cupcakes" that the store could have sold. We don't know how many 6-cupcake packages it sold, but it doesn't matter. There's more than one answer to this question. Since we've already taken care of the 6-cupcake package that we know of, we can just divide the remaining 44 cupcakes by 4:

$$\frac{44}{4} = 11$$

So 11 is one possible answer. On the test, there's no reason to find the other answers, but let's see how you might go about it. Since the store sold "at least one large package", we know that they could have sold more than one. Let's see what happens if we assume they sold two large packages.

Two large packages of 6 cupcakes each is 12 total cupcakes. Subtract that from our total of 50:

$$50 - 12 = 38$$

We can divide by 4 to see how many of the small packages they sold:

$$\frac{38}{4} = 9.5$$

This is a problem. We can't sell half of a package, so this answer does not work. We need a number that is evenly divisible by 4 (doesn't have a remainder). Let's see what happens if we assume the store sold three large packages, which would be 18 cupcakes:

$$50 - 18 = 32$$

$$\frac{32}{4} = 8$$

The math checks out, and 8 is another possible answer. We could keep going, and we'd find that the other possible answers are 5 and 2.

Basic Arithmetic — The Basics

Find a starting point or total. Write it down.

Look for any rules or conditions that you need to take care of first. If they leave something open-ended or vague, it's okay to make assumptions so you can continue to solve.

The Twists

Example 2

This question isn't all that different from the last example. There's a clear starting point: Betsy can't spend more than $42.

There's also a rule that we need to take care of. The question says that Betsy must pay the entrance fee of $15. Let's remove that amount from our total:

$$42 - 15 = 27$$

The question wants to know how many $4 rides Betsy can go on with the money she has left. Let's divide to find out:

$$\frac{27}{4} = 6.75$$

Once again, we don't want a remainder because Betsy can't go on a fraction of a ride. We can ignore the decimal and focus on the fact that 4 goes into 27 6 times. **So the answer is 6.** Betsy can spend $24 on rides, but the remaining $3 are not enough to buy another ticket for another ride.

Basic Arithmetic — The Twists

Be careful of remainders. Sometimes you need to ignore decimals and find a whole number.

Answers: Basic Arithmetic

#1 — Answer = 4150
Multiply 550 miles per hour by the 5 hours to get 2,750 miles. Add in the 1,400 miles already traveled to get a total of 4,150 miles.

#2 — Answer = anything from 8 to 14
Divide 112 cars by 14 cars per hour to get 8 hours. Or divide 112 cars by 8 cars per hour to get 14 hours. Either answer works, and so would any number in between. In this case, decimals are okay because you can have fractions of an hour.

#3 — Answer = 5 or 6
If you start with $59, you'll first subtract out the $10 for the one entree, leaving you with $49. Divide that by $8 per appetizer to find the value of a. You'll get 6.125, but you can't have a fraction of an appetizer, so the answer would be 6. If you start with $49, subtracting out the one entree leaves you with $39. Divide that by $8 per appetizer to get 4.875. This time, you have to round up because you started with a minimum, and you don't want to end up below the minimum, so the other answer is 5.

#4 — Answer = 5

Guess & Check. Pick a number of workers that divides evenly into 150. If there were 10 workers originally, each would inspect 15 widgets (150 ÷ 10 = 15). When 2 workers are out sick, there are 8 workers left to inspect the same number of widgets, but that does not divide evenly (150 ÷ 8 = 18.75). You can't have a worker inspect a fraction of a widget, so you need to try a different number. If there were 5 workers originally, each one would inspect 30 widgets (150 ÷ 5 = 30). If 2 workers were out sick, each of the remaining 3 workers would inspect 50 widgets (150 ÷ 3 = 50), which is 20 additional widgets, exactly what the question wants.

#5 — Answer = 13

The twist is that the number of mice does not matter. Focus on the number of snakes. Let x = the number of snakes. Create an equation using the given information. One side will be 3x + 5 (three mice per snake plus five extra mice). Set that equal to 4x − 8 (four mice per snake, but eight mice short). Solve for x to find that Fletcher has a ridiculous 13 snakes.

Ratios and Units lesson

The Basics

It's very easy to stick to a pattern with Ratios questions. Notice that, in all of the examples, the process is pretty much the same, even when the wording is different.

Example 1

Start by creating a fraction that captures the rate, or the two values that we want to compare:

$$\frac{\$23}{2 \text{ hours}}$$

Set this fraction equal to another ratio that compares the same types of values. We don't know the $ amount, but we do know the number of hours. Make sure your units are consistent:

$$\frac{\$23}{2 \text{ hours}} = \frac{\$x}{7 \text{ hours}}$$

Cross multiply:

$$2x = 161$$

Divide to get x by itself:

$$x = \$80.50$$

So Choice B is the answer.

Example 2

This question uses some advanced math vocabulary, "directly proportional", to ask the same thing. We're clearly dealing with rates and comparisons, so we'll use ratios again. Start by creating a fraction that captures the rate:

$$\frac{15 \text{ years}}{65 \text{ apples}}$$

Set this fraction equal to another ratio that compares the same types of values:

$$\frac{15 \text{ years}}{65 \text{ apples}} = \frac{21 \text{ years}}{x \text{ apples}}$$

Cross multiply, and divide:

$$15x = 1{,}365$$

$$x = 91 \text{ apples}$$

That's it! **The answer is 91.**

Ratios and Units — The Basics

Use fractions to compare rates. Make sure your units are consistent across the tops and bottoms of the fractions.

Cross multiply and divide to solve for x.

The Twists

Example 3

Let's use the same pattern we did for the basic examples. Start by identifying an easy rate:

$$\frac{4 \text{ miles}}{7 \text{ minutes}}$$

Now look for a similar rate that we can compare it to by setting them equal. In this case, speed is a rate that we could write as a fraction:

$$\frac{4 \text{ miles}}{7 \text{ minutes}} = \frac{x \text{ miles}}{1 \text{ hour}}$$

As you can see, the units are not correct. Let's convert hours to minutes:

$$\frac{4 \text{ miles}}{7 \text{ minutes}} = \frac{x \text{ miles}}{60 \text{ minutes}}$$

Cross-multiply and divide:

$$7x = 240$$

$$x = 34.28571429 \text{ miles}$$

Rounding to the nearest tenth means the answer is 34.3.

In this case, it was easy to change the units so they matched, but it's going to get harder. We can anticipate the twist by using multiple fractions to get the units the same. Remember that you can reduce fractions when you have the same number on the top and bottom:

$$\frac{5x}{5y} = \frac{\cancel{5}x}{\cancel{5}y} = \frac{x}{y}$$

The same is true for units. When the same unit is on the top and the bottom, we can cancel them out. We can use this property to get rid of the units that don't match and get new units that do match:

$$\frac{4 \text{ miles}}{7 \text{ minutes}} = \frac{x \text{ miles}}{1 \text{ \cancel{hour}}} \cdot \frac{1 \text{ \cancel{hour}}}{60 \text{ minutes}}$$

For more complex Ratios and Units questions, we'll keep multiplying by rates until the units match up with the other side of the equation. In fact, this strategy will help you keep track of all the information because it checks itself — you'll know you're done when all the "bad" units are gone.

Example 4

Start with whatever rate you find in the problem. Some people start at the end because the question usually gives you some sort of rate. But you can also start at the beginning:

$$\frac{\$95}{7 \text{ cakes}}$$

The question wants to know how much was spent on Kevin's share of cake, so that already matches up one of the units — dollars to dollars.

$$\frac{\$95}{7 \text{ cakes}} = \frac{\$x}{5 \text{ pieces}}$$

But the bottom units don't match. Find a rate that contains one of the bottom units. It doesn't matter what you choose, as long as you put the new ratio on the same side of the equals sign as the fraction that has the unit you're trying to cancel. In this case, we'll work from the start of the question again and use the left side of the equation:

$$\frac{1 \text{ cake}}{4 \text{ quarters}} \cdot \frac{\$95}{7 \text{ cakes}} = \frac{\$x}{5 \text{ pieces}}$$

We can cancel the "cakes", but we don't want "quarters" either. Luckily, there's one more ratio:

$$\frac{1 \text{ \cancel{quarter}}}{3 \text{ pieces}} \cdot \frac{1 \text{ \cancel{cake}}}{4 \text{ \cancel{quarters}}} \cdot \frac{\$95}{7 \text{ \cancel{cakes}}} = \frac{\$x}{5 \text{ pieces}}$$

We know we're done because we have "dollars" in both numerators and "pieces" in both denominators. Now we multiply all the numbers to get back to the simple proportion that we had with the basic examples. Remember that when fractions are on the <u>same side</u> of an equals, we multiply all the tops and all the bottoms.

$$\frac{1 \times 1 \times 95}{3 \times 4 \times 7} = \frac{x}{5}$$

$$\frac{95}{84} = \frac{x}{5}$$

When fractions are on <u>opposite sides</u> of an equals, we cross multiply top to bottom and bottom to top:

$$84x = 475$$

Divide:

$$x = \$5.654761905$$

We need to round to the nearest cent, so $5.65 is the correct answer.

Was this complicated? Absolutely! But if you write out the units, you can go step by step in an organized way. And you could have just as easily put the ratios on the other side:

$$\frac{\$95}{7 \text{ cakes}} = \frac{\$x}{5 \text{ pieces}} \cdot \frac{3 \text{ pieces}}{1 \text{ quarter}} \cdot \frac{4 \text{ quarters}}{1 \text{ cake}}$$

$$\frac{95}{7} = \frac{12x}{5}$$

$$84x = 475$$

$$x = \$5.65$$

Same answer!

Ratios and Units — The Twists

Always write your units. You won't necessarily know if they matter when you read the question, but it'll be obvious when the ratios don't match.

When a unit appears in the numerator and denominator on the same side of an equals, you can cancel it out. Find ratios in the question that eliminate "bad" units so that you're left with what you want.

Once your units match, multiply along the tops and bottoms to condense your ratios into a simple proportion. Cross-multiply and divide, as usual.

Answers: Ratios and Units

#1 — Answer = 1925

Set up a ratio: $\frac{550 \text{ shirts}}{2 \text{ days}} = \frac{x \text{ shirts}}{7 \text{ days}}$. Cross-multiply and divide to find that x equals 1,925 shirts.

#2 — Answer = D

Set up a ratio: $\frac{2 \text{ apples}}{5 \text{ oranges}} = \frac{10 \text{ apples}}{x \text{ oranges}}$. Cross-multiply and divide to find that x equals 25 oranges.

#3 — Answer = B

Set up a ratio: $\frac{3 \text{ girls}}{2 \text{ boys}} = \frac{x \text{ girls}}{30 \text{ students}}$. The twist is that the units don't match. You need to adjust the ratio so that the units are consistent. Add the 2 boys and 3 girls to find that there are 3 girls for every 5 students. This is a common fix when the units don't match up — add the two parts to get a whole. The new ratio should be: $\frac{3 \text{ girls}}{5 \text{ students}} = \frac{x \text{ girls}}{30 \text{ students}}$. Cross-multiply and divide to find that x equals 18.

#4 — Answer = 147

Here's one way to set up the ratios:
$$\frac{1 \text{ phone}}{34 \text{ mg}} = \frac{x \text{ phones}}{5 \text{ grams}} \cdot \frac{1 \text{ gram}}{1,000 \text{ mg}}$$
Multiply along the tops to get: $\frac{1}{34} = \frac{x}{5,000}$

Cross-multiply and divide to get x equals 147.06, so the maximum number of phones is 147.

#5 — Answer = 9

The twist is that there is information in the chart that you won't need to use, which is very rare on the SAT. Focusing on the units will help you figure out what matters: $\dfrac{x \text{ days}}{1 \text{ trip}} = \dfrac{1 \text{ day}}{6 \text{ hours}} \cdot \dfrac{1 \text{ hour}}{45 \text{ miles}} \cdot \dfrac{2{,}416 \text{ miles}}{1 \text{ trip}}$. Multiply along the fractions to find the proportion: $\dfrac{x}{1} = \dfrac{2{,}416}{270}$. Divide to get 8.95 days, which rounds up to 9.

#6 — Answer = 1.47

The Dodgers are the first place team because they have the most wins (45 home + 49 away = 94 total). The D-backs are the last place team because they have the fewest wins (33 home + 31 away = 64 total). The question wants the ratio of the first place team to the last place team, so the fraction is $\dfrac{94}{64}$, which is 1.47 as a decimal.

#7 — Answer = 25

"Same rate" means you need a ratio. Since you're only asked about home games, focus only on the first two columns. The total number of home games is 81 (45 wins + 36 losses). The ratio should compare the win rate for those 81 games to the win rate for the 45 games described in the question: $\dfrac{45 \text{ wins}}{81 \text{ games}} = \dfrac{x \text{ wins}}{45 \text{ games}}$. Cross-multiply and divide to find that x is equal to 25 wins.

#8 — Answer = B

This is a made up stat, so just follow instructions. Create a ratio for each team: $\dfrac{\text{wins at home}}{\text{wins away}}$. The question wants the team with a ratio that is closest to 1. The Dodgers' ratio is 0.92. The Giants' is 1.05. The Padres' is 1.66. The D-backs' is 1.06. The Giants' ratio is closest to 1.

#9 — Answer = 110

They've twisted the standard Ratios question so that it's hard to know what's going on. There are two key ideas that pop off the page that help us know that we need to use ratios. One is that they're clearly asking us to compare two types of values — dollars and months. The other is that the increase is <u>constant</u>, which tells us that we can set our two fractions equal to each other. Just be careful that you capture the <u>change</u> in the dollar amount by subtracting: $2{,}056 - 1{,}000 = 1{,}056$. Your ratios should be: $\dfrac{\$c}{5 \text{ months}} = \dfrac{\$1{,}056}{4 \text{ years}} \cdot \dfrac{1 \text{ year}}{12 \text{ months}}$. Simplify the ratios to: $\dfrac{c}{5} = \dfrac{1{,}056}{48}$. Cross-multiply and divide to find c is 110.

#10 — Answer = 30

It doesn't matter that one of the ratios includes a fraction within a fraction. Just turn it into a decimal: $\dfrac{2.6 \text{ acres}}{2 \text{ years}} = \dfrac{39 \text{ acres}}{x \text{ years}}$. Cross-multiply and divide to get that x is equal to 30 years.

#11 — Answer = 9324

Set up the ratios: $\dfrac{18 \text{ feet}}{13.9 \text{ sec}} = \dfrac{x \text{ feet}}{2 \text{ hours}} \cdot \dfrac{1 \text{ hour}}{60 \text{ min}} \cdot \dfrac{1 \text{ min}}{60 \text{ sec}}$. Simplify to $\dfrac{18}{13.9} = \dfrac{x}{7{,}200}$. Cross-multiply and divide to get 9,323.7, which rounds to 9,324.

#12 — Answer = A

Set up the ratios: $\dfrac{1 \text{ snark}}{14.1 \text{ ounces}} = \dfrac{7 \text{ snarks}}{1 \text{ blerg}} \cdot \dfrac{30 \text{ blergs}}{x \text{ pounds}} \cdot \dfrac{1 \text{ pound}}{16 \text{ ounces}}$. Simplify to $\dfrac{1}{14.1} = \dfrac{210}{16x}$. Cross-multiply and divide to get that x is equal to 185.0625.

#13 — Answer = D

The twist here is that only 85 percent of the tickets are sold. You're probably better off not using ratios. Take 85% of 1,200 to find the number of tickets sold, which is 1,020. Divide $24,000 by 1,020 to find the cost per ticket, which is approximately $23.53. If you want to use ratios, you can incorporate the 85%, but you'll have to be clever: $\dfrac{\$x}{\text{ticket sold}} = \dfrac{\$24{,}000}{1{,}200 \text{ tickets available}} \cdot \dfrac{100 \text{ tickets available}}{85 \text{ tickets sold}}$

#14 — Answer = 19.2

Set up the ratios:

$$\frac{x \text{ acres}}{72 \text{ bags}} = \frac{1\frac{1}{3} \text{ acres}}{1 \text{ field}} \cdot \frac{\frac{1}{5} \text{ field}}{1 \text{ bag}}$$

The twist is that you have fractions in fractions. Luckily, both fractions are over 1, so you can just drop the denominators. Convert the mixed number to $\frac{4}{3}$ to make things easier. Multiply and divide to get 19.2 acres.

#15 — Answer = 7.7

Set up the ratios:
$$\frac{4 \text{ miles}}{14 \text{ min}} = \frac{x \text{ meters}}{1 \text{ sec}} \cdot \frac{1 \text{ mile}}{1,609 \text{ meters}} \cdot \frac{60 \text{ sec}}{1 \text{ min}}$$
Simplify to $\frac{4}{14} = \frac{60x}{1,609}$. Cross-multiply and divide to get x equal to 7.6619, which rounds to 7.7.

Percentages lesson

The Basics

Remember that decimals and percentages are really the same thing. To convert a percentage to a decimal, you move the decimal point two spaces to the left:

$$12\% = 0.12$$
$$112\% = 1.12$$
$$1.2\% = 0.012$$

The first four of these short questions are probably pretty easy, but you might have been stumped by the last two. We'll use the **OPEN** formula at the bottom of the page to solve all of these questions too:

What is 12% of 275?

$$(O)(P) = N$$

$$(275)(0.12) = N$$

$$33 = N$$

What is 4% of 340?

$$(O)(P) = N$$

$$(340)(0.04) = N$$

$$13.6 = N$$

What is 200% of 68?

$$(O)(P) = N$$

$$(68)(2.00) = N$$

$$136 = N$$

What is 1.9% of 320?

$$(O)(P) = N$$

$$(320)(0.019) = N$$

$$6.08 = N$$

42 is what percent of 175?

$$(O)(P) = N$$

$$(175)(P) = 42$$

$$P = \frac{42}{175}$$

$$P = 0.24 = 24\%$$

63.84 is 76% of what number?

$$(O)(P) = N$$

$$(O)(0.76) = 63.84$$

$$O = \frac{63.84}{0.76}$$

$$O = 84$$

It's important to be able to convert quickly between percentages and decimals. Be careful that you don't confuse 40% and 4%. They should be written as 0.4 and 0.04, respectively. For the second to last question, remembering that decimals and percentages blend together was important. Otherwise, we might have thought that the answer was 0.24%. Just think about it — could 42 be 0.24% of 175? No way! 0.24% is a very, very small part of a number, so 42 is too big. We need to convert our decimal back to a percentage, and 24% makes much more sense.

The SAT really likes to twist Percentages questions so that you're dividing instead of multiplying, just like in the last two examples above. The **OPEN** formula is just one way to prevent the common mistake of multiplying when you're supposed to divide. Another way to prevent it is to reread the question once you have your answer. If you had multiplied 63.84 and 0.76, you'd have gotten 48.5. Does it make sense for 63.84 to be 76% of 48.5? No! The question suggests that we should get a number bigger than 63.84, not smaller. This method of checking your answer is even easier when you have a story.

Example 1

In this case, it's easy to see how the story fits into the OPEN formula. We're looking for the original number of trees in the grove. And don't forget to write 21.4% as a decimal.

$$(O)(P) = N$$

$$(O)(0.214) = 199$$

$$O = \frac{199}{0.214}$$

$$O = 929.9 \approx 930$$

Rounding will get you an answer of 930. Notice that our answer makes sense with the story. Only 21.4% of the trees are infected, so we'd expect 199 to be considerably smaller than our answer, which is supposed to be all of the trees in the grove. If we had multiplied instead, we would have gotten an answer of approximately 43, which wouldn't make sense — if 199 trees in the grove are infected, how could there

be only 43 total trees in the grove? Most people are too lazy to check whether their Percentages answers make sense with the question, especially because the wrong answer choices will almost always include the common mistakes. Don't be lazy and you could save yourself 10 points!

Percentages — The Basics

You can think of percentages as decimals. Move the decimal point two places to the left to turn a percentage into a decimal. Be careful:
- 80% would be 0.8
- 8% would be 0.08
- 1.8% would be 0.018
- 800% would be 8.0

When you convert percentage questions into equations, be careful with variables that represent the percentage. Divide the variable by 100, or double check if you've solved for the variable in its percentage form or decimal form.

Use the OPEN formula so you don't get tricked by the SAT's percentage questions:

<u>O</u>riginal times <u>P</u>ercentage <u>E</u>quals <u>N</u>ew

$$(O)(P) = N$$

The Twists

Example 2

Some people might use the percent/increase formula here, and that's totally fine:

$$\% \text{ inc/dec} = \frac{\text{new} - \text{old}}{\text{old}} \times 100$$

But we're going to try the **OPEN** formula instead:

$$(O)(P) = N$$

$$(916)(P) = 958$$

$$P = \frac{958}{916}$$

$$P = 1.046 = 104.6\%$$

That's weird. How could we have 104.6%? That seems like a lot. Actually, this is a much better way to think about percentages than you're used to from school. You're used to taking a percentage and then adding or subtracting it from your original amount. Think about how you calculate the tip at a restaurant — you probably take 20% and then add it to the bill.

$$\$18 \text{ bill} \times 20\% \text{ tip}$$

$$18 \times 0.20 = 3.60$$

$$\text{total} = \$18 + \$3.60 = \$21.60$$

A more efficient way to do this is to just multiply the bill by 1.2, which is 120%. In other words, you're paying 100% of the bill, plus an additional 20%.

$$\$18 \times 1.20 = \$21.60 \text{ bill and tip}$$

Something similar is happening with these babies. This year, there were 104.6% of the babies as last year. In other words, there were 100% of the babies as last year, plus an additional 4.6% of last year's babies. **Since the question is asking about the increase, the answer is D.**

If you can get comfortable with this way of thinking, Percentages will be easy on the SAT and in life in general. Whenever you're dealing with percent change, you can think of the percentage as a change from 100%. You can adjust the **OPEN** formula to reflect that:

$$(O)(1 \pm P) = N$$

The 1 represents 100% of the original, and you'd choose plus or minus depending on whether you were calculating a percent increase or decrease.

$$(916)(1 + P) = 958$$

$$1 + P = \frac{958}{916} = 1.04585$$

$$P = 0.04585 \approx 4.6\%$$

Example 3

The hardest part about percent increase/decrease is figuring out which thing is the "original" and which is the "new". If you switch them, you'll get the wrong answer. But in this case, I think it's pretty clear — Todd is the original because Kim has 30% more than he does. In other words, Kim's fries are based on Todd's. So we could plug all of this information into the modified **OPEN** formula:

$$(O)(1 \pm P) = N$$

$$(T)(1 + 0.30) = K$$

$$T(1.3) = 65$$

$$T = \frac{65}{1.3}$$

$$T = 50$$

And that makes sense. We know that Kim is supposed to have more fries than Todd. **So Choice C is the correct answer.**

But if we had accidentally switched the original and new values, we should have been able to catch our mistake. Here's what would have happened:

$$(65)(1.3) = T$$

$$84.5 = T$$

That's close enough to Choice D that you might pick it. But if you take a second to pause and think about the story, you should catch your mistake. The question says Kim should have 30% more fries than Todd, but that wouldn't make sense if Todd had 85 fries and Kim only had 65. Taking 10 seconds to check your answer against the story could save you 10 points!

Another common mistake occurs when you take 30% of Kim's fries and then subtract:

$$65 \times 0.30 = 19.5$$

$$65 - 19.5 = 45.5$$

This is very similar to the example above about paying a bill in a restaurant. Your instinct is to do percentages in two steps, so this mistake feels very natural. The problem is that you're treating Kim's fries like they're the original amount. You might be thinking, "why does it matter? Isn't Todd plus 30% the same as Kim minus 30%?" Unfortunately, no. And until you realize this, you'll continue to struggle on Percentages questions. Let's look at it this way:

You go to a store to buy a new phone. The phone costs $100. You have a coupon for a 10% discount. How much do you pay after the discount? You can probably do the math in your head — $90 for the phone. But let's say that there's a 10% tax on the discounted price. How much do you pay in total after the tax is added to the $90?

Some people think it's back to $100. After all, you took 10% off with the coupon and added 10% back on with the tax. Seems like it all evens out.

Wrong! You would actually pay $99 for the phone. How is that possible? Where did the extra dollar go?

$100	original cost of phone
−$10	10% discount ($100 \times 0.10 = 10$)
$90	new price/original
+$9	10% tax ($90 \times 0.10 = 9$)
$99	final cost

As you can see, the value of 10% changes because the base amount that we're taking 10% of also changes. Percentages are dependent on the original amount. So to bring it back to the Example, 30% of Todd's fries is not the same as 30% of Kim's fries. You need to accept this or you'll keep making mistakes on Percentages questions!

Answers: Percentages

#1 — Answer = B
It's easy to use the OPEN formula here because they're directly asking you for the original amount. And since it's a tax, you can test out your new understanding of percentages. You're paying 107% of the fee. $(O)(1 + 0.07) = 63.13$. Solve and you'll get 59 exactly. You could also Guess & Check. The answer choices represent the original cost of the service before the fee. Multiply each answer choice by 1.07 to find the cost after the 7% fee is added. ($1.07 \times 59.00 = 63.13$)

#2 — Answer = B
Match the fruit to the correct percentage. 6% of the 129 watermelons (129×0.06) is 7.74, or 8 watermelons left. 3% of the 369 apples (369×0.03) is 11.07, or 11 apples. Add them together to get 19 pieces of fruit.

#3 — Answer = B
This is a great example of how the modified OPEN formula can save you points. Since Mars is based on Earth, Earth is the original and Mars is the new. And since it's "less than", you'll use subtraction: $(E)(1 - P) = M$. Putting in the numbers, you'll see that the percentage actually changes into something you might not expect: $(160)(0.40) = M$. That's a very common twist because the SAT knows that percent decrease is a little counterintuitive. Multiply 160 by 0.40 to get that a person's weight on Mars is 64 pounds. Watch out for this twist. It helps to think

about it in terms that you're more familiar with. If a store offers a "10% off" sale, you don't pay 10% of what an item costs. You pay 90% of what it costs.

#4 — Answer = D

This is more like a Read the Chart question. Focus on the denominator first. They're only asking about cars sold in 2010, so the denominator is 365. The numerator is red cars sold in 2010, which is 197. Divide 197 by 365 to get 0.54, which is 54%. You can also use the OPEN formula, where the original number of cars is 365 and the new is just the 197 red ones.

#5 — Answer = A

A perfect opportunity to use the modified OPEN formula: $(168)(1 - P) = 128$. Solving for P gets you 24%. But be careful. If you use the OPEN formula without the 1, you'll get that P is 76%, which is an answer. That's because, like with #3, the number of green cars in 2015 is 76% of the number in 2010, but that's a decrease of 24%. Just remember that when they talk about percent decrease, you're going to want to get that negative into the formula so you don't fall for the trap.

Statistics lesson

The Basics

You <u>must</u> memorize these words. Here are some helpful tricks to remember them:

The **mean** is the average, but it's also sometimes called the "arithmetic mean". It's <u>mean</u> that so many words <u>mean</u> average.

The **median** is the middle number, but the set has to be arranged in order. If you're just learning to drive, you probably know that the <u>median</u> is the barrier in the <u>middle</u> of the road.

The **mode** is the most common number. Both mode and most start with <u>mo-</u>.

The **range** is the biggest number minus the smallest number. A singer's range is the highest note she can sing to the lowest note she can sing.

You will never need to calculate **standard deviation** on the SAT, but you still need to know what it is. Focus on the word "deviation". If you deviate from a path, you wander off of it. Essentially, standard deviation is a measurement of how far the data points wander from the path. The more they wander, the greater the standard deviation. Let's look at the dot plots in Example 1 to see standard deviation in action.

Example 1

Compare the two test results. The grades on the History test are all over the place. They wander a lot. But the grades on the Chemistry test bunch together. It looks like they're following the same path.

Since the History test grades deviate more from the middle, this dot plot shows a greater standard deviation. The grades on the Chemistry test have a low standard deviation. The SAT will only ever ask you to compare two sets of values. One will clearly deviate more than the other.

Statistics — The Basics

Know the definitions of mean, median, mode, range, and standard deviation. You will be asked to compare values and understand the difference between these terms.

Memorize the average formula:

$$\text{average} = \frac{\text{sum of the numbers}}{\text{how many numbers}}$$

The Twists

Example 2

The twist is almost always that they list the data values by frequency. For some reason, a lot of students struggle to make sense of this. This Example presents the data as a **histogram**. Another twist is that the values of the rolls are very similar to the frequencies, so it's hard to even know what you're looking at. Let's break it down.

The first bar says that the number 1 was rolled 4 times total. The second bar says that the number 2 was rolled 3 times total. The number 3 wasn't rolled at all. The number 4 was rolled once. Both 5 and 6 were rolled twice each.

So the x-axis is just listing all of the possible rolls on a 6-sided die. The y-axis is telling us how many times each value came up. The mode will be the most common number, which means we need to find the tallest bar. **In this case, the mode is 1.**

The median is the middle number, but we need to take into account that there are multiples of each roll. We could just create a list with four 1s, three 2s, etc:

$$\{1,1,1,1,2,2,2,4,5,5,6,6\}$$

Cross off from each end until you get to the middle number:

$$\{\cancel{1},\cancel{1},\cancel{1},\cancel{1},\cancel{2},2,2,\cancel{4},\cancel{5},\cancel{5},\cancel{6},\cancel{6}\}$$

When we eliminate five numbers from each side, we're left with two 2s. Normally, we'd need to take the average when there are two middle numbers, but **since they're the same, we know that the median is 2.** If we're careful, we could have found the median by crossing off on the graph directly. Just remember that you need to cross off 1 four times, and so on:

Values of 12 Die Rolls

The mean is the most annoying of the three to find. Again, we can't forget that there are four 1s. You should fill out the average formula like this:

$$average = \frac{\text{sum of the numbers}}{\text{how many numbers}}$$

$$average = \frac{4(1) + 3(2) + 1(4) + 2(5) + 2(6)}{12}$$

We're still adding the numbers, but we're multiplying as well. You can read the numerator like this: there are four 1s, three 2s, (we left out the 3s because there are none), one 4, two 5s, and two 6s. We divide by 12 because there were 12 rolls. Simplify:

$$average = \frac{4 + 6 + 4 + 10 + 12}{12}$$

$$average = \frac{36}{12} = 3$$

The mean is 3. This may seem strange since 3 wasn't ever rolled, but it doesn't matter. The mean is the average, which is a calculation, not an actual data point.

Example 3

Histograms come up on the SAT once in a while, but **frequency charts** are very common. They give the same information. In this case, the left column corresponds to the x-axis on our histogram — it lists our values. The right column corresponds to the y-axis on the histogram — it gives the frequency, or how many times each age should be counted.

The mode is still easy to find. It's the value with the highest frequency, so **the mode is 30.**

The median requires careful attention. We can "cross off" values like we did on the histogram, but it's a little harder since we don't have a graph. If we add up all the frequencies, we'll see that there are 15 players on the team. That means the median will be the 8th number in the set, no matter which way you count. Count from both ends just to be safe:

Ages of Softball Team Members

Age	Frequency	
19	1	1
23	1	2
25	2	3, 4
28	1	5
29	2	6, 7
30	4	5, 6, 7, **8**
32	1	4
33	1	3
35	1	2
48	1	1

Notice that we're counting Age 25 twice. We need to make sure we don't forget about the frequency of the values. **So the eighth number and the median are 30.**

We should calculate the average the same we did before, multiplying the value by the frequency:

$$avg = \frac{1(19) + 1(23) + 2(25) + 1(28) + 2(29) + 4(30) + 1(32) + 1(33) + 1(35) + 1(48)}{15}$$

Simplify:

$$avg = \frac{19 + 23 + 50 + 28 + 58 + 120 + 32 + 33 + 35 + 48}{15}$$

$$avg = \frac{446}{15}$$

$$avg = 29.7\overline{33}$$

So the average is approximately 29.73.

Statistics — The Twists

The most common twist is that you'll be given the list of data in a frequency chart or histogram. Don't forget that the frequency of each value needs to be taken into account when you find the median and mean. Stay organized, and don't do all the steps in your calculator. Writing them down will help you catch mistakes.

Answers: Basic Statistics

#1 — Answer = 37

This is just a simple list of values, but they're not in order. It's easier to find the median if they're organized from least to greatest: {25, 32, 36, 37, 41, 48, 48}. The middle number is 37.

#2 — Answer = D

The SAT is trying to slow you down. You don't actually need to calculate all of these values if you know your Statistics terms. The number 23 is so far away from the rest of the numbers that removing it won't affect the median, mean, or mode significantly. The range, however, changes a lot. It goes from 23 days to 6 days.

#3 — Answer = A

Standard deviation measures how spread out the data values are. East Springfield has an even spread, but West Springfield bunches around 8 hours of sleep. In other words, East Springfield has greater deviation from the "path" than West Springfield.

#4 — Answer = 3.6

Don't forget to take the frequencies into account. Your average formula should be:

$$avg = \frac{47(4) + 8(3) + 2(2) + 0(1) + 3(0)}{60}$$. That

simplifies to $\frac{216}{60}$, which is 3.6.

#5 — Answer = 1

Since each group has 60 members, the median will be the average of the 30th and 31st numbers. You can count from either direction. The median of Group A is 3, and the median of Group C is 2. The difference is 1.

#6 — Answer = A

Box plots are annoying. They tell you 5 things. The easiest is that the lines outside the box mark the (1) minimum and (2) maximum of the set. In this case, that doesn't really help us. The line inside the box is (3) the median of the set, which would eliminate choices B and C, since the median of Group D is 3. The ends of the box tell us (4) the first quartile and (5) the third quartile.

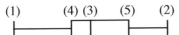

Basically, the quartiles are like the medians of the median. The regular median divides a set into two halves. The quartiles are the medians of each of the two halves. In this case, the first quartile would be the average of the 15th and 16th numbers, and the third quartile would be the average of the 45th and 46th numbers. (We take the average because the halves contain an even number of numbers.) Both the 15th and 16th numbers (starting from 0) would be in the 1 star column for Group D, so the first quartile is 1, which matches with Choice A. Luckily, box plots do not appear on the SAT very often.

#7 — Answer = B

Be careful! Even though the x-axis of the chart includes values from 0 to 60, the range is only the values in the set. So the maximum is at 50, and the minimum is at 10. The range is the difference between these: $50 - 10 = 40$.

#8 — Answer = B

If you picked Choice A, you fell for the oldest trick in the SAT book — hard questions shouldn't be easy! Is it really going to be the case that solving this question comes down to seeing that $6 = 6$? No way! There's clearly something more complicated going on here. In fact, the story tells us that Roger surveyed 125 patients in 2010, but he surveyed 250 patients in 2011. So even though 6 people responded with a 10-minute wait time in each year, those 6 people represent different proportions of the survey. In 2010, you could represent the 10-minute wait times as $\frac{6}{125}$. In 2011, it would be $\frac{6}{250}$. You could get the fractions to have the same denominator to compare them more easily. You'd see that twice as many people

responded with a 10-minute wait time in 2010: $\frac{6}{125} = \frac{12}{250}$. That means that Choice B is the answer. We'd expect that a larger portion of the 2,000 patients had 10-minute wait times in 2010 because those 6 people represent a larger portion of the 125 person sample. Always pay attention to where you are in the test — at the least, you could probably eliminate Choice A and take a better guess if you are aware that it's too easy to be correct on a hard question.

#9 — Answer = B

Unfortunately, all of the choices show a median of 30, so that doesn't help. Choice A is wrong because the maximum and minimum are incorrect. Choice B is correct because the first quartile occurs at 25 (average of the 31st and 32nd numbers) and the third quartile occurs at 35 (average of the 94th and 95th numbers). See #6 for more details on box plots.

Mystery Averages

Example 4

Mystery averages aren't particularly hard, but students have trouble because there's a lot of information. You'll almost always have to do the average formula twice. Start with the set where you have all the values:

$$\text{Meg's avg} = \frac{9.8 + 10.4 + 10.1 + 9.5}{4}$$

$$\text{Meg's avg} = \frac{39.8}{4} = 9.95$$

The question says that Meg's average is 0.9 pounds greater than AJ's:

$$9.95 - 0.9 = 9.05$$

Now build another average equation for AJ's cats with the data we have:

$$9.05 = \frac{x + 8.7 + 9.3 + 9.0}{4}$$

Multiply both sides by 4 to eliminate the fraction:

$$36.2 = x + 8.7 + 9.3 + 9.0$$

Add everything up, then subtract to get x by itself:

$$36.2 = x + 27$$

$$36.2 - 27 = x$$

$$9.2 = x$$

AJ's mystery cat weighs 9.2 pounds.

Example 5

This one is twisted because we don't have the specific values for Josephine's test scores. But here's a little trick: they don't matter. Let's see why by using our average formula:

$$\text{average} = \frac{\text{sum of the numbers}}{\text{how many numbers}}$$

We know two of these pieces:

$$86 = \frac{\text{sum of the numbers}}{5}$$

The question tells us that Josephine's average on 5 tests is 86. Multiply by 5 to find the sum:

$$430 = \text{sum of the numbers}$$

You can think of this as the total points that Josephine earned on all the tests combined. As we said earlier, Mystery Averages usually involve two average formulas, so let's set it up again, but this time we need to factor in a 6th exam:

$$88 \le \frac{430 + x}{6}$$

So the 88 is the new average that Josephine needs to get. The 6 tells us that we're now finding the average of 6 exams. She still has the same 430 points that she earned on the last 5 exams, but we're adding x points on the 6th. We need to find x, which is her score on the 6th exam.

Multiply by 6 to eliminate the fraction:

$$528 \le 430 + x$$

Subtract to find x:

$$528 - 430 \le x$$

$$98 \le x$$

So Josephine needs a 98% on her sixth exam to bring up her average.

Mystery Averages — Summary

If you need to find a missing value, you'll probably need to use the average formula twice. It's okay if you feel like you're stumbling through this process. Just set up the formula and plug in the numbers that you know. You only need 2 of the 3 values to keep moving through the question.

There might also be circumstances where you need to make up some values. Sometimes there are rules to follow, but other times you can make up whatever numbers you want by Arithmetizing. (HINT: this will help on the Exercise!)

Answers: Mystery Averages

#1 — Answer = 9.3
Start by finding the total number of strikeouts for the first 4 games. Use the average formula to stay organized. You'll multiply the average by the number of games (8 x 4) to find the sum of the strikeouts (32). Do the same thing for the next 2 games. Multiply the average by the number of games (12 x 2) to find the sum of the strikeouts in those 2 games (24). Now find the average for the 6 games by adding the two sums (32 + 24) and dividing them by 6 (56 ÷ 6) to get an average of 9.3 strikeouts per game.

#2 — Answer = 24
This is a very twisted question. Start with the basics. You can find the sum of the first 3 cards using the average formula: $9 = \frac{\text{sum}}{3}$. The sum of the first 3 cards is 27. Use a new average formula to account for

all 6 players: $9 = \dfrac{27 + x + y + z}{6}$. In order for Hans's number to be as high as possible, the other players should have numbers as low as possible. And remember that no two players can write the same number. The formula should be: $9 = \dfrac{27 + 1 + 2 + z}{6}$. Solve to find that Hans's card is 24.

#3 — Answer = A

Arithmetize. Let $x = 1$. The average of 1 and 7 would make $a = 4$. The average of 4 and 3 would make $b = 3.5$. The average of 1 and 8 would make $c = 4.5$. The average of 4, 3.5 and 4.5 is 4. Plug 1 in for x in all the choices. Only Choice A gives you 4. If you do this algebraically, there's a high chance that you get it wrong and pick Choice C, so use the strategies.

Surveys

Example 6

Survey questions are barely math. They involve a lot of reading, and one word can make all the difference, so pay attention.

This question requires deep understanding of the difference between mean and median. Both are measures of the "center" of the data, but they are different definitions of the center. Why would the mean value ($10,000) be less than the median value ($16,000)? Let's look at another hypothetical situation to better understand the difference between mean and median.

Imagine a seesaw:

The seesaw has a midpoint. The triangle represents the hinge, or fulcrum, that lets the seesaw tilt. The triangle is the median. It's a fixed midpoint because both sides have the same length of seesaw. Remember that the median is the middle number, so if there are 5 numbers on one side of the median, there have to be 5 numbers on the other side. In seesaw-terms, if there are 5 feet of seesaw on the left side, there has to be 5 feet of seesaw on the right side.

But let's visualize the midpoint a different way. The mean is represented by a ball that we place in the middle when we start. If we have two people on the seesaw who are about the same weight, then the seesaw will be balanced. It won't want to tilt in either direction.

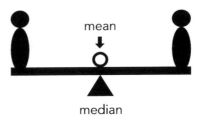

When this happens, the mean/average will be pretty close to the middle. The ball won't roll toward either side. But what if a fat person sat on one side?

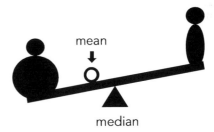

The median is still fixed in the middle of the seesaw because we haven't changed the length of either side. But he have changed the weight, and the ball rolls toward the fat person. In other words, the median doesn't care about the values of the data — it's the middle number no matter what the numbers are. But the mean <u>does</u> care about the values — it gets pulled toward the side that has the more extreme values.

Let's replace our people with the values from the Example. We'll also say that the dealership has 100 cars on the lot, just so we can visualize it better.

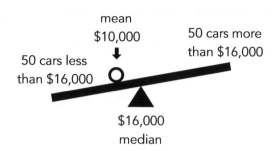

mean
$10,000

50 cars more
than $16,000

50 cars less
than $16,000

$16,000
median

There's still the same length of seesaw on both sides of the hinge. The median is the middle, so the "length" of the set is the same on each side, which is why there are 50 cars on each side.

But the mean is $10,000, which is closer to the "less than $16,000" side. The principle is the same as when we were using fat and skinny people — the ball is rolling toward the side that has more extreme values. In other words, the 50 cars on the left cost a lot less than $16,000, but the 50 cars on the right cost only a little more than $16,000.

To sum up, the median tells us that the dealership has 50 cars that cost less than $16,000 and 50 cars that cost more than $16,000. But the mean tells us that the 50 cars that are less than $16,000 are <u>way less</u> than $16,000. The side with smaller values actually has a greater "weight", which pulls the mean down.

This matches with Choice C, which is the correct answer. If you're still a little confused, that's okay. This is a really hard question and concept.

Example 7

This question is a little easier because it's less about numbers and more about words. We need to be careful of strong words that take the survey's conclusion too far. Let's go choice-by-choice:

A) The word "exactly" is a problem. The survey found that 68% prefer chocolate, but it wasn't a survey of the entire town. Only 250 people got asked. It <u>might</u> be the case that 68% of the 10,000 residents also prefer chocolate, but is it really that hard to imagine 67% or 70% of them preferring chocolate? A survey gives us an

estimate, but it's not exact. <u>In general, the more people you ask (the greater the sample size), the more accurate the result (the lower the margin of error).</u>

B) This choice is tempting, but "all" is a strong word. Go back to the survey. They didn't ask every type of person. They only asked "people over the age of 30". That means that the results of the survey only apply to people over the age of 30. Maybe kids really like vanilla. We just don't know, so we can't jump to conclusions about what everybody in the town would think. <u>In general, a survey should ask a group of people that represents the overall makeup of the town (a random sample of the residents).</u> When a survey is limited, we have to also limit our conclusions.

C) This choice seems okay. "Approximately" is a good word because it leaves some room on either side in case our survey is slightly off. And the conclusion is limited to residents over the age of 30, just like the survey. **Let's keep this choice.**

D) This is identical to Choice C, except it says that 68% like ice cream. That's not what our survey asked. Maybe some of the people who said they prefer chocolate don't actually like ice cream. They might just pick chocolate if they were forced to eat ice cream. If given the choice, they might not eat either flavor. Just like with Choice B, we can't jump to conclusions that go beyond the scope of the survey. We need to stick to what was asked.

Choice C is the correct answer because it basically just restates the survey. We don't jump to any conclusions, and we leave some wiggle room in case the survey is a little off.

Read carefully. Eliminate answer choices that are too strong. Don't jump to conclusions that aren't supported by the survey.

The **sample size** is the number of people who were surveyed. The larger the sample size, the more accurate the survey.

Ideally, a survey should ask a **random sample** of the population that represents the overall population.

Bias is bad. It means the survey might be inaccurate because it did not ask a random sample. For example, if you asked a group of old people if they have a smartphone, you'd probably get a very different result than if you asked a random sample of the population. For various reasons, old people are probably less likely to have a smartphone than the average person, so the results of the survey would be biased.

Biased results have a high **margin of error**, which is a measurement of the accuracy of a survey or poll. A larger sample size means a lower margin of error.

Answers: Surveys

#1 — Answer = C
Go through the choices. Choice A is not necessarily true. It's possible that Parkville has a higher income because only a few residents have much higher incomes than everyone else, which would pull up the mean. Choice B is not necessarily true because everyone in Floraltown could earn $55,000 and everyone in Parkville could earn $60,000. Choice C must be true because the sample size for Floraltown was less than the sample size for Parkville. In general, the greater the sample size, the smaller the margin of error.

#2 — Answer = C
Look for wrong answers. Choice B is definitely wrong because the population size would not affect the accuracy of the survey. Choice D is tempting. The distance probably affects the result of the survey, but

it does not affect its accuracy. Choice A is second best because sample size does usually affect the accuracy of a survey. But 150 people seems like a good number. More importantly, the time the survey was given is a big problem. A Tuesday morning is a very odd time if you're looking to get a sense of what a random sample of your customers think. Most people would be at work during that time. The Tuesday morning shoppers might have strange schedules that would allow them to travel to a different location more easily. In general, you want a survey to sample a group of people who represent the overall population.

#3 — Answer = D
This survey is biased because it is only asking people who work at the factory. It's understandable that they would oppose taxing the factory. It might cost them their jobs. And since the survey only asked factory workers, you can't draw conclusions about what the entire city might think. People who don't work at the factory might support the tax.

Essential Algebra lesson

The Basics
In general, when solving for x, work your way toward the variable—from the outside in.

Example 1

Subtract 15 from both sides:

$$
\begin{array}{rr}
6x + 15 = & 27 \\
- 15 & - 15 \\
\hline
6x = & 12
\end{array}
$$

Divide both sides by 6:

$$\frac{6x}{6} = \frac{12}{6}$$

$$x = 2$$

That's not the answer! The SAT almost always wants something else, so go back to the question. In this case, they want the value of 2x + 5, so plug our value for x back in:

$$2x + 5 = 2(2) + 5$$
$$= 4 + 5$$
$$= 9$$

The correct answer is 9. If you're clever with algebra, you might notice that there's a shortcut. A lot of SAT algebra questions have one. If we divide our original equation by 3, we get straight to the answer:

$$\frac{6x + 15 = 27}{3}$$

$$2x + 5 = 9$$

It's not necessary to use these shortcuts, but try to look for them. You'll get better at finding them, and they might help a lot on twisted questions.

Example 2

Divide both sides by 2:

$$\frac{2a}{2} = \frac{14}{2}$$

$$a = 7$$

Plug back into the expression they want:

$$4a + 8 = 4(7) + 8$$
$$= 28 + 8$$
$$= 36$$

The answer is 36. But once again, there's a shortcut:

$$2(2a = 14)$$

$$4a = 28$$

$$4a + 8 = (28) + 8$$
$$= 36$$

Example 3

We could add 16 to both sides, then take the square root:

$$x^2 - 16 = 0$$
$$\underline{+ 16 \quad + 16}$$
$$x^2 \quad = \quad 16$$

$$\sqrt{x^2} = \sqrt{16}$$

$$x = 4$$

But you might also want to get in the habit of factoring when you have x^2 terms:

$$x^2 - 16 = 0$$

$$(x + 4)(x - 4) = 0$$

So technically x could be 4 or –4, but the question says x > 0, so **only +4 works.**

Essential Algebra — The Basics

Show your work.

Work toward the variable, usually by adding/subtracting first, then multiplying/dividing. But each situation is different.

Pay attention to what they're asking for. The SAT knows that you're used to being done once you've solved for x. They will try to trick you by asking for something else. This final step will be easy, but it will also be easy to miss if you're not in the habit of rechecking the question.

Look for shortcuts. You might be able to manipulate the equation to get to your answer faster.

The Twists

Example 4

The twist is that this is not an equation. Untwist it by turning the words into equations. The first one is straightforward:

$$2n + 8 = 6$$

Read it back to be sure: two times n plus 8 equals 6. That matches our original question pretty well. Now solve for n:

$$
\begin{aligned}
2n + 8 &= \quad 6 \\
-8 &\quad -8 \\
\hline
2n &= -2 \\
\frac{2n}{2} &= \frac{-2}{2} \\
n &= -1
\end{aligned}
$$

Now go back to the question. What do they want? If you skip this step, you'll pick Choice A, which is wrong. They want you to do one more thing:

$$
\begin{aligned}
4n + 20 &= 4(-1) + 20 \\
&= -4 + 20 \\
&= 16
\end{aligned}
$$

So Choice D is the correct answer.

Example 5

Combine like terms. The twist is that they're counting on you to forget how to combine variables with exponents. But don't let them make you second guess yourself! Just think about it for a second. What's x + x ?

$$x + x = 2x$$

$$(x)(x) = x^2$$

The same rules apply here. We add the coefficients, not the exponents:

$$
\begin{aligned}
2x^2 - 6x + 1 \\
+4x^2 - 3x - 8 \\
\hline
6x^2 - 9x - 7
\end{aligned}
$$

Choice A is the answer.

Essential Algebra — The Twists

This is the math section, so when they twist questions by describing math with words, you need to untwist them by creating equations. Always double check that your equation matches the text.

Know how to combine like terms. The wrong answer choices will make you second guess yourself:

$$2x^2 + 3x^2 = 5x^2$$

The exponents don't change when you're adding and subtracting.

Answers: Essential Algebra

#1 — Answer = B
Use the first values of x and y to find the value of c: $36 = c(9)$. So c = 4. Use the value of c to find the other value of y: $y = (4)(2)$. So y = 8.

#2 — Answer = C
Turn the words into an equation: $9 + 6t = 28 - 7$. The twist is that "7 less than" is hard to place. Subtraction is almost always at the end of the equation. Solve the equation to find that $t = 2$. But the question wants the value of 3t, which is 6.

#3 — Answer = A
When you add the two expressions together, the 3 and –3 cancel out, leaving just $y^2 + 2y$.

#4 — Answer = A
You do not need to solve for a or b. Divide both sides by 5 to find that $a - b = -\dfrac{8}{5}$.

#5 — Answer = A
Turn the words into an equation: $3n + 13 = 9$. Solve for n, which is $-\dfrac{4}{3}$. But the question wants the value of 6n, which is –8. You could also see that if 3n is –4, then 6n would be double that.

#6 — Answer = B

Combine like terms and the equation should simplify to: $4x + 5 = 2x - 3$. Solve for $x = -4$.

#7 — Answer = 13

When you add the equations together, you should get: $4x^2 - 6x + 15$. Add the coefficients to get 13.

#8 — Answer = 29

Turn the words into an equation: $20 - 2x = 14$. Solve and you'll get that x = 3. The question wants the value of $8x + 5$, which is $24 + 5 = 29$.

Distribution lesson

The Basics

One of the most common mistakes on the SAT is distributing incorrectly. These mistakes are unacceptable. They're incredibly easy to prevent, especially now that you know the SAT is looking to catch you making them.

Example 1

Distribute to both parts:

$$2(x + 5) + 6(x - 9) = 4x$$

$$2x + 10 + 6x - 54 = 4x$$

Combine like terms:

$$8x - 44 = 4x$$

Solve for x:

$$\begin{array}{r} 8x - 44 = 4x \\ -8x -8x \\ \hline -44 = -4x \end{array}$$

$$\frac{-44}{-4} = \frac{-4x}{-4}$$

$$11 = x$$

The correct answer is 11.

Example 2

Distribute to both parts:

$$4(x + 3) - 8$$

$$4x + 12 - 8$$

Combine like terms:

$$4x + 4$$

The correct answer is Choice B. You could also Arithmetize if you want:

Let $x = 0$

$$\begin{aligned} 4(x + 3) - 8 &= 4((0) + 3) - 8 \\ &= 4(3) - 8 \\ &= 12 - 8 \\ &= 4 \end{aligned}$$

- A) $12(0) - 8 = -8$ X
- B) $4(0) + 4 = 4$ ✓
- C) $4(0) - 5 = -5$ X
- D) $4(0) - 20 = -20$ X

Example 3

You might be tempted to factor these expressions, but notice that the answer choices are all written without parentheses. That probably means we should get rid of the parentheses, not add more. Distribute the negative to both parts of the second term:

$$(x^2 - 8) - (-5x^2 + 3)$$

$$x^2 - 8 + 5x^2 - 3$$

Combine like terms:

$$6x^2 - 11$$

The correct answer is Choice A.

The Twists

Example 4

The twist here is that they sometimes throw a lot of similar-looking variables at you. They're just trying to confuse you. If you're organized, it shouldn't matter.

Distribute the negative to all parts:

$$(2ab^2 + 5a^2 - 4a^2b) - (-2ab^2 - a^2b + 5a^2)$$

$$2ab^2 + 5a^2 - 4a^2b + 2ab^2 + a^2b - 5a^2$$

Combine like terms:

$$2ab^2 + 2ab^2 + 5a^2 - 5a^2 - 4a^2b + a^2b$$

$$4ab^2 - 3a^2b$$

Choice A is the correct answer.

Example 5

If you're confused by the wording of this question, that's okay. It's just a twist to scare you. If it looks like algebra, do algebra. You know how to clean up the left side of the equation. Distribute to all parts:

$$3x(4x - 2) - 5(4x - 2)$$

$$12x^2 - 6x - 20x + 10$$

Combine like terms, and you'll get:

$$12x^2 - 26x + 10 = ax^2 + bx + c$$

The equation and the question are both saying that the numbers in front of the variables line up with a, b, and c. Put them on top of each other to see:

$$12x^2 - 26x + 10$$
$$ax^2 + bx + c$$

All this talk about "constants" just means that:

$$a = 12$$
$$b = -26$$
$$c = 10$$

Finish the question by following the remaining instructions. What is the value of a + b ?

$$a + b = 12 + (-26)$$
$$= 12 - 26$$
$$= -14$$

The correct answer is Choice A.

Answers: Distribution

#1 — Answer = A
Distribute to all parts and you should get: $4x^2y - 12xy^2 - 3x^2y - xy^2$. Combine like terms. The x^2y terms cannot be combined with the xy^2 terms. They have different exponents, so they're not actually "like" terms.

#2 — Answer = C
Ignore the right side for now. Distribute to all parts on the left side to get: $x^2 - 5x + 2x + 10 - 5$. Combine like terms to get: $x^2 - 3x + 5$. The coefficients of the terms on the left match up with the terms on the right, so c is 5.

#3 — Answer = D

Distribute to all parts to get: $5t - 5 - 2t - 4 = 2t$. Combine like terms: $3t - 9 = 2t$. Solve for t to get that t equals 9.

#4 — Answer = 955

Distribute to all parts: $400x^2 + 1095 - 640 + 100x^2$. Combine like terms: $500x^2 + 455$. The twist is that you need to add the coefficients: $500 + 455 = 955$.

#5 — Answer = A

Distribute the negative to all parts: $-x^2 - 9 - 6 - 3x + 3x^2$. Combine like terms: $2x^2 - 3x - 15$.

#6 — Answer = 10

Distribute to all parts: $2x^2 - 8 - 3x^2 - 3x$. Combine like terms: $-x^2 - 3x - 8$. Subtract the coefficients as instructed: $-1 - (-3) - (-8) = 10$. Remember that you can't have negative answers in the Grid-ins, so if you get one, you know you've made a mistake.

Fractions lesson

The Basics

If you're confused by fractions, it's probably because you vaguely know there are rules you're supposed to follow, but you don't remember what the rules are. The SAT mostly focuses on multiplication:

> ### Example 1

The second equation tells us the value of y, so plug it into the first equation so you're only dealing with one variable:

$$\frac{x + 3}{4} = 5$$

To eliminate a fraction, multiply both sides by the denominator (bottom number).

$$\left(\frac{\cancel{4}}{1}\right)\frac{x + 3}{\cancel{4}} = 5\left(\frac{4}{1}\right)$$

$$x + 3 = 20$$

Solve for x:

$$x = 17$$

Choice C is the correct answer.

> ### Example 2

Notice that in the first example, I eliminated the 4 by multiplying by 4, but I wrote it as a fraction. That's because we are essentially eliminating fractions by multiplying by their reciprocals (reversing the top and bottom). We'll do the same thing here:

$$\frac{2}{7}t = \frac{3}{2}$$

$$\left(\frac{\cancel{7}}{\cancel{2}}\right)\frac{\cancel{2}}{\cancel{7}}t = \frac{3}{2}\left(\frac{7}{2}\right)$$

Multiplying the top by 7 eliminates the 7 on the bottom, and multiplying the bottom by 2 eliminates the 2 on the top. Now simplify the right side by multiplying across the tops and bottom of the fractions:

$$t = \frac{3 \times 7}{2 \times 2}$$

$$t = \frac{21}{4}$$

The answer is Choice A.

Fractions — The Basics

Eliminate fractions by multiplying by the reciprocal (the fraction flipped upside-down).

When you multiply fractions together, multiply across the numerators and denominators.

The Twists

> ### Example 3

The SAT loves this type of question for some reason. The easiest way to solve it is by

Arithmetizing. Pick numbers for x and y that would make the first equation true.

$$\frac{x}{y} = 3$$

Let $x = 3$ and $y = 1$

$$\frac{3}{1} = 3$$

Now put those numbers into the other expression:

$$\frac{12y}{x} = \frac{12(1)}{(3)}$$

$$= \frac{12}{3}$$

$$= 4$$

Choice B is the correct answer. You could also solve this algebraically if you know how to manipulate fractions. You can essentially flip the first equation upside down:

If $\frac{x}{y} = 3$, then $\frac{y}{x} = \frac{1}{3}$.

The second expression can be rewritten to emphasize the variables so you can substitute:

$$\frac{12y}{x} = \left(\frac{12}{1}\right)\left(\frac{y}{x}\right)$$

$$= \left(\frac{12}{1}\right)\left(\frac{1}{3}\right)$$

$$= \frac{12}{3}$$

$$= 4$$

Knowing how to flip fractions upside-down will help you on some harder questions, but Arithmetize when you can.

Example 4

Surprisingly, adding fractions is harder than multiplying them. We can add the left side no problem:

$$\frac{3}{7}x + \frac{2}{7}x$$

$$\frac{5}{7}x$$

But the right side can't be added easily because we don't have a common denominator. We can get a common denominator by multiplying, but notice that the process is different this time. Both the numerator and denominator are multiplied by the same number. This lets us change how the number looks without changing its value. Since $\frac{4}{4}$ is equal to 1, we're not actually changing the value of the term.

$$\frac{3}{8} + \frac{1}{2}$$

$$\frac{3}{8} + \frac{1}{2}\left(\frac{4}{4}\right)$$

$$\frac{3}{8} + \frac{4}{8}$$

$$\frac{7}{8}$$

Solve for x by eliminating the fraction on the left just like we did in Example 2:

$$\frac{5}{7}x = \frac{7}{8}$$

$$\left(\frac{7}{5}\right)\frac{5}{7}x = \frac{7}{8}\left(\frac{7}{5}\right)$$

$$x = \frac{49}{40}$$

Choice A is the correct answer.

Fractions — The Twists

You can Arithmetize on many Fractions questions (especially when you don't actually have to solve for x). Just make sure that the numbers you pick follow the rules/equations in the question.

When you add or subtract fractions, you <u>must</u> have a common denominator. Add or subtract the tops, but keep the bottom the same.

Multiplying the top and bottom of the fraction by the same number lets you change how a fraction looks without changing its value because you're really only multiplying by 1.

Answers: Fractions

#1 — Answer = D
Substitute 28 in for b in the first equation. Multiply to get that a is equal to 21. But that's not the answer. Plug 21 into the expression they ask for:
$2(21) + 1 = 43$.

#2 — Answer = 10
Substitute 2 in for x. Solve for c by subtracting 2 from both sides, then multiplying both sides by –5.

#3 — Answer = A
Multiply the second equation by 2 to solve for $y = 12$. Substitute 12 in for y in the first equation. Solve for $x = -3$. Multiply x and y as instructed to get –36.

#4 — Answer = A
Even though this fraction has variables, you can still multiply both sides by the denominator to eliminate it. If you multiply both sides by $a + 4$, you'll get $a + 2 = 6(a + 4)$. Distribute, then get all the variables on the same side. You should solve for a equals $-\dfrac{22}{5}$.

#5 — Answer = B
Cross-multiply to get: $9x = 3x + 36$. Solve to find that $x = 6$. But the question wants the value of $\dfrac{x}{3}$, so the answer is 2.

#6 — Answer = D
Arithmetize. Let x =1 and y = 2. Substitute those values into the second expression to get $\dfrac{32}{1}$.

#7 — Answer = 27/8
Eliminate the fraction by multiplying both sides by $\dfrac{9}{4}$, the reciprocal of $\dfrac{4}{9}$. You'll get that h is equal to $\dfrac{27}{8}$.

Inequalities lesson

The Basics
Inequalities tend to make people forget everything they know about algebra. But they shouldn't! All of the same rules apply, except the equals sign is replaced with a less than or greater than sign.

Example 1

Whenever possible, Guess & Check. It's absolutely the easiest way if you have the option:

$$2(-1) + 1 \leq 5(-1) - 2$$
$$A) \quad -2 + 1 \leq -5 - 2$$
$$-1 \leq -7 \text{ X}$$

That's it! **Choice A is the correct answer.** This inequality doesn't make sense because –1 is not less than –7, but the question wants us to find a value that doesn't work: "which of the following numbers is NOT a solution". Even though the NOT is in capital letters, it's easy to miss once you start doing the math. It's a good idea to underline it so you don't forget about it.

If you want to solve this algebraically, you would do the exact same steps as if it were an equals sign. Start by getting all the x's on one side:

$$
\begin{array}{rcl}
2x + 1 & \leq & 5x - 2 \\
-2x & & -2x \\
\hline
1 & \leq & 3x - 2 \\
+2 & & +2 \\
\hline
3 & \leq & 3x
\end{array}
$$

$$\frac{3}{3} \le \frac{3x}{3}$$

$$1 \le x$$

Since x has to be greater than or equal to 1, Choice A would be the only answer that doesn't fall in that range.

Example 2

You could also solve this one with Guess & Check. You'd need to try different numbers to eliminate the wrong answers. But if you solve algebraically, you need to take into account the ONLY thing that's strange about Inequalities. It starts out the same:

$$6 \le \quad 1 - x$$
$$\underline{-1 \quad -1}$$
$$5 \le \quad -x$$

From here, we have to be careful. We should divide by –1 to get x by itself. But when we do, we have to reverse the inequality sign:

$$5 \le -x$$

$$\frac{5}{-1} \le \frac{-x}{-1}$$

$$-5 \ge x$$

Notice that the inequality sign used to open to the right, but now it opens to the left. To make our answer match the choices, we can flip it once more, but this time we're reversing the entire inequality:

$$x \le -5$$

Choice C is the correct answer. If you're unsure, use Guess & Check to confirm:

Let $x = -6$

$$6 \le 1 - (-6)$$

$$6 \le 1 + 6$$

$$6 \le 7 ✓$$

–6 works, which we'd expect based on our answer. But let's try –4 also. This guess should not work:

Let $x = -4$

$$6 \le 1 - (-4)$$

$$6 \le 1 + 4$$

$$6 \le 5 \ X$$

As expected, x is less than –5, but not greater than –5.

Inequalities — The Basics

Don't confuse the inequality signs. Remember that the larger side faces the side with the greater value:
- $4 < 5$
- $5 > 4$

Guess & Check is usually the most efficient way to solve Inequalities questions. Just be careful if they ask for a number that does NOT satisfy the inequality.

The rules of Algebra still apply to Inequalities. Solve for x the same way you normally would.

The only exception is when you divide by a negative number. You <u>must</u> switch the direction of the inequality sign.

The Twists

Example 3

You know that Inequalities give you a range of values. This question is twisted to make you think that you need to find one specific value within a very wide range, but it's actually really easy. The greatest possible value will occur at the "equals" part of this "less than or equal to" inequality.

Let's start by looking at what we have and what we want:

$$3a - 1 \leq 5 \qquad 3a + 1\ ?$$

You could solve for a, but you're much better off using a shortcut to go directly from question to answer. Add 2 to both sides of the inequality:

$$
\begin{array}{rcl}
3a - 1 & \leq & 5 \\
+2 & & +2 \\
\hline
3a + 1 & \leq & 7
\end{array}
$$

So the greatest possible value of 3a + 1 is 7 because the expression has to be less than or equal to 7. **The correct answer is Choice C.**

Example 4

This question is even more confusing because you have two inequalities, but we can trust that the signs will behave as if they were equals signs. Both inequalities have wide ranges, but the "greatest possible value" part tells us that those ranges overlap at one point that is greater than all the others. That point is where the lines intersect.

Substitute 3 in for y:

$$y \geq 3$$

$$x + 3 \leq 10$$

Now solve for x:

$$
\begin{array}{rcl}
x + 3 & \leq & 10 \\
-3 & & -3 \\
\hline
x & \leq & 7
\end{array}
$$

So the greatest possible value of x is 7. **And the correct answer is Choice B.**

Inequalities — The Twists

When the SAT asks for greatest or least possible values on Inequalities questions, they're almost always asking for a point of intersection. You can pretend the inequality signs are just equals signs.

HOWEVER, there might be hard questions where this is a bad assumption that gets you in trouble, so pay attention to where you are in the Math section. If it's supposed to be a hard question, double check your math by graphing the inequalities.

Answers: Inequalities

#1 — Answer = C
Add 7 to both sides, then divide by 2 to get that $x < 9$.

#2 — Answer = A
Guess & Check. Plugging in 0 for x gives the inequality: $-1 < 0$. This is true, so Choice A is the answer.

#3 — Answer = C
Divide the inequality by 2, and you'll get:
$4x - 3y \leq 13$.

#4 — Answer = C
Guess & Check. Start with the smallest number since the question is asking for the least possible value. Plugging in Choice D gives $-17 \geq -12$, which is not true. Choice C gives $-12 \geq -12$, which is true.

#5 — Answer = D
It's difficult to Guess & Check because the answer choices do not represent the value of x. Subtract 5, then divide by 2 to simplify the first inequality to $x \leq -3$. The greatest possible value of x is –3, so plug –3 in for x in the second expression. You'll get that x is equal to 3.

#6 — Answer = C
Solve for x by adding 4x and 1 to both sides to get: $6 > 6x$. Divide by 6 to get $1 > x$. The twist is that this inequality is backwards, and it's easy to jump to the

wrong conclusion and pick Choice D. When you flip the inequality, you have to flip the sign: $x < 1$.

Factor & FOIL lesson

The Basics

Hopefully you've taken Algebra 2 and have become a pro at both of these operations. But if not, we'll see that you can also Arithmetize on many Factor & FOIL questions.

Example 1

First, distribute the 2. It only gets distributed to one of the parenthetical terms (one of the binomials). When we FOIL, we'll technically be distributing it to the other term as well:

$$2(x + 1)(3x + 4)$$

$$(2x + 2)(3x + 4)$$

Now you can FOIL. Remember what it stands for: First, Outer, Inner, Last. You should get:

$$6x^2 + 8x + 6x + 8$$

If you want, you can use the Box Method to FOIL instead:

	$3x$	$+ 4$
$2x$	$6x^2$	$8x$
$+ 2$	$6x$	8

Add the terms:

$$6x^2 + 8x + 6x + 8$$

$$6x^2 + 14x + 8$$

So Choice C is the answer. As I said, you can also Arithmetize:

Let $x = 0$

$$2(x + 1)(3x + 4) = 2\big((0) + 1\big)\big(3(0) + 4\big)$$
$$= 2(1)(4)$$
$$= 8$$

Which choices also equal 8 when x is 0?

A) $6(0)^2 + 8 = 8$ ✓

B) $6(0)^2 + 11(0) + 4 = 4$ X

C) $6(0)^2 + 14(0) + 8 = 8$ ✓

D) $12(0)^2 + 28(0) + 16 = 16$ X

That eliminates Choices B and D, but we need to Arithmetize with a new number to choose between A and C:

Let $x = 1$

$$2(x + 1)(3x + 4) = 2\big((1) + 1\big)\big(3(1) + 4\big)$$
$$= 2(2)(7)$$
$$= 28$$

Which choice (of A and C only) equals 28 when x is 1?

A) $6(1)^2 + 8 = 6 + 8 = 14$ X

C) $6(1)^2 + 14(1) + 8 = 6 + 14 + 8 = 28$ ✓

Once again, Choice C is the correct answer. Knowing how to FOIL is definitely the better way to solve, but Arithmetizing gives you another tool that should guarantee you this question.

Example 2

In this case, Arithmetizing is probably the better way to solve. Pick smart numbers:

Let $x = 2$ and $y = 1$

$$\left(\frac{x}{2} + y\right)^2 = \left(\frac{2}{2} + 1\right)^2$$
$$= (1 + 1)^2$$
$$= (2)^2$$
$$= 4$$

Which choice also equals 4?

A) $\dfrac{(2)^2}{2} + (1)^2 = \dfrac{4}{2} + 1 = 3$ ✗

B) $\dfrac{(2)^2}{4} + (1)^2 = \dfrac{4}{4} + 1 = 2$ ✗

C) $\dfrac{(2)^2}{4} + \dfrac{(2)(1)}{2} + (1)^2 = \dfrac{4}{4} + \dfrac{2}{2} + 1 = 3$ ✗

D) $\dfrac{(2)^2}{4} + (2)(1) + (1)^2 = \dfrac{4}{4} + 2 + 1 = 4$ ✓

Choice D is the correct answer. Is the algebra faster? Probably. But it's easy to make a mistake, so make sure you FOIL correctly:

$$\left(\frac{x}{2} + y\right)^2$$

$$\left(\frac{x}{2} + y\right)\left(\frac{x}{2} + y\right)$$

$$\frac{x^2}{4} + \frac{xy}{2} + \frac{xy}{2} + y^2$$

$$\frac{x^2}{4} + \frac{2xy}{2} + y^2$$

$$\frac{x^2}{4} + xy + y^2$$

Same answer, but you've got to know how to multiply and add fractions. Also, make sure you don't forget to FOIL. Many students mistakenly pick Choices A or B because they just square each term. That's a common algebra mistake! Write out both terms so you can actually FOIL them correctly, without losing the middle term.

Factor & FOIL — The Basics

FOIL when you have two binomials.
- multiply the First terms
- multiply the Outer terms
- multiply the Inner terms
- multiply the Last terms
- combine like terms (usually in the middle)

Remember that squaring a binomial means you have to FOIL, so write out both the terms so you don't forget. This is a very common mistake:

$$(x + y)^2 = x^2 + y^2 \text{ ✗}$$

There's going to be a middle term:

$$(x + y)^2 = x^2 + 2xy + y^2 \text{ ✓}$$

If you don't trust yourself to FOIL correctly, Arithmetize so you can still get these questions right.

The Twists

Example 3

The twist is factoring because it takes a little more effort than FOILing. In this question, they're also twisting the exponents to make you second guess yourself. Basically, we can eliminate Choices B and D right from the start. If those binomials were to the 4th power, we'd have a very complicated answer with a LOT of terms. In this case, it makes sense that squaring a square gets you a 4th power. Here's a simpler version:

$$\left(x^2\right)^2 = \left(x^2\right)\left(x^2\right)$$
$$= (x)(x)(x)(x)$$
$$= x^4$$

The coefficient 2 in front of the x would also be squared, so **the correct answer is Choice A.** We can FOIL it out to be sure:

$$\left(2x^2 - y^2\right)^2 = \left(2x^2 - y^2\right)\left(2x^2 - y^2\right)$$
$$= 4x^4 - 2x^2y^2 - 2x^2y^2 + y^4$$
$$= 4x^4 - 4x^2y^2 + y^4 \text{ ✓}$$

Example 4

The SAT loves this type of twisted Factor & FOIL question! If I didn't tell you that it involves factoring and FOILing, how would you know? In other words, what would you do if you saw a question like this in the midst of the real SAT?

My hope is that the squared terms in the first equation would pop off the page. You would see it, and instantly be reminded of factoring & FOILing because they almost always involve a squared term. It's just a matter of learning the pattern and turning it into a reflex. Once Factor & FOIL are on your mind, you should do what you can:

$$a^2 - b^2 = (a + b)(a - b)$$

This is the DOTS rule (Difference of Two Squares). It's just a special kind of factoring that you need to memorize. When you have a squared term minus a squared term, they can be factored just like we did above.

Now substitute what we know.

If $a^2 - b^2 = x$ and $a + b = y$, then we can substitute:

$$a^2 - b^2 = (a + b)(a - b)$$
$$x = y(a - b)$$

Pay attention to the question. They're asking for the value of a – b, so we're almost done. Just divide both sides by y to get a – b alone:

$$\frac{x}{y} = \frac{y(a - b)}{y}$$

$$\frac{x}{y} = a - b$$

So Choice C is the correct answer. If that was confusing, that's okay. You can still get this right by Arithmetizing:

Let $a = 5$ and $b = 3$

$$a^2 - b^2 = x$$

$$5^2 - 3^2 = x$$

$$25 - 9 = x$$

$$16 = x$$

Remember that result. We'll use it later. But let's find y from the other equation:

$$a + b = y$$

$$5 + 3 = y$$

$$8 = y$$

Now we can find the value of a – b:

$$a - b = 5 - 3$$

$$a - b = 2$$

Which answer choice also gives us 2, when we put 16 in for x and 8 in for y?

A) $16 - 8 = 8$ X

B) $(16)(8) = 128$ X

C) $\dfrac{16}{8} = 2$ ✓

D) $\dfrac{8}{16} = \dfrac{1}{2}$ X

Only Choice C works.

Factor & FOIL — The Twists

Raising a binomial to the 3rd or 4th power is a mess, so it's usually not the answer. Don't let the higher exponents scare you. Use logic to find an answer, but FOIL it out to test it.

If a question involves a squared term, it probably involves factoring or FOILing. Maybe it's a pure algebra question, or maybe it involves graphing quadratics. Either way, get in the habit of immediately jumping to Factor & FOIL in your mind when you see a squared term, especially if the question seems really hard.

When in doubt, Arithmetize.

Answers: Factor & FOIL

#1 — Answer = C
Arithmetize. Let x = 0. Plugging in gives you $3(-2)(-5)$, which is 30. Only Choice C also equals 30 when you substitute 0 in for x.

#2 — Answer = A
Arithmetize. Since there are radicals in several answers, let k = 4. This also makes the original equation the easily-factorable $x^2 - 16$, which is equivalent to $(x-4)(x+4)$. If you plug 4 in for k in all the answer choices, only Choice A is equivalent.

#3 — Answer = D
Arithmetize. Let p = 1 and q = 2. That makes the original expression equal to 25. Only Choice D also equals 25 when you substitute. You could also FOIL, which is probably easier.

#4 — Answer = D
FOIL the left side to get that $a = 16$.

#5 — Answer = D
Arithmetize. You can tell from the choices that picking 0 will not eliminate everything, so let x = 1. The original expression will equal 12. Only Choice D also equals 12.

#6 — Answer = C
You might try to Arithmetize, but the numbers don't work out. Instead, FOIL the last expression: $(a+b)^2 = a^2 + 2ab + b^2$. Rearrange the expression, and you'll see that you have everything you need: $a^2 + b^2 + 2(ab)$. Substitute: $12 + 2(4)$. Simplify to get 20.

Radicals lesson

The Basics
The rules of algebra still apply. Show your work, and stay organized.

Example 1

Do what the question says and substitute for x:

$$\sqrt{a-1} - 3 = 1$$

Add 3 to both sides. Remember that you want to solve toward the variable, from the outside in. Don't start squaring things just yet. The 3 is further away from the variable, so we should deal with that first:

$$\sqrt{a-1} - 3 = 1$$
$$\underline{\quad + 3 \quad +3}$$
$$\sqrt{a-1} \quad = \quad 4$$

Now you can square both sides to get rid of the square root:

$$\left(\sqrt{a-1}\right)^2 = 4^2$$

$$a - 1 = 16$$

Solve for a:

$$a = 17$$

Choice C is the correct answer. You also could have Guess & Checked if you wanted to.

Example 2

Start by going from two equations to one. Substitute the first equation in for x in the second equation:

$$3\left(4\sqrt{3}\right) = \sqrt{3y}$$

$$12\sqrt{3} = \sqrt{3y}$$

You could square both sides here, but you have to make sure you square everything correctly. Instead, let's break apart what we have into separate terms:

$$12 \cdot \sqrt{3} = \sqrt{3} \cdot \sqrt{y}$$

As you can see, both sides have a root 3. Eliminate them:

$$12 = \sqrt{y}$$

Now it's easier to solve by squaring:

$$12^2 = \left(\sqrt{y}\right)^2$$

$$144 = y$$

Choice D is the correct answer.

Radicals — The Basics

Obey the normal rules of algebra.

Don't start squaring things until you have to.

Sometimes it's better to break apart radicals so that you can understand what's really going on.

The Twists

Example 3

There is absolutely no reason to solve this algebraically. In fact, doing so would make it very likely that you get this question wrong. You only have a handful of possible values of x, so just Guess & Check them!

First, let's get rid of k by substituting as instructed:

$$\sqrt{x + 3} = x - 3$$

Let $x = 1$

$$\sqrt{1 + 3} = 1 - 3$$

$$\sqrt{4} = -2$$

$$2 = -2 \text{ X}$$

This doesn't work, so we can cross off Choices A and B. Sometimes you need to include the negative root, but this is not one of those times. I'm honestly not really sure why, except that the SAT doesn't want you to include it here. I guess because then the original equation wouldn't be a function? (If you know the reason, definitely email me!) If you have no idea what I'm talking about, then don't worry about it! It doesn't matter. Let's keep checking:

Let $x = 3$

$$\sqrt{3 + 3} = 3 - 3$$

$$\sqrt{6} = 0 \text{ X}$$

Looks like Choice D will be the answer, but let's make sure:

Let $x = 6$

$$\sqrt{6 + 3} = 6 - 3$$

$$\sqrt{9} = 3$$

$$3 = 3 \checkmark$$

Choice D is the correct answer.

Example 4

This question is very easy, but it's also very easy to make a careless mistake. The SAT is really trying hard to trick you here. Start by getting rid of the radicals:

$$\sqrt{x} - \sqrt{16} = \sqrt{25}$$

$$\sqrt{x} - 4 = 5$$

Add 4 to both sides to get the x alone:

$$\sqrt{x} = 9$$

Now be careful! A lot of students pick Choice A here because they're moving too quickly. They see a square root and a 9, and their brains just really want the answer to be 3. It's not!

$$\left(\sqrt{x}\right)^2 = 9^2$$

$$x = 81$$

The correct answer is Choice D. What a mean little twist that question was!

Radicals — The Twists

If the answers are solution sets, don't bother solving algebraically. Just Guess & Check the choices.

Be very careful when working with square roots. It's very easy to skip steps because you're moving too quickly. Be thorough. Show your work. Stay organized.

Answers: Radicals

#1 — Answer = B

Guess & Check. Substitute 8 in for k. Choice B gives $\sqrt{36 + 28} - 8 = 0$, which simplifies to $\sqrt{64} - 8 = 0$. If you choose to solve algebraically, add 8 to both sides before you square both sides.

#2 — Answer = B

Guess & Check. If $x = -2$, then $\sqrt{16} + 4 = 0$, which is not true (the SAT does not include the negative root). This eliminates every choice except Choice B. Check it anyway to be sure: $\sqrt{49} + 4 = 11$.

#3 — Answer = C

Simplify the radical on the right by breaking apart the 18 into two radicals: $9\sqrt{2} = x\sqrt{9} \cdot \sqrt{2}$. Simplify further: $9\sqrt{2} = 3x\sqrt{2}$. The value of x is 3.

#4 — Answer = A

Square both sides: $2a = b^2$. Divide by 2: $a = \dfrac{b^2}{2}$.

#5 — Answer = B

Guess & Check. Substitute 4 in for k. Check 0 first: $0 = 2 + \sqrt{4}$. This doesn't work (the SAT does not include the negative root), so Choice B is the answer. Check it to be sure: $3 = 2 + \sqrt{1}$.

Exponent Rules lesson

The Basics

Unfortunately, you have to memorize these. It's guaranteed that they'll test at least one of these rules at least once per test. Since you'll be working with high exponents or weird combinations of exponents, Arithmetizing probably won't work. If you want a top score, spend some time on Khan Academy drilling these rules over and over and over again until you're comfortable with them.

Exponent Rules — The Basics

Learn the rules.

The Twists

Example 1

Almost every question will at least *feel* twisted. And the answer choices will be so similar that you won't have a good sense whether you're right or wrong. Try to go one step at a time so that you don't miss anything:

$$\sqrt[4]{\frac{1}{b}}$$

Start by turning the radical into a fractional exponent:

$$\left(\frac{1}{b}\right)^{\frac{1}{4}}$$

When a fraction is raised to an exponent, both the numerator and denominator are raised to that exponent:

$$\frac{1^{\frac{1}{4}}}{b^{\frac{1}{4}}}$$

But since 1 to any exponent is still 1, we're really looking at an expression like this:

$$\frac{1}{b^{\frac{1}{4}}}$$

We can move the b-term from the denominator to the numerator by negating the exponent.

$$b^{-\frac{1}{4}}$$

Choice B is the correct answer.

Example 2

This is a twisted mess. Since we're dividing, we should start by subtracting exponents. You should write out the subtraction because there are a lot of negatives, and it's easy to lose one.

$$\frac{x^3 y^{-\frac{1}{2}}}{x^{-\frac{3}{2}} y^2}$$

$$x^{\left(3-\left(-\frac{3}{2}\right)\right)} \; y^{\left(-\frac{1}{2}-2\right)}$$

$$x^{\left(3+\frac{3}{2}\right)} \; y^{\left(-\frac{5}{2}\right)}$$

$$x^{\left(\frac{9}{2}\right)} \; y^{\left(-\frac{5}{2}\right)}$$

It's still pretty twisted. Since the y's are clearly in the denominator, we should eliminate the negative exponent by moving the y-term to the denominator:

$$\frac{x^{\frac{9}{2}}}{y^{\frac{5}{2}}}$$

Now let's turn these fractional exponents into radicals. The denominators of the exponents tell us that these are square roots, and the numerators tell us the exponent of the variable under the radical:

$$\frac{\sqrt{x^9}}{\sqrt{y^5}}$$

We're so close! At this point, you can probably eliminate Choice A, so that's something. For the next part, we should play around with the variables and exponents to make it easier to see what happens. Since we're using a square root, we should break apart the x's and y's so that we have squared terms. Something like this:

$$\frac{\sqrt{x^2} \cdot \sqrt{x^2} \cdot \sqrt{x^2} \cdot \sqrt{x^2} \cdot \sqrt{x}}{\sqrt{y^2} \cdot \sqrt{y^2} \cdot \sqrt{y}}$$

Count up the exponents, and you'll see that we still have 9 x's on top and 5 y's on the bottom. Now it's easy to get rid of most of the square roots:

$$\frac{x \cdot x \cdot x \cdot x \cdot \sqrt{x}}{y \cdot y \cdot \sqrt{y}}$$

Recombine those x's and y's so that we once again have exponential terms:

$$\frac{x^4 \sqrt{x}}{y^2 \sqrt{y}}$$

Choice D is the correct answer. There are other ways to break apart the radicals, but I wanted to play it as safely as I could. If I were doing this question on the test, I'd probably check all my steps again to make sure I didn't lose a variable, negative, or exponent somewhere along the way.

Exponent Rules — The Twists

Go one step at a time. Write down everything you do so that you can easily check your work.

Good luck!

Answers: Exponent Rules

#1 — Answer = C

Divide both sides by 2. Raise each side to the –3 to cancel out the $-\dfrac{1}{3}$ (since you multiply the exponents, and this would make the exponent on the x equal to 1). You should have: $x = \left(\dfrac{k}{2}\right)^{-3}$. The exponent gets "distributed" to both the numerator and denominator: $x = \dfrac{k^{-3}}{2^{-3}}$. You can make the negative exponents positive by flipping the fraction: $x = \dfrac{2^3}{k^3}$. Simplify by raising 2 to the third power, which is 8.

#2 — Answer = 3, 4, 6, or 12

You have no choice but to Arithmetize. Pick values for x that would get you to 81 when raised to an exponent. The easiest is probably x = 81. That means that the exponent needs to simplify to 1, which happens when y = 3 because $81^{\frac{3}{3}} = 81$. As another example, if x = 9, the exponent must be 2, which means that y must equal 6 because $9^{\frac{6}{3}} = 81$. You can get y = 12 when x = 3, and y = 4 when x = 27.

#3 — Answer = D

Rewrite the fractional exponent as a radical: $\sqrt[3]{4^2}$. Simplify to 16, then break it apart into factors: $\sqrt[3]{8} \cdot \sqrt[3]{2}$. The first term is a perfect cube that can be simplified to 2, so $2\sqrt[3]{2}$ is the answer.

#4 — Answer = D

Rewrite the fractional exponent as a radical: $\sqrt[3]{a^4}$. There's no need to simplify further.

#5 — Answer = A

Start by using the rules of exponents. When you multiply exponential numbers with the same base, you add the exponents, so $x^{a^2-b^2} = x^{12}$. Since the bases are the same, you can focus on the exponents: $a^2 - b^2 = 12$. This should make you instantly think of factoring. Use the Difference of Two Squares rule to get: $(a - b)(a + b) = 12$. Since we're told that $a - b = 4$, we can substitute and solve: $4(a + b) = 12$. So $a + b = 3$.

#6 — Answer = A

Focus on the second part. You can reduce the fraction, but first you need to get both the numerator and denominator to have the same base: $\dfrac{3^a}{3^{2b}}$. When you are dividing exponential numbers, you subtract the exponents: 3^{a-2b}. It's no coincidence that the exponent is the exact same expression that they gave you at the beginning of the question. Just substitute to find the answer: 3^{24}.

Absolute Value lesson

The Basics

The mathematical definition of Absolute Value is a little confusing. Technically, the absolute value of a number is its distance from 0. Basically, it's the positive version of a number:

$$|4| = 4$$

$$|-4| = 4$$

It's helpful to think of absolute value bars as "special" parentheses that magically turn a number positive. But there's one thing that you <u>cannot</u> do:

$$|x - 7| = x + 7 \quad \text{X}$$

No! They don't work like that. They turn the <u>result</u> positive. So we'd need to put a number in for x to see what's really going on:

$$|3 - 7| = |-4| = 4$$

Luckily, most Absolute Value questions can be solved by using Guess & Check or Arithmetize, which means you're usually putting in numbers anyway.

Example 1

You're given three possible values of x. Try them!

Let $x = -2$

$$\left|(-2) - 2\right| - 2 = 0$$

$$\left|-4\right| - 2 = 0$$

$$4 - 2 = 0 \ X$$

Cross out Choice A. Let's try B:

Let $x = 0$

$$\left|(0) - 2\right| - 2 = 0$$

$$\left|-2\right| - 2 = 0$$

$$2 - 2 = 0 \ ✓$$

That's it! No need to check anything else. **Choice B is the correct answer.**

Absolute Value — The Basics

Absolute Value bars are like "special" parentheses that turn the <u>result</u> positive. As always, solve for whatever is in those parentheses first, then do the absolute value.

The Twists

Example 2

The question is worded in a confusing way, but essentially it's asking which graph will have only positive values of y (because y ≥ 0).

You should be able to use your knowledge of graphs to see that Choices A, B, and C will all dip below the x-axis because they all have a y-intercept of (0, –3).

But if we put 0 in for x in Choice D, we see that it does not have a negative value:

$$y = \left|0 - 3\right|$$

$$y = \left|-3\right|$$

$$y = 3$$

In fact, Choice D is correct because an absolute value function cannot be negative. Remember, it turns whatever result we get positive, so even negative values of x will become positive. The graph of Choice D looks like this:

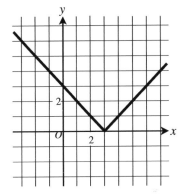

Absolute Value — The Twists

Absolute value graphs "bounce" off the x-axis because they cannot be negative.

Answers: Absolute Value

#1 — Answer = B
You can Arithmetize with a few numbers to test out the choices. But if you understand absolute value, Choice B is the only possible answer. The absolute value bars make the value inside them positive. The only way to get the entire expression equal to 0 is with subtraction.

#2 — Answer = 9/2 or 4.5

To solve absolute value equations, you need to create two equations that represent the positive and negative values. If you solve $x - 5 = \frac{1}{2}$, you'll get that $x = \frac{11}{2}$. But you also need to solve $x - 5 = -\frac{1}{2}$ to find x when the absolute value is negative. You will get the answer, which is $x = \frac{9}{2}$.

#3 — Answer = B

Arithmetize. But you'll need to be clever. If $n = 10$, then both x = 6 and 14 should satisfy the inequality. Since 6 doesn't work in Choices A and C, you can eliminate them. Try negative values next. If $n = -10$, then both x = –6 and –14 should satisfy the inequality. Choice D doesn't work when x = –6: $|-6| - (-10) < 5$ can be simplified to $6 + 10 < 5$. It works in Choice B, though.

Must Be True lesson

The Basics

The SAT used to have a lot of these questions. The ACT still does, but they mostly test Geometry. Essentially, these are perfect Arithmetize questions. Having real numbers is much better than trying to think about the situation using only logic. Remember, the SAT is trying to trick you, so you shouldn't really trust your logic. At least support your theory with numerical proof.

Example 1

Pick some easy-to-use numbers. Just make sure you obey any rules that they give you. In this case, a must be positive, and b must be negative.

Let $a = 1$ and $b = -2$

$$x = \frac{a}{b - a}$$

$$= \frac{1}{-2 - 1}$$

$$= \frac{1}{-3}$$

$$x = -\frac{1}{3}$$

So x is negative. **That matches with Choice C, which is the correct answer.** See how easy these are if you use numbers?

Must Be True — The Basics

Arithmetize. Obey the rules in the question.

The Twists

Example 2

Different kinds of numbers will behave differently when you put them into equations. Exponents, in particular, make things tricky. Compare:

positive number greater than 1

$$x = 2$$
$$x^2 = 4 \qquad \text{Numbers get bigger.}$$
$$x^3 = 8$$

positive number less than 1

$$x = \frac{1}{2}$$
$$x^2 = \frac{1}{4} \qquad \text{Numbers get smaller!}$$
$$x^3 = \frac{1}{8}$$

negative number less than –1

$$x = -2$$
$$x^2 = 4 \qquad \text{Numbers all over the place!}$$
$$x^3 = -8$$

And this question is telling us to work with a negative number that's greater than –1:

Let $x = -\frac{1}{2}$

I. $-\frac{1}{2} < \frac{1}{4}$ ✔

II. $\dfrac{1}{4} < -\dfrac{1}{8}$ X

III. $-\dfrac{1}{2} < -\dfrac{1}{8}$ ✓

So the correct answer is Choice C. Notice how unexpected the result was. This is why picking numbers is so helpful!

Must Be True — The Twists

Different types of numbers behave in different ways, so it's best to try a variety and eliminate choices as you go. Try positive and negative integers and fractions.

Answers: Must Be True

#1 — Answer = B
Plug Points Into Equations. You have the values for x and y, so substitute into the parabola:
$0 = a(-1)^2 + b(-1) + c$. This simplifies to:
$0 = a - b + c$. Add b to both sides to get Choice B.

#2 — Answer = B
Arithmetize. Try different kinds of numbers to prove each of the numerals wrong. If $a = 1$ and $b = -1$, then the original equation is true, but numerals I and II are not. Since numeral III can be rewritten as $\dfrac{1}{a^2} = \dfrac{1}{b^2}$, it must be true because we already know that $a^2 = b^2$.

#3 — Answer = C
If you subtract x from both sides, you'll eliminate the x's and simplify the inequality to $y > 0$, which is Choice C.

Point of Intersection lesson

The Basics
Usually we think of a Point of Intersection on a graph, but most of the SAT questions that test this idea will not use a graph at all. That's why the Point

of Intersection questions are considered Algebra and not Linear Properties.

Example 1

If you Plug Points Into Equations, make sure you test the point in <u>both</u> equations:

Choice A
$$4(1) - (16) = -12$$
$$4 - 16 = -12$$
$$-12 = -12 ✓$$
$$2(1) + 3(16) = -34$$
$$2 + 48 = -34 \text{ X}$$

This is why you check both points! The SAT loves to trick you by making the point work in one equation, but not the other. If you know they're trying to trap you like this, it's easy to avoid the mistake.

Choice B
$$4(-1) - (8) = -12$$
$$-4 - 8 = -12$$
$$-12 = -12 ✓$$
$$2(-1) + 3(8) = -34$$
$$-2 + 24 = -34$$
$$22 = -34 \text{ X}$$

Once again, the point works in the first equation, but not in the second equation.

Choice C
$$4(-5) - (-8) = -12$$
$$-20 + 8 = -12$$
$$-12 = -12 ✓$$

$$2(-5) + 3(-8) = -34$$

$$-10 - 24 = -34$$

$$-34 = -34 \checkmark$$

Now we're done. **Choice C is the correct answer because the point satisfies both equations.** There's no need to check Choice D since we've already proven that Choice C works.

If you want a faster way to solve, use the "stack" method to get rid of one of the variables. You need to have a positive and negative version of the same variable so that you can add the equations and cross them out. Start by multiplying the first equation by 3 so that we can get a –3y to match the +3y in the second equation:

$$3\left[4x - y = -12\right]$$

I know it's weird to see an equals sign in parentheses, but I think it helps you remember to distribute the 3 to all parts:

$$12x - 3y = -36$$

Now we can "stack" the equations and add them together:

$$
\begin{aligned}
12x - \cancel{3y} &= -36 \\
+ \ 2x + \cancel{3y} &= -34 \\
\hline
14x &= -70
\end{aligned}
$$

Divide by 14:

$$\frac{\cancel{14}x}{\cancel{14}} = \frac{-70}{14}$$

$$x = -5$$

Since Choice C is the only answer where x is –5, you don't need to plug back in to solve for y. Sometimes you will, though. In general, the "stack" method is the fastest way to solve most Point of Intersection questions. Unless…

Example 2

…there's an easy way to substitute. This example gives us equations that have an x or y all by itself. We should substitute one equation in for the variable in the other equation. But first, it's a good idea to eliminate things that make our lives complicated. Solve the fraction problem now and it won't cause headaches later on:

$$\frac{x}{3} = y$$

$$x = 3y$$

This is much easier to work with. You can substitute 3y in for x in the second equation:

$$1 + 2(y + 2) = 3y$$

Distribute and combine like terms:

$$1 + 2y + 4 = 3y$$

$$2y + 5 = 3y$$

Subtract:

$$
\begin{aligned}
2y + 5 &= 3y \\
-2y &= -2y \\
\hline
5 &= y
\end{aligned}
$$

No need to solve for x. **Choice A is the correct answer.** It's worth pointing out, however, that Choice C is the value of x. The SAT does this a lot. They want you to solve for the wrong variable, and then be so excited that you forget to check back with the question. Get in the habit of rereading the question so that you are sure that you've solved for the correct variable.

The Twists

Example 3

The fractions do a good job of twisting this Point of Intersection question so that it looks hard to solve. Untwist it by getting rid of the fractions:

First equation:

$$4\left[\frac{1}{4}x + \frac{1}{2}y = 7\right]$$

$$x + 2y = 28$$

Second equation:

$$4\left[x - \frac{1}{4}y = 10\right]$$

$$4x - y = 40$$

Let's re-stack them so we can get a better look:

$$x + 2y = 28$$
$$4x - y = 40$$

We should try to eliminate a variable. We can easily eliminate the y's if we multiply the bottom fraction by 2, but I'm going to do it the hard way to show you something else. If we want to eliminate the x's instead, we'll need to multiply the top equation by

negative 4. That means we need to also distribute the negative to the entire equation:

$$-4\left[x + 2y = 28\right]$$

$$-4x - 8y = -112$$

Re-stack the equations, and add them together:

$$\begin{array}{r} \cancel{-4x} - 8y = -112 \\ + \cancel{4x} - y = 40 \\ \hline -9y = -72 \end{array}$$

Divide by –9:

$$\frac{\cancel{-9}y}{\cancel{-9}} = \frac{-72}{-9}$$

$$y = 8$$

Another twist here is that they don't want the value of x or y. We need both to find the value of x over y. Plug 8 in for y so that we can find x. It's easier to use the second equation:

$$x - \frac{1}{4}(8) = 10$$

$$x - 2 = 10$$

$$x = 12$$

Now find the value of the expression:

$$\frac{x}{y} = \frac{12}{8}$$

$$\frac{x}{y} = \frac{3}{2}$$

So $\frac{3}{2}$ or **1.5 are both correct answers.** This definitely seems like a hard question, but it's not significantly different from the basic Point of Intersection questions. In fact, the process for solving these is almost always the same. With practice, you should be able to get these questions right every time without much effort.

Example 4

This one looks different. Or does it? There are two equations, and the question seems to be asking when they're equal to each other. That's exactly what a point of intersection is! Follow instructions by setting f equal to g. We'll also replace the x's with a's, since that's what we're supposed to do with functions:

$$a^2 - 8a + 16 = a - 2$$

The squared term tells us that we're probably going to need to factor. We usually factor when everything is on one side of the equation and the other side is equal to 0. Let's move everything over to the left side:

$$
\begin{array}{r}
a^2 - 8a + 16 = a - 2 \\
-a + 2 \quad -a + 2 \\
\hline
a^2 - 9a + 18 = 0
\end{array}
$$

Factor:

$$a^2 - 9a + 18 = 0$$

$$(a - 6)(a - 3) = 0$$

So our solutions are:

$$a = 6 \text{ and } a = 3$$

Both 6 and 3 are correct answers.

Point of Intersection — The Twists

Make equations easier to work with. Eliminate fractions by multiplying to Get Back to Basics.

Whenever they give you two equations, it's probably a Point of Intersection question. Sometimes they use functions or weird phrasing to confuse you. Basically, if you're looking for where two equations equal each other, it's a Point of Intersection question.

Answers: Point of Intersection

#1 — Answer = C
Guess & Check. The only point that works in both equations is (3, –1). You can also use the "stack" method by multiplying the first equation by 4 and eliminating the y-terms.

#2 — Answer = 0
Use the "stack" method. Multiply the first equation by 2 so you can eliminate the y-terms.

#3 — Answer = 7
Substitute the first equation in for the y-term in the second equation. After you distribute the 2, you should get: $2x^2 + 2 - 5 = 9 - 2x$. Since this is a quadratic, you move the terms so that everything is on one side and equal to 0. You should get: $2x^2 + 2x - 12 = 0$. You can divide by 2 to make it easier to factor: $x^2 + x - 6 = 0$. The factors are –3 and 2, but the question wants only positive values of x, so x = 2. Substitute 2 in for x into the first equation to find that y = 5. Add 2 and 5 as instructed to get that $x + y = 7$.

#4 — Answer = C
The easiest way to solve this is by graphing a rough sketch. Even without a calculator, you should be able to see that the line has a y-intercept of 1, and the parabola has a y-intercept of –6. Since the parabola opens upward, the line must intersect it twice. Solving algebraically is very long, and the numbers don't work out nicely. You could set the equations equal to each other, and then manipulate so one side is equal to 0. Use the discriminant to find the number of solutions (see Quadratic Properties Twists).

#5 — Answer = C
You could easily graph a rough sketch, but you'd still need to find the point of intersection. Simplify the second inequality: $x > 3$. Substitute 3 in for x in the first inequality. Since 3 is the minimum value of x, you'd be finding all of the y-values where x is greater than 3. You should get $y > -3$.

#6 — Answer = B
Guess & Check. Choice A works in the first inequality, but not in the second. Choice B works in both.

Advanced Algebra lesson

The Basics

Use the SAT math strategies to solve if you're not comfortable with algebra. Mostly, you just need to be clever.

Example 1

There's absolutely no reason to do this algebraically. Watch how easy it is to Arithmetize:

Let $x = 0$

$$\frac{1}{\frac{1}{(0)+1} + \frac{1}{(0)-4}}$$

$$\frac{1}{\frac{1}{1} - \frac{1}{4}}$$

$$\frac{1}{\frac{3}{4}}$$

Remember that dividing by a fraction is the same as multiplying by its reciprocal:

$$1 \times \frac{4}{3} = \frac{4}{3}$$

So our answer choice should also be $\frac{4}{3}$ when we put 0 in for x. This part should be quick:

A) $2(0) - 3 = -3$ ✗

B) $(0)^2 - 3(0) - 4 = -4$ ✗

C) $\frac{2(0) - 3}{(0)^2 - 3(0) - 4} = \frac{3}{4}$ ✗

D) $\frac{(0)^2 - 3(0) - 4}{2(0) - 3} = \frac{4}{3}$ ✓

You could probably see that Choice D would be the correct answer just by looking at the expressions. This is by far the best way to answer this

question. Using 0 makes it very simple, and there's no rule that says we can't.

But here's the algebra in case you're curious:

$$\frac{1}{\frac{1}{x+1} + \frac{1}{x-4}}$$

Start by getting a common denominator for the bottom fractions:

$$\frac{1}{\left(\frac{x-4}{x-4}\right)\frac{1}{x+1} + \frac{1}{x-4}\left(\frac{x+1}{x+1}\right)}$$

$$\frac{1}{\frac{x-4}{(x+1)(x-4)} + \frac{x+1}{(x+1)(x-4)}}$$

We can now add the two fractions, and while we're at it, we should FOIL the two binomials:

$$\frac{1}{\frac{2x-3}{x^2-3x-4}}$$

Once again, dividing by a fraction is the same as multiplying by the reciprocal, so we'll end up flipping the bottom fraction upside-down:

$$\frac{x^2-3x-4}{2x-3}$$

We still got that Choice D is the correct answer. But there's a lot to keep track of. Arithmetizing is better.

Example 2

This is a very hard question. Your instinct is probably to subtract 12 and get the whole equation equal to 0. Not a bad idea, but it's basically impossible to factor cubic functions (x^3).

There's not much else you can do except try different things and see what happens. Maybe if we moved the negative term to the other side:

$$x^3 + 3x = 4x^2 + 12$$

Hmm... We can factor out some stuff:

$$x(x^2 + 3) = 4(x^2 + 3)$$

Whoa. That worked out well. Divide out the common term to make the answer obvious:

$$x \; \cancel{(x^2 + 3)} = 4 \; \cancel{(x^2 + 3)}$$

$$x = 4$$

The correct answer is 4. This is why you shouldn't give up on a question just because you don't see a clear path to the solution. It might be a question you skip at first so that you don't run out of time on the section, but you could return to it and just keep trying different things.

Even Guess & Check will work here. The SAT usually picks small numbers for these Advanced Algebra questions. It's unlikely that you'll end up with a fractional answer on such a hard question. But who knows? The point is, don't be afraid to try things. Sometimes you'll have no idea what you're doing until the answer just falls into your lap. Even after taking countless SATs and seeing thousands and thousands of math questions, I still find myself stumped occasionally. I just play with the equation a bit, trusting that something will happen that gets me closer to the answer. The SAT likes to trick you, but there's only so much they can do. Persistence will eventually beat them.

Advanced Algebra — The Basics

Arithmetize! It can make a lot of the tough algebra much much easier.

Don't give up so easily. Try some simple manipulations so you can see the equation in a slightly different way. Eventually something will pop and you'll know what to do.

The Twists

Example 3

If you haven't learned function notation yet, these questions can seem impossible. But we can follow our Plug Points Into Equations strategy. The only difference is that the point is written a little differently than we're used to. The first sentence of this question actually gives us a point:

$$h(3) = 14$$

This is really the point (3, 14). The 3 goes in place of x because that's just how function notation works. We often say that f(x) = y, and so we can see how that would give us an (x, y) coordinate:

$$f(x) = y$$
$$f(1) = 2$$

$$(1, 2)$$

The f is not a variable. It's kind of like a definition, just like the question says. In this Example, they're telling us that they've made up an equation, and they're calling it h:

$$h(x) = 2x^2 + c$$

The problem is that we don't know part of the equation because they used c instead of a number. But we can figure out what c is because they also gave us a point that works in the equation. Let's take the point (3, 14) and plug it into the function:

$$14 = 2(3)^2 + c$$

$$14 = 2(9) + c$$

$$14 = 18 + c$$

$$-4 = c$$

Once again, Plugging Points Into Equations makes our lives much easier. The rest of the question tells us to find the y-value when x is −3. Here's how it would look with function notation, but remember that the −3 on the left is really only instructions that tell us to put –3 in for x. We can also replace c with –4 now that we know its value:

$$h(-3) = 2(-3)^2 - 4$$

$$h(-3) = 2(9) - 4$$

$$h(-3) = 18 - 4$$

$$h(-3) = 14$$

So Choice A is the correct answer.

Example 4

This is a very twisted functions problem, but we should trust our strategies. We're still being given a point, but it's weird because it has a variable in it:

$$g(k - 2) = 0$$

$$(k - 2, 0)$$

As always, Plug Points Into Equations, even if they're really weird. In this case, $x = k - 2$:

$$0 = (k - 2)^2 - 4(k - 2) + 3$$

FOIL and distribute:

$$0 = k^2 - 4k + 4 - 4k + 8 + 3$$

Combine like terms:

$$0 = k^2 - 8k + 15$$

Factor:

$$0 = (k - 5)(k - 3)$$

The possible values of k are 5 and 3. Either would be a correct answer. Once you recognize that they're giving you a point and an equation, this very difficult question becomes pretty easy to untwist.

Answers: Advanced Algebra

#1 — Answer = B
You could Guess & Check by trying the three easy answers. When they don't work, you're left with Choice B. To solve algebraically, put the left side over 1, and cross-multiply to get $(x - 2)^2 = 8$. Take the square root of both sides, then simplify the resulting radical.

#2 — Answer = D
To get $g(4)$, plug 4 in for x, which makes the second equation $g(4) = 5 - f(8)$. Find $f(8)$ using the first equation. You should get –6. Use that value in the second equation: $g(4) = 5 - (-6)$. Don't lose the negative, and you'll get 11.

#3 — Answer = 5/4 or 1.25
Just plug 2 in for x. There's no need to try to factor or anything. This is Advanced Algebra because it's about functions, not because the math is particularly difficult.

#4 — Answer = C
You can Arithmetize, but you'll have to be very organized. To solve algebraically, factor the second equation: $g(x) = 3x(x^2 - x - 5)$. It's no coincidence that one of the factors is exactly the same as $f(x)$. The correct answer will be a function that is divisible by both $x^2 - x - 5$ and $2 - 3x$. If you're clever with algebra, you can multiply these two factors together to better understand what the correct answer will be composed of: $(2 - 3x)(x^2 - x - 5) = 2(x^2 - x - 5) - 3x(x^2 - x - 5)$. The second term is the exact same as $g(x)$. The first term is simply 2

times $f(x)$. You can rewrite this as $2f(x) - g(x)$, which is Choice C.

#5 — Answer = 7/3

Plug Points Into Equations. The first part tells us that the point $(6, -11)$ is included in the function. Plug it in: $-11 = a(6) - 3$. Solve to find that $a = -\dfrac{4}{3}$. Now that you know the full function, you can find $f(-4)$. Plug the values into the function: $-\dfrac{4}{3}(-4) - 3$. You should get $\dfrac{7}{3}$.

Dividing Polynomials lesson

The Basics

First, you should remember how to do regular long division:

$$3\overline{)475}$$

3 goes into 4 once:

$$\begin{array}{r} 1 \\ 3\overline{)475} \end{array}$$

Multiply 3 by 1:

$$\begin{array}{r} 1 \\ 3\overline{)475} \\ 3 \end{array}$$

Subtract:

$$\begin{array}{r} 1 \\ 3\overline{)475} \\ -3 \\ \hline 1 \end{array}$$

Drop down the 7:

$$\begin{array}{r} 1 \\ 3\overline{)475} \\ -3 \downarrow \\ \hline 17 \end{array}$$

Divide 17 by 3:

$$\begin{array}{r} 15 \\ 3\overline{)475} \\ -3 \downarrow \\ \hline 17 \end{array}$$

Multiply by 5:

$$\begin{array}{r} 15 \\ 3\overline{)475} \\ -3 \downarrow \\ \hline 17 \\ -15 \end{array}$$

Subtract and drop the 5:

$$\begin{array}{r} 15 \\ 3\overline{)475} \\ -3 \downarrow \\ \hline 17 \\ -15 \\ \hline 25 \end{array}$$

Divide 3 into 25, and finish the long division:

$$\begin{array}{r} 158 \\ 3\overline{)475} \\ -3 \downarrow \\ \hline 17 \\ -15 \\ \hline 25 \\ -24 \\ \hline 1 \end{array}$$

There's still a 1 left, but here's where we'll stop. Your calculator would keep diving and give you a decimal, but we want the 1 as a remainder. When we use long division on polynomials, we'll always have a remainder. The process is similar to long division of numbers, but there are a few quirks that make it even harder:

Example 1

Set it up like this:

$$x - 2\overline{)x^3 - 4x^2 + 2x + 5}$$

Even though we have two numbers on the outside, we only use the first one in the division process. How many times does x go into x^3?

$$x - 2\overline{)x^3 - 4x^2 + 2x + 5}$$

with x^2 above.

Just like before, we multiply, but now we'll use the entire x – 2 term:

$$\begin{array}{r} x^2 \\ x - 2\overline{)x^3 - 4x^2 + 2x + 5} \\ x^3 - 2x^2 \end{array}$$

This part is where everybody messes up. Just like before, we need to subtract, but we need to make sure that we subtract the <u>entire</u> term. That means we'll need to distribute a negative:

$$\begin{array}{r} x^2 \\ x - 2\overline{)x^3 - 4x^2 + 2x + 5} \\ -(x^3 - 2x^2) \end{array}$$

That $-2x^2$ is going to become positive after we distribute, so our subtraction will end with:

$$\begin{array}{r} x^2 \\ x - 2\overline{)x^3 - 4x^2 + 2x + 5} \\ -x^3 + 2x^2 \\ -2x^2 \end{array}$$

If you're confused, that's totally okay. We'll look at another way to solve these afterward, but top scorers need to know how to do this the hard way. Just like before, we'll drop down the next term:

$$\begin{array}{r} x^2 \\ x - 2\overline{)x^3 - 4x^2 + 2x + 5} \\ -x^3 + 2x^2 \downarrow \\ -2x^2 + 2x \end{array}$$

How many times does x go into $-2x^2$?

$$\begin{array}{r} x^2 - 2x \\ x - 2\overline{)x^3 - 4x^2 + 2x + 5} \\ -x^3 + 2x^2 \downarrow \\ -2x^2 + 2x \end{array}$$

Multiply x – 2 by –2x, and subtract. Make sure you don't forget to distribute the negative:

$$\begin{array}{r} x^2 - 2x \\ x - 2\overline{)x^3 - 4x^2 + 2x + 5} \\ -x^3 + 2x^2 \downarrow \\ -2x^2 + 2x \\ -(-2x^2 + 4x) \\ -2x \end{array}$$

Bring down the 5:

$$\begin{array}{r} x^2 - 2x \\ x - 2\overline{)x^3 - 4x^2 + 2x + 5} \\ -x^3 + 2x^2 \downarrow\downarrow \\ -2x^2 + 2x \downarrow \\ -(-2x^2 + 4x) \downarrow \\ -2x + 5 \end{array}$$

Divide –2x by x:

$$\begin{array}{r} x^2 - 2x - 2 \\ x - 2\overline{)x^3 - 4x^2 + 2x + 5} \\ -x^3 + 2x^2 \downarrow\downarrow \\ -2x^2 + 2x \downarrow \\ -(-2x^2 + 4x) \downarrow \\ -2x + 5 \end{array}$$

Multiply and subtract:

$$\begin{array}{r} x^2 - 2x - 2 \\ x - 2\overline{)x^3 - 4x^2 + 2x + 5} \\ -x^3 + 2x^2 \downarrow\downarrow \\ -2x^2 + 2x \downarrow \\ -(-2x^2 + 4x) \downarrow \\ -2x + 5 \\ -(-2x + 4) \\ 1 \end{array}$$

We're out of terms to drop, and x does not divide into 1. So just like before, we have a remainder. Here's how we'd write this result as an expression:

$$x^2 - 2x - 2 + \frac{1}{x-2}$$

So the main answer is just a polynomial, but the remainder is a fraction, where the denominator is the same denominator as our original expression. **The correct answer is Choice A.**

As you can see, Dividing Polynomials questions are a nightmare. You won't always be able to Arithmetize, but it can make things much much easier:

Let $x = 0$

$$\frac{(0)^3 - 4(0)^2 + 2(0) + 5}{(0) - 2}$$

$$\frac{0 - 0 + 0 + 5}{0 - 2} = -\frac{5}{2}$$

Now we have a value that our answer choices should equal when x is 0:

Choice A

$$(0)^2 - 2(0) - 2 + \frac{1}{(0) - 2}$$

$$-2 - \frac{1}{2}$$

$$-\frac{5}{2} \checkmark$$

Remember, we have to check all the choices. We wouldn't know that the answer is A if we hadn't done it the long way first. So let's keep going:

Choice B

$$(0)^2 - 2(0) + 6 - \frac{7}{(0) - 2}$$

$$6 + \frac{7}{2} \ \text{X}$$

Choice B is clearly wrong. Notice that Arithmetizing is still hard. It's very easy to lose a negative near the fraction.

Choice C

$$(0)^2 - 6(0) - 10 + \frac{25}{(0) - 2}$$

$$-10 - \frac{25}{2} \ \text{X}$$

That's going to be way less than $-\frac{5}{2}$. Keep going.

Choice D

$$(0)^2 - 6(0) + 14 - \frac{23}{(0) - 2}$$

$$14 + \frac{23}{2} \ \text{X}$$

Doesn't work. **So only Choice A gave us a valid answer, and now we can confidently choose it.** Arithmetizing is still a pain, but that's because Dividing Polynomials questions are among the most difficult on the SAT. Anything we can do to make them a little easier is worthwhile, and Arithmetizing is probably safer than long division because there are fewer negatives to lose.

There's one other way to solve these. You may have learned about synthetic division in school. Personally, I find the process confusing and error prone, but if you're already comfortable with it, you can use it to solve instead of long division. If you've never heard of it before, don't worry about it. Learning it isn't worth it for this one question. Just Arithmetize!

Dividing Polynomials — The Basics

First of all, don't do this unless you have to. If you can factor, that's definitely the best solution. But you'll know when you hit a true Dividing Polynomials question because it will look almost exactly like the Example.

Try to Arithmetize, but remember to check all the choices, and be careful with negatives, especially around the fraction at the end.

If you can, learn how to do the long division. You might not be able to Arithmetize on certain twisted versions of these.

The Twists

Example 2

This one looks like we won't be able to Arithmetize because there are no answer choices, but actually we can! The x carries through the whole equation, so we can pick a number.

Let $x = 0$

$$\frac{4(0)^2 - 3(0) + 7}{(0) + 2} = 4(0) - 11 + \frac{k}{(0) + 2}$$

$$\frac{7}{2} = -11 + \frac{k}{2}$$

$$11 + \frac{7}{2} = \frac{k}{2}$$

$$\frac{22}{2} + \frac{7}{2} = \frac{k}{2}$$

$$\frac{29}{2} = \frac{k}{2}$$

$$29 = k$$

Wow! That wasn't bad at all. **The correct answer is 29.** This is another great question to stress the idea that sometimes things on the SAT just work out if you let them. Try something! Don't let a confusing question paralyze you. Even if you Arithmetize and it doesn't work, you probably won't waste much time, especially if you're using 0.

In case you're curious, here's how the work for the long division would look:

$$\begin{array}{r} 4x - 11 \\ x + 2\overline{)4x^2 - 3x + 7} \\ -(4x^2 + 8x) \\ \hline -11x + 7 \\ -(-11x - 22) \\ \hline 29 \end{array}$$

Since 29 is the remainder, we'd write our answer like this:

$$4x - 11 + \frac{29}{x + 2}$$

And the 29 is exactly where our k was in the original equation.

Dividing Polynomials — The Twists

Even when they twist the question by removing the choices or introducing another variable, there's still a chance you can Arithmetize. If you've got the time, try something!

Answers: Dividing Polynomials

#1 — Answer = 23

Arithmetize. If $x = 0$, then the equation simplifies to $-\frac{5}{3} = 6 - \frac{A}{3}$. Solve for A, and you'll get 23. You can also do long division, and the remainder will be –23, but the negative is included in the equation already, in front of the fraction.

#2 — Answer = C

You have to do this the long way. When you divide, you should get $x + 3 + \frac{12}{x - 7}$. The remainder would be 12.

#3 — Answer = 4

This is much easier than it looks. Focus on the division. What would you need to divide $20x^2$ by in order to get $5x$? The value of k would have to be 4. You could do the long division to test it. You could also Arithmetize from the start. You can't pick 0 for x because that would eliminate the k term. But if you make $x = 1$, the equation becomes $\frac{26}{k+2} = 2 + \frac{14}{k+2}$. Subtract the fraction to get: $\frac{12}{k+2} = 2$. Cross-multiply: $12 = 2k + 4$. Solve, and you'll find that $k = 4$.

#4 — Answer = B

Arithmetize. If $x = 0$, the equation becomes: $-\frac{12}{b} = -5 - \frac{17}{b}$. Get the b's on the same side: $\frac{5}{b} = -5$. Solving will get you $b = -1$. You can solve algebraically using a similar process as question #3, but it's harder because you have to be very comfortable with long division.

Imaginary Numbers lesson

The Basics

There are two very distinct types of Imaginary Numbers questions. One is much easier than the other, so the Basics/Twists difference is very obvious. If you see imaginary numbers in a question, take note of where you are in the section. If you're near the beginning, it's probably the easy kind. If you're near the end, it's probably a little twisted. Luckily, both types follow a fairly repetitive pattern to solve.

Example 1

Follow instructions by writing these two expressions as a sum:

$$7 + 4i + 3 + 8i$$

Combine like terms:

$$10 + 12i$$

That's it. **Choice C is the correct answer.** Easy Imaginary Numbers questions will really be about combining like terms. You can pretend the i is a variable. Yet another example of how the SAT throws weird things at you just to make you doubt yourself.

Example 2

This is also mostly standard Algebra. Distribute that negative to both parts:

$$(9 + 6i) - (4i^2 - 8i)$$

$$9 + 6i - 4i^2 + 8i$$

Here's the rare case where we need to actually use i to solve. This is why:

$$i = \sqrt{-1}$$
$$i^2 = \left(\sqrt{-1}\right)^2$$
$$i^2 = -1$$

We need to make this substitution:

$$9 + 6i - 4(-1) + 8i$$

There are a lot of negatives, so we need to be careful:

$$9 + 6i + 4 + 8i$$

Combine like terms:

$$13 + 14i$$

Choice D is the correct answer.

Imaginary Numbers — The Basics

i doesn't usually matter on easy questions. Just combine like terms.

If you have an i^2, replace it with –1. But make sure you don't lose any negatives.

The Twists

Example 3

Hard Imaginary Numbers questions will be easy to recognize. They almost always have i in the denominator of a fraction. We need to get it out of there. In math, we want to avoid having i in the denominator for a reason that isn't really important. Just learn this process.

We need to multiply the top and bottom by the conjugate, which is kind of like an opposite version of a binomial. As the directions say, $3 + 5i$ and $3 - 5i$ are conjugates. Here's how we multiply:

$$\frac{2}{3+5i}\left(\frac{3-5i}{3-5i}\right)$$

Notice that we're really just multiplying by 1. This is how we change the way the fraction looks without actually changing its value. Let's rewrite it so it's easier to see the next few steps:

$$\frac{2(3-5i)}{(3+5i)(3-5i)}$$

The numerator is easy. Just distribute:

$$\frac{6-10i}{(3+5i)(3-5i)}$$

The denominator isn't as tricky as it seems. You might recognize that it's the factored form of a Difference of Two Squares (DOTS) situation. FOIL it out to be sure:

$$\frac{6-10i}{9-15i+15i-25i^2}$$

As we'd expect with DOTS, there's no middle term because the $15i$'s cancel:

$$\frac{6-10i}{9 \,\cancel{-15i} \,\cancel{+15i}\, -25i^2}$$

$$\frac{6-10i}{9-25i^2}$$

Remember that we can replace i^2 with -1. That will completely remove the i from the denominator:

$$\frac{6-10i}{9-25(-1)}$$

As always, watch those negatives when we combine the terms:

$$\frac{6-10i}{9+25}$$

$$\frac{6-10i}{34}$$

The answer choices split apart the numerator, which we can do by dividing each piece by 34:

$$\frac{6}{34}-\frac{10i}{34}$$

Reduce:

$$\frac{3}{17}-\frac{5i}{17}$$

Choice D is the correct answer. Even though this is definitely more twisted than the basic questions, it's actually not that different from regular algebra. So even if this is the first time you've ever worked with imaginary numbers, you should be able to apply your other algebra skills to these questions and get them right. Just watch those negatives!

Imaginary Numbers — The Twists

When there's an imaginary number in the denominator of a fraction, multiply both the top and bottom by the conjugate to eliminate it.

Answers: Imaginary Numbers

#1 — Answer = B
Distribute the negative to both parts to get:
$1 + 4i - 5 + 2i$. Combine like terms. The i doesn't really matter.

#2 — Answer = D

Product means multiply: $(3 + 5i)(2 - i)$. FOIL to get: $6 - 3i + 10i - 5i^2$. Replace the i^2 with –1, then combine like terms. Don't lose the negative!

#3 — Answer = C

Multiply the numerator and denominator by the conjugate, which is $4 - 6i$. You'll have to FOIL. You should get: $\dfrac{20 - 30i - 4i + 6i^2}{16 - 36i^2}$. Replace the i^2 with –1, then combine like terms to get: $\dfrac{14 - 34i}{52}$. Reduce and break apart the fraction.

#4 — Answer = C

Multiply the numerator and denominator by the conjugate, which is $2 + 5i$. After you FOIL, you'll get: $\dfrac{20 + 50i - 6i - 15i^2}{4 - 25i^2}$. Replace the i^2 with –1, which makes both terms positive. Combine like terms to get: $\dfrac{35 + 44i}{29}$. As the question says, the b term is the one in front of the i. You can break apart the fraction to get it: $\dfrac{35}{29} + \dfrac{44i}{29}$.

#5 — Answer = B

In order to add fractions, you need a common denominator, which is $4i$ in this case. Multiply the first fraction by $\dfrac{2}{2}$ and the second fraction by $\dfrac{i}{i}$. You should get: $\dfrac{6 - 8i + i + 2i^2}{4i}$. Replace the i^2 with –1, then combine like terms: $\dfrac{4 - 7i}{4i}$. You can't have i in the denominator, so you have to multiply both the numerator and denominator by i for the same reason that you usually multiply by the conjugate. You'll get: $\dfrac{4i - 7i^2}{4i^2}$. Replace the i^2's with –1 to get: $\dfrac{4i + 7}{-4}$. Divide each term by –4 to separate the two terms: $-i - \dfrac{7}{4}$, which can be rearranged into Choice B.

Linear Properties lesson

The Basics

There's such a wide variety of SAT questions that involve lines that students often feel like there's too much that they need to memorize. In fact, almost everything boils down to y=mx+b. When they give you lines in other formats, Get Back To Basics.

Example 1

This is very transparently about y=mx+b. I prefer to start with the b because it's a little easier to find on a graph. Let's compare:

$$y = mx + b$$
$$y = 3x - 1$$

The y-intercept is –1. That means we can eliminate Choices B and D.

The slope is 3, which means we'll rise 3 boxes and run (to the right) 1 box. **Choice C is the correct answer.** Choice A has a slope of $\dfrac{1}{3}$, which is a common way the SAT tries to trick you. It's very important that you remember that <u>slope is rise over run.</u> Remember it this way: first you need to rise in the morning, then you can go for your run. If you run first, you're just sleepwalking!

Example 2

If you want, you can manipulate this equation until it's back into y=mx+b form. But the easier way to solve this is to use the Plug Points Into Equations strategy. Whenever we're talking about intercepts, we already know one half of the point. In this case, the y-intercept will have an x-coordinate of 0 (because it intercepts the y-axis). Plug 0 in for x:

$$\frac{2}{3}(0) - \frac{3}{4}y = -2$$

$$-\frac{3}{4}y = -2$$

Multiply by the reciprocal to eliminate the fraction:

$$\left(-\frac{4}{3}\right) \bullet -\frac{3}{4}y = -2\left(-\frac{4}{3}\right)$$

$$y = \frac{8}{3}$$

There's nothing else you need to do. **The correct answer is $\frac{8}{3}$.**

Example 3

Get Back to Basics. This question has a lot of steps, but you can find your way through this mess by continuously bringing yourself back to y=mx+b.

We start with 2 points that lie on a line. When you have 2 points, find the slope between them. Don't worry about why. Just know that it'll probably be important because lines are all about slopes and intercepts:

$$points = (1, 11) \text{ and } (-1, 9)$$

$$slope = \frac{y_1 - y_2}{x_1 - x_2}$$

$$= \frac{11 - 9}{1 - (-1)}$$

$$= \frac{2}{2}$$

$$slope = 1$$

Let's start filling in our y=mx+b:

$$y = (1)x + b$$

It's not much, but it's a start. Now what? Well, what else can we plug into this linear equation? We have 2 points, and we have an equation. Use our strategy—Plug Points Into Equations:

$$11 = (1)(1) + b$$

$$11 = 1 + b$$

$$10 = b$$

And just like that, we now have the equation for our first line:

$$y = x + 10$$

Move on to the second line, again focusing on y=mx+b. We are told the slope and a point on the line. Plug in what you know:

$$y = mx + b$$

$$2 = (-2)(1) + b$$

$$2 = -2 + b$$

$$4 = b$$

So our second line has the equation:

$$y = -2x + 4$$

The question wants the point of intersection, so we can set the two lines equal to each other (because they'll have the same y-value at the intersection point).

$$x + 10 = -2x + 4$$

Solve for x:

$$\begin{array}{rcl} x + 10 &=& -2x + 4 \\ +2x - 10 && +2x - 10 \\ \hline 3x &=& -6 \end{array}$$

$$\frac{3x}{3} = \frac{-6}{3}$$

$$x = -2$$

We're so close. We have the x-coordinate of the point of intersection (which the question tells us is a), but we need the y-coordinate. Pick an equation and Plug Points Into Equations:

$$y = x + 10$$
$$y = (-2) + 10$$
$$y = 8$$

The point of intersection is (–2, 8), but the question wants the value of $b - a$, so we have one last step:

$$b - a = 8 - (-2)$$

$$b - a = 10$$

The correct answer, after a very long process, is 10. This is a long question, but it's not particularly hard if you stay focused on lines and y=mx+b.

Linear Properties — The Basics

Everything revolves around y=mx+b. When in doubt, return to this standard.

m is the slope. You must memorize the various slope formulas. First you have to rise in the morning, then you can go for your run. If you run, then rise, you're sleepwalking!

$$\text{slope} = \frac{\text{rise}}{\text{run}} = \frac{\Delta y}{\Delta x} = \frac{y_1 - y_2}{x_1 - x_2}$$

b is the y-intercept, which always has an x-coordinate of 0.

(x, y) are points on the line. Don't forget one of our most essential strategies: Plug Points Into Equations.

The Twists

Example 4

It's important that you become familiar with all of the terms and ideas described in The Twists. The rules about parallel lines tend to be the most important. Yes, they have the same slope, but a lot of questions ask about parallel lines without explicitly saying so. When they talk about "infinitely many" or "no solutions", they're really talking about parallel lines.

When lines have no solution, they must have the same slope, but different intercepts. When they have infinitely many solutions, they must have the same slope and the same intercepts.

In Example, 4 we should try to get the equations to look exactly the same because they're supposed to be the same line. The first problem is that 15 does not equal 75. Let's fix that:

$$5 \left[3x + 5y = 15\right]$$

$$15x + 25y = 75$$

If these equations have infinitely many solutions, then the coefficients also need to be equal:

$$15x + 25y = 75$$
$$ax + by = 75$$

$$a = 15$$
$$b = 25$$

It's really that simple. Now just finish up by finding the value of the expression:

$$\frac{a}{b} = \frac{15}{25}$$

$$\frac{a}{b} = \frac{3}{5}$$

So $\frac{3}{5}$ or 0.6 are both valid answers. This is a good example of a question where the math is relatively easy. The difficulty comes from understanding what they're asking.

Example 5

This is the rare case where you actually need to graph the inequalities. Some of my students are very methodical when they graph lines. They draw out the axes and make little boxes or tick marks. If you have to graph something on the SAT without a calculator, chances are the little details won't matter much, so don't waste time making a pretty graph when a rough sketch will do.

To start, ignore the inequality signs. Just graph these as lines, focusing on slopes and intercepts. It should look something like this:

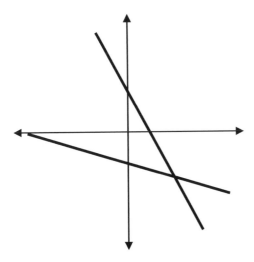

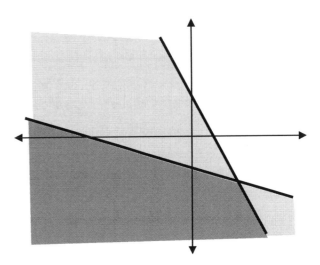

The top equation has a positive y-intercept and a steep negative slope. The bottom equation has a negative y-intercept and a flatter negative slope. They should clearly intersect in the 4th Quadrant.

Now we have to shade the solution sets. Both equations have a y< shading so we need to shade where the y's are less than the line. In other words, shade down:

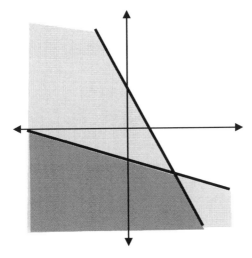

The two shaded regions overlap in the bottom left, and that's what we want. Solutions to the system will be shaded by both inequalities. So there are definitely solutions in Quadrants III and IV.

The benefit of a rough sketch is that you can adjust it as needed. It's unclear at first, but if we extend our lines, we'll see that there are also solutions in Quadrant II:

So the correct answer is Choice A. There are no solutions in Quadrant I, mostly because our second line never passes through that quadrant.

One other thing to note: technically our first line should be dashed because it uses the < symbol, and not the ≤ symbol. In other words, the solution set does not include the line itself, and we normally use a dashed line to show that. But it doesn't matter for this question. Again, rough sketches are usually all you need.

Linear Properties — The Twists

We normally think of solutions as points of intersection, but some Linear Properties questions involve twists that require a deeper understanding of how lines work.

Parallel lines have no solutions.

…unless they are exactly the same line. In that case, the lines have infinitely many solutions.

Inequalities intersect, but they also have shaded solution sets that overlap. Graph the lines normally, but shade either up or down depending on whether y is > or < the rest of the equation.

Answers: Linear Properties

#1 — Answer = D

Plug Points Into Equations. First, you have to make the equation. The y=mx+b equation of this line is $y = -\dfrac{2}{5}x$. There's no b because the line passes through the origin. The only point that works is Choice D.

#2 — Answer = D

Parallel lines have the same slope. Find the slope of the line p by using the slope formula. The slope is $\dfrac{1}{2}$. Use the slope formula a second time for line q: $\dfrac{1}{2} = \dfrac{0 - (-4)}{k - 0}$. Simplify and solve for k.

#3 — Answer = 240

Treat the inequalities like equals signs, and set them equal to each other: $12x = -6x + 360$. Solve for x.

#4 — Answer = C

Plug Points Into Equations. The line becomes: $b = ka + c$. Since k represents the slope, you can just rearrange the equation to solve for k. Subtract c and divide by a to get Choice C.

#5 — Answer = D

Lines have no solutions when they are parallel. You can rearrange the two equations so that they're in y=mx+b form. The first equation would be: $y = -\dfrac{5}{a}x + \dfrac{2}{a}$. The second equation would be: $y = -\dfrac{4}{3}x + 2$. Only the slopes matter. Parallel lines have the same slope, so set the two slopes equal to each other: $\dfrac{-5}{a} = \dfrac{-4}{3}$. Cross-multiply and divide to solve for a.

#6 — Answer = B

Arithmetize. If $a = 1$, then the points are (1, 0) and (0, 1). Sketch them on a rough graph, and you'll see that the slope is clearly negative.

#7 — Answer = C

Get Back to Basics. Perpendicular lines have negative reciprocal slopes. The safest way to answer this question is to get each of the equations back into basic y=mx+b form. The original equation should be $y = \dfrac{4}{5}x - 4$. The perpendicular slope would be $-\dfrac{5}{4}$. Only Choice C has the that slope.

#8 — Answer = D

Plug Points Into Equations. First, create the equation of this line. You don't know the slope, so the best you can do is say that the equation won't have a b because the line passes through the origin: $y = mx$. You can plug one of the points into the equation: $4 = mc$. You still don't know the slope, but you can use the origin and the other point to find it: $\dfrac{c - 0}{36 - 0}$. Plugging the result in for m changes the equation to: $4 = \dfrac{c}{36}c$. This simplifies to $144 = c^2$. Solve for $c = 12$.

#9 — Answer = 14

First, find the slope of the graph of f(x). You can count the boxes, and you'll see that the slope is $\dfrac{2}{3}$. The question says that g(x) has a slope that is 3 times larger, which would be 2. Using the slope and the given x-intercept, you can use y=mx+b to find the equation of g(x): $0 = (2)(-1) + b$. Solving for b, you'd get that $g(x) = 2x + 2$. Now find that $g(6) = 2(6) + 2$, which is 14.

Quadratic Properties lesson

The Basics

Hopefully, the first page of this packet gives you a good summary of the most essential quadratic ideas. It's really important to know all of the different vocabulary since they'll constantly switch the words they use just to confuse you. The Vertex Form tends to be the one that people have the most trouble with. For some reason, it's more important on the SAT than it was in school.

Example 1

The root form is usually the easiest place to start. This graph has x-intercepts at –3 and 1, so:

Root Form

$$y = (x + 3)(x - 1)$$

You can't really get the entire standard form from the graph. You can only find that the y-intercept (c-term) is –3. You'll have to FOIL the root form for the rest:

$$y = (x + 3)(x - 1)$$

$$y = x^2 - x + 3x - 3$$

Standard Form

$$y = x^2 + 2x - 3$$

You can get the vertex form just by looking at the vertex of the graph. The vertex is at (–1, –4). Plug those points into the right places, remembering that the x-value will be negated (in this case the two negatives make a positive):

Vertex Form

$$y = (x + 1)^2 - 4$$

You can also find the vertex form by completing the square with the standard form. Just to show you how it's done:

$$y = x^2 + 2x - 3$$

$$y = (x^2 + 2x) - 3$$

$$y = (x^2 + 2x + 1) - 3 - 1$$

$$y = (x + 1)^2 - 4$$

Completing the square is an important skill on the SAT. It's a quick way to switch between different versions of a quadratic equation, and it'll be essential for Circle Properties questions. Completing the square is described in more detail right before the Exercise.

The **range** of any function is the set of possible y-values. For a parabola, the limit will be the vertex, which is also the maximum or minimum. In this case, the range can be expressed as:

$$y \geq -4$$

The parabola turns when y is –4, but it continues on toward infinity on either side. It does so symmetrically, meaning that the two sides of the parabola are mirror images of each other across the vertex, or axis of symmetry. Notice that (–2, –3) and (0, –3) are both the same "distance" from the turning point. You go one unit up and one unit over on each side of the vertex. The next easily recognizable points are (–3, 0) and (1, 0), which are both 4 units above and 2 units over from the vertex. That's symmetry!

Quadratic Properties — The Basics

Know the three versions of a quadratic equation.
- Root Form gives the x-intercepts, but remember that the values on the graph are negated in the equation.
- Standard Form gives the y-intercept (the c-term), and tells you whether the graph opens up (+a) or down (–a). Standard form is the y=mx+b of quadratics. When in doubt, get back to this form.
- Vertex Form gives the vertex, or turning point, of the parabola. Remember that the x-value is negated in the equation.

Factor, FOIL, and complete the square to move between forms.

Parabolas are symmetrical across the vertex.

Answers: Convert Quadratics

#1 — Answer = $x^2 - 3x - 10$

#2 — Answer = $x^2 - 9$

#3 — Answer = $2x^2 + 7x - 4$

#4 — Answer = $(x - 7)(x - 1)$

#5 — Answer = $(x - 8)(x - 3)$

#6 — Answer = $2(x - 9)(x + 1)$

#7 — Answer = $(x - 4)^2 + 5$

#8 — Answer = $(x + 1)^2 + 4$

#9 — Answer = $(x - 3)^2 - 29$

#10 — Answer = $(x + 1)^2 - 10$

#11 — Answer = $(x - 5)^2 - 1$

Answers: Graphs of Quadratics

#1 — Answer = C

Factor this equation into $y = (x - 1)(x - 5)$. The x-intercepts are the roots.

#2 — Answer = D

FOIL to get this equation into $y = x^2 - 2x - 3$. Complete the square to get the equation into vertex form: $y = (x - 1)^2 - 4$.

#3 — Answer = B

The minimum value is the vertex, which is halfway between the two roots. Since the equation is given in root form, you just need to know that the roots are 7 and 3. The vertex will be between 7 and 3, specifically at 5. Choice B includes that value.

#4 — Answer = A

The question gives you two pieces of information. Focus on the zeros first. Only Choices A and B have zeros at 2 and –4. The range of the function must be less than or equal to 9. Choice A is the answer because the maximum occurs at y = 9.

#5 — Answer = B

The solutions are –4 and 9. Add them together to get 5.

#6 — Answer = 6

Factor into $(x - 6)(x + 1) = 0$. The solutions are 6 and –1. Since the question wants a positive solution, the answer is 6.

#7 — Answer = C

Complete the square: $(x - 2)^2 + 7$. You can also Arithmetize, but you should really learn how to complete the square.

#8 — Answer = B

Get Back to Basics. The twist is that the squared term has a 7. Divide the whole equation by 7 in order to get back to the standard form: $x^2 - 3x - 10 = 0$. Factor into $(x - 5)(x + 2) = 0$. The solutions are –2 and 5.

#9 — Answer = C

Sketch a parabola that roughly lines up with the dots. You'll see that the y-intercept is around 650. Since it's positive, you can eliminate the choices with negative c-terms, which are Choices B and D. Since the parabola opens downward, the a-term must be negative, so Choice C is the answer.

#10 — Answer = B

This question has a huge twist! Most people pick Choice D because they see that the new equation has a negative a-term and a negative c-term. If you did, you didn't use the graph at all. That's a big problem! Remember that the SAT rarely gives you information that you don't use. The graph is of a parabola with the equation $y = ax^2 + bx + c$. It opens upward, so the a-term is clearly positive. When it becomes negative in the new equation, the new parabola will open downward, which lets you eliminate Choices A and C. But the y-intercept of the original graph is negative, which means that the original value of the c-term is also negative. Arithmetize to make this easier to understand. The y-intercept in the graph could be –2, which would make $c = -2$. When that is plugged into the new equation, the c-term becomes negative, but it's a double negative! Arithmetize: $y = ax^2 + bx - (-2)$. Two negatives make a positive, which means that the y-intercept of our new graph will also be positive.

The Twists

Example 2

If you want a top score, you need to memorize quadratic formula. Questions that use it are rare, but it's basically impossible to get them right without it.

First, be clear about what your values are. This equation is in standard form, so it's easy:

$$x^2 + 4x + 1 = 0$$

$$a = 1$$
$$b = 4$$
$$c = 1$$

Plug those values into the quadratic formula:

$$x = \frac{-b \pm \sqrt{b^2 - 4ac}}{2a}$$

$$x = \frac{-(4) \pm \sqrt{(4)^2 - 4(1)(1)}}{2(1)}$$

$$x = \frac{-4 \pm \sqrt{16 - 4}}{2}$$

$$x = \frac{-4 \pm \sqrt{12}}{2}$$

$$x = \frac{-4 \pm \sqrt{4} \cdot \sqrt{3}}{2}$$

$$x = \frac{-4 \pm 2\sqrt{3}}{2}$$

$$x = -2 \pm \sqrt{3}$$

The correct answer is Choice A. A common mistake is dividing by 2 before you've simplified the radical. Remember that the plus/minus means the two terms on the top are "connected". We have to divide into both.

Example 3

Most students have seen the axis of symmetry formula at some point, and it's another way of finding the vertex if you can't complete the square. But the discriminant confuses people and isn't taught as thoroughly in school. Here's the simplest explanation so that you can understand why it tells us the number of solutions.

Let's look at the quadratic formula, but I'm going to ignore the denominator just to make things easier:

$$x = \frac{-b \pm \sqrt{b^2 - 4ac}}{2\cancel{a}}$$

$$x = -b \pm \sqrt{b^2 - 4ac}$$

It's important to remember that the plus/minus is the real reason we can get <u>two</u> solutions out of one equation. Essentially, we can split this into two equations:

$$x = -b + \sqrt{b^2 - 4ac}$$

$$x = -b - \sqrt{b^2 - 4ac}$$

If the discriminant is a positive number (>0), then we'll have two real solutions because we'll be adding and subtracting a number. So for example, you could have solutions that look like this:

$$x = 5 + \sqrt{4}$$

$$x = 5 - \sqrt{4}$$

In this case, the discriminant is 4, and the solutions would be 7 and 3. <u>A positive discriminant means two solutions.</u>

But if the discriminant is 0, then we'll only have one solution because our two equations will end up being the same:

$$x = 5 + \sqrt{0}$$

$$x = 5 - \sqrt{0}$$

In this case, 5 + 0 and 5 − 0 are both 5. So even though the plus/minus gives us two equations, the two equations give us the same answer. <u>When the discriminant is 0, we'll only have one solution.</u>

If the discriminant is less than 0, things will get weird:

$$x = 5 + \sqrt{-4}$$

$$x = 5 - \sqrt{-4}$$

You can't take the square root of a negative number. Technically, this quadratic would still have two solutions, but they would be imaginary solutions:

$$x = 5 + 2i$$

$$x = 5 - 2i$$

This parabola would not cross the x-axis. <u>So when the discriminant is less than 0, we have no real solutions</u> because we can't take the square root of a negative number.

Now let's get to the actual question for Example 3. We have a quadratic, but it's not in standard form, so we should move these variables to the left side:

$$4x^2 = 8x + c$$

$$4x^2 - 8x - c = 0$$

$$a = 4$$
$$b = -8$$
$$c = -c$$

This is still confusing! c = –c ? What? This is one of the SAT's favorite twists on quadratics. They know that negatives are already a problem, so they use them to confuse you about what the actual values are. Just know that c is a constant here. It could be a positive or a negative number. We don't yet. But we do know that moving it to the left side is changing how it looks, and we need to reflect that change throughout the question.

Let's put our values into the discriminant expression. And since we want "no real solutions", we should create an inequality where the discriminant is less than 0:

$$b^2 - 4ac < 0$$

$$(-8)^2 - 4(4)(-c) < 0$$

Start simplifying:

$$64 + 16c < 0$$

Let's solve for c:

$$16c < -64$$

$$c < -4$$

This means that we'll have 0 solutions when c is less than –4. **The only choice that satisfies our inequality is Choice D, so it must be the correct answer.** As we said before, the –c is still weird. Our actual quadratic equation with Choice D would be:

$$4x^2 - 8x - (-5) = 0$$

$$4x^2 - 8x + 5 = 0$$

So technically our c was negative all along, but the c-term in the standard form is actually positive because the two negatives make a positive. Watch out for twists like this.

Quadratic Properties — The Twists

Memorize quadratic formula:

$$x = \frac{-b \pm \sqrt{b^2 - 4ac}}{2a}$$

Be comfortable with the discriminant:
- If $b^2 - 4ac > 0$, then 2 real solutions
- If $b^2 - 4ac = 0$, then 1 real solution
- If $b^2 - 4ac < 0$, then 0 real solutions

Pay attention to negatives when working with the a, b, and c constants in the quadratic's standard form. The SAT likes to twist these around so that the negatives are hidden within the constants.

Answers: Advanced Quadratics

#1 — Answer = C

Start by setting the equations equal to each other, then subtracting k so you have: $0 = 5x^2 + 1 - k$. Use the discriminant to find the number of solutions. There's one solution when the discriminant equals 0. Use the a, b, and c-terms in the equation to fill in the discriminant: $a = 5$, $b = 0$, and $c = 1 - k$. The twist is that there is no b-term because there's no term with just one x. The c-term is $1 - k$ because both are numbers that are not attached to an x. Plugging these values into the discriminant gives you $0 - 20(1 - k) = 0$, which simplifies to $-20 + 20k = 0$. Solve for k, which equals 1. This question is so much easier with a calculator because you can just graph the two equations, using Guess & Check for the value of k.

#2 — Answer = A

Get Back to Basics. Start by dividing the equation by 2 so that you can work with the quadratic more easily: $x^2 + 3x - 5 = 0$. You can't factor, so you'll have to use the quadratic formula. Plug the a, b, and c-terms into the equation:

$x = \dfrac{-3 \pm \sqrt{3^2 - 4(1)(-5)}}{2(1)}$. The solutions simplify to

$x = \dfrac{-3 \pm \sqrt{29}}{2}$. Break the +/– into the two solutions, and break the fraction up while you're at it:

$\dfrac{-3}{2} + \dfrac{\sqrt{29}}{2} + \dfrac{-3}{2} - \dfrac{\sqrt{29}}{2}$. Now you can see that the radical terms cancel each other out. Add the other two terms: $\dfrac{-3}{2} + \dfrac{-3}{2} = \dfrac{-6}{2}$. Reduce to –3.

#3 — Answer = B

Guess & Check. The projectile will hit the ground when the height is 0. Since the answer choices are approximations, you won't get 0 exactly, but only Choice B will be close when you plug it in for t. If you want to solve directly, you'll have to use a calculator. You can graph the quadratic and use the CALC button to find the zero, or you can use quadratic formula.

#4 — Answer = D

This is a very twisted FOIL question. Start by FOILing the left side: $6x^2 + 3bx + 2ax + ab$. You can match these terms up with the corresponding terms on the right side of the equation. The two terms without an x are going to give you important information: $ab = 28$. There are not very many possible values for a and b. Try the most obvious first: $a = 4$ and $b = 7$. You can test these numbers in the other equation: $4 = 11 - 7$. You can also match up the x-terms in the two quadratics: $3bx + 2ax = cx$. Plug in the values for a and b: $3(7)x + 2(4)x = cx$. Simplify, and you'll find that $c = 29$. Only Choice D includes that value. You can also get 26 by switching the values of a and b so that $a = 7$ and $b = 4$.

#5 — Answer = C

Get Back to Basics. Start by eliminating the fractions. They only complicate things. You can multiply the entire equation by 4 to make it easier to work with: $4x^2 + 2m = nx$. You also need to move all the variables to one side: $4x^2 - nx + 2m = 0$. Plug $a = 4$, $b = -n$, and $c = 2m$ into the quadratic formula. Don't lose the negatives with the n. The result will simplify to Choice C. You can also Arithmetize so you don't need to worry about the variables, but you may end up doing more work than needed with all the plugging in.

Function Properties lesson

The Basics

Like most topics on the SAT, functions sound harder than they actually are. If you haven't taken Algebra 2, some of this may seem very advanced, but a lot of it is just definitions.

> Example 1

The basics of Function Properties are very similar to the basics of Quadratic Properties. You know that x-intercepts, roots, and factors are all basically the same. If you had a quadratic with x-intercepts of 5 and –6, then it would be factored as:

$$y = (x - 5)(x + 6)$$

Notice that the factors have the opposite sign (+/–) as the x-intercept. The same rule applies to "higher order" functions and polynomials:

In this case, we would expect a function that has x-intercepts at –2, 1, and 4 to have factors:

$$y = (x + 2)(x - 1)(x - 4)$$

Only one of these is an answer choice. **The correct answer is Choice C.**

Example 2

As the text says, they ask the same question multiple ways, just like with quadratics. In Example 1, they asked about x-intercepts. Now they're asking about roots. It's the same thing!

A function with roots at 0, –2, and 2 would look like:

$$f(x) = x(x - 2)(x + 2)$$

Choice A is the correct answer.

Function Properties — The Basics

Like quadratics, longer polynomials also have roots, x-intercepts, zeros, and factors. The same rules apply.

The Twists

Example 3

There's one extra thing you should know about roots and factors. It also applies to quadratics, but it's mostly tested with functions like this one.

As you can see, this function has x-intercepts at 3, 0, and –2. We would expect that the function would have factors that look like:

$$y = x(x + 2)(x - 3)$$

But that's not quite it. The one extra thing is that functions "bounce" off the x-axis when they have the same factor twice. Notice that the function dips down to touch the axis at –2, but it barely touches it before going back up. That's a "bounce", and it means that –2 is a double root, so the factor is squared:

$$y = x(x + 2)^2(x - 3)$$

The correct answer is Choice D. In general, if the exponent is even (2, 4, 6…), then the function will bounce. If it's odd (1, 3, 5…), then the function will pass through the axis like it does on this graph at 0 and 3.

Example 4

It's unclear why the SAT likes to test this rule. It has almost no relation to anything else on the test. It's also extremely confusing, which can make it hard to memorize. Here's what helps me:

They don't tell us the equation for g(x), but we can imagine a simple one that includes the point they give us: (–2, 7). How about:

$$g(x) = x + 9$$

It includes the point:

$$g(-2) = -2 + 9 = 7$$

But is it a polynomial? Well, if we cheat a little, we can get it to have a lot more variables without affecting the value:

$$g(x) = 0x^3 + 0x^2 + x + 9$$

But let's just stick with the simple version:

$$g(x) = x + 9$$

Now go through the choices. Choices A and B are clearly not true. The only factor is $x + 9$. A longer polynomial might have those factors, but the question says, which "must" be true. Cross off those choices.

For Choices C and D, we actually need to divide:

$$\begin{array}{r} 1 \\ x+2\overline{)x+9} \\ -(x+2) \\ \hline 7 \end{array}$$

Which means that:

$$\frac{x+9}{x+2} = 1 + \frac{7}{x+2}$$

So Choice C is true. The remainder is 7. And that matches with the example versions of the rule:

If $f(a) = b$, then b is the remainder when $f(x)$ is divided by $(x - a)$.

If $f(3) = 5$, then 5 is the remainder when $f(x)$ is divided by $(x - 3)$.

If $g(-2) = 7$, then 7 is the remainder when $g(x)$ is divided by $(x + 2)$.

Choice C is the correct answer. But we could try D just to make sure:

$$\begin{array}{r} 1 \\ x-2\overline{)x+9} \\ -(x-2) \\ \hline 11 \end{array}$$

Nope! Honestly, this rule is not very important. It comes up occasionally, so it's worth paying attention to if you're looking for a top score, but most people can ignore remainder theorem without worrying.

Function Properties — The Twists

A function "bounces" off the x-axis when it has an even number of the same root. Usually the factor is squared.

Remainder theorem doesn't come up often, but it states:

If $f(a) = b$, then b is the remainder when $f(x)$ is divided by $(x - a)$.

Answers: Functions and Factors

#1 — Answer = C

If x is a factor, then f(x) will equal 0. That happens when x = –1. But the factor itself will be $x + 1$, just like with the zeros of quadratics.

#2 — Answer = A

A function with zeros at –5, 1, and 5 will have factors $x + 5$, $x - 1$, and $x - 5$, respectively. Choice A has those factors.

#3 — Answer = C

The question is asking for the graph that intersects the x-axis 4 times. Only Choice C has 4 x-intercepts.

#4 — Answer = B

The first expression in the question is the rare case where the SAT gives extra information that you don't need. Focus on the second expression, which gives the factors… almost. The $(p^2 - 4)$ term must be factored further using Difference of Two Squares: $(p - 2)(p + 2)$. The fully factored form of the expression is $(p + 1)^2(p - 2)(p + 2)$, which means the polynomial has x-intercepts at –1, 2, and –2, which is Choice B.

Function Values

If you're new to function notation, these questions can seem really hard. But even if you have used function notation before, it's very easy to make a careless mistake. These questions are all about the x- and y-axes. Which one are they asking about?

Example 5

In the Roman numerals, all of the values are in the x position, so we should go to those values on the x-axis. Then go up to where y = 3. Do we intersect the function at that point?

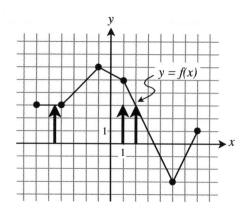

I. $f\left(-\dfrac{9}{2}\right) = 3$ ✓

II. $f(1) = 3$ X

III. $f(2) = 3$ ✓

Only I and III are true, so **Choice C is the correct answer.** The value of f(1) is 5, not 3.

Example 6

This question is slightly more confusing. It's asking about the minimum, so let's find that first. According to the graph, the minimum occurs at (5, –3).

Of course, both numbers are answer choices. The SAT is trying to trick you. They want you to be confused about x versus y.

But go back to the question. It's clear if you just read: "For what value of x…" They're asking for the x-coordinate of the minimum, which is 5. **So Choice A is the correct answer.**

Function Values — Summary

These questions are entirely about x versus y. Pay attention to which value they give you and which value they ask for. Here are the two most common situations:

- If $f(3)$ is given, then $x = 3$. Find y.
- If $f(x) = 3$ is given, then $y = 3$. Find x.

Answers: Function Values

#1 — Answer = C

The question is asking for the x-value when y = 2. The x-coordinate is 4.

#2 — Answer = B

Guess & Check. The question is really asking for the y-value that has exactly two x-values. In other words, draw a horizontal line at each of the numbers in the choices. Choice C is wrong because $y = 2$ only intersects the graph once. Choice D is wrong because $y = 4$ intersects the graph 3 times. Choice A is wrong because $y = -5$ intersects the flat line at the bottom of the graph. It may look like two points, but it's really an infinite number of intersections because you have to include all the decimals in between (–2, –5) and (–4, –5). Choice B is correct because $y = -3$ intersects the graph exactly twice.

#3 — Answer = D

Guess & Check. Only Choice D works because $f(-1) = -3$ and $g(-1) = 3$.

Undefined

You can't divide by 0. Just try it in your calculator. You'll get an error.

Example 7

The question is clear as long as you know what "undefined" means. Just set the denominator of the fraction equal to 0:

$$x^2 - 6x + 8 = 0$$

$$(x - 4)(x - 2) = 0$$

$$x = 4 \text{ and } x = 2$$

Choice C is the correct answer.

Undefined — Summary

A function is undefined when the denominator of the fraction is 0. Find the values that would make the denominator equal 0.

Translations

There are a few rules that dictate how functions "move" in the xy-plane. You could memorize them, but usually you can figure out the translation without the rules. One way is to graph the two functions and see how they compare. Another is to focus on a known point, which is basically our Plug Points Into Equations strategy.

Example 8

We have two equations. Do they remind you of anything? Hint—they both have a squared term…

$$f(x) = (x - 2)^2 + 13$$
$$y = (x + 5)^2 + 13$$

They're both quadratics! And they're both in vertex form. We know the vertex of each, and we can see how it changes.

Starting vertex: $(2, 13)$

Translated vertex: $(-5, 13)$

The difference is 7, so the correct answer is 7.

Translations — Summary

Instead of thinking about the entire function, focus on one point and see how it changes.

If you want, you can memorize the rules for translations of a function $f(x)$:
- $f(x) + 2$ = translation up 2
- $f(x) - 2$ = translation down 2
- $f(x + 2)$ = translation left 2
- $f(x - 2)$ = translation right 2

Answers: Special Function Values

#1 — Answer = D
Ignore the numerator. The question wants the denominator equal to 0. You could easily Guess & Check, but it might be faster to solve algebraically.

FOIL and distribute: $0 = x^2 + 4x + 4 - 8x - 16 + 16$. Combine like terms: $0 = x^2 - 4x + 4$. Factor and you'll find that the solution is $x = 2$.

#2 — Answer = A
Plug Points Into Equations. This question is very easy if you just focus on the easiest point, which is the y-intercept (0, 10). The new equation is the negative version of the graph, so it should include the point (0, –10). Only Choice A includes that point.

Circle Properties lesson

The Basics

Just like lines and quadratics, circles have a standard equation. Memorize it.

Example 1

$$(x - 3)^2 + (y + 2)^2 = 4$$

center: $(3, -2)$

radius: 2

point on the circle: (3, 0)

Points that lie on the circle will fit the equation:

$$(3 - 3)^2 + (0 + 2)^2 = 4$$

$$0^2 + 2^2 = 4$$

$$4 = 4 \checkmark$$

We knew that (3, 0) would lie on the circle because the center is (3, –2) and the radius is 2. Just go 2 units in any direction. So (3, –4), (1, –2), and (5, –2) are all on the circle. Let's graph it:

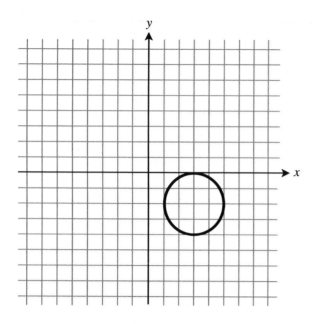

Properties. The only big difference is that, with circles, we maintain balance by adding the number to both sides of the equation instead of adding it and subtracting it to the same side. The point is you have to keep things equal.

Circle Properties — The Twists

Get Back to Basics with weird circle equations by completing the square.

Answers: Circle Properties

#1 — Answer = C
Work backwards by starting with the equation of the circle described: $(x - 9)^2 + (y + 4)^2 = 25$. FOIL both terms to get the equation to look like the choices: $x^2 - 18x + 81 + y^2 + 8y + 16 = 25$. Combine like terms, and subtract the 25 to get Choice C.

#2 — Answer = A
Plug Points Into Equations. But first, eliminate Choices B and D because they do not have the right center point. The point $\left(1, -\dfrac{12}{5}\right)$ can be plugged into the two remaining choices to see if it's a point on the circle. The arithmetic is tricky because of all the fractions, but Choice A works.

#3 — Answer = C
Plug Points Into Equations. But this has a twist. Points that lie on the circle will work in the equation. Points that lie inside the circle will work in this inequality: $(x - 4)^2 + (y - 5)^2 < 9$. Think about it logically. This inequality is saying that the distance from the center is less than the radius. Only Choice C works in the inequality. You could also draw a graph of the circle and plot the choices as points.

#4 — Answer = A
Get Back to Basics. Group the terms, then complete the square twice:
$(x^2 - 2x + 1) + (y^2 - 12y + 36) = -12 + 1 + 36$.
Simplify and you'll get: $(x - 1)^2 + (y - 6)^2 = 25$.
Remember that 25 is not the radius. It's the radius squared, so take the square root to find that the radius is 5.

Circle Properties — The Basics

Memorize the standard circle equation:

$$(x - h)^2 + (y - k)^2 = r^2$$

The center is (h, k).

The radius is r.

Points that lie on the circle are (x, y).

The Twists

Example 2

The SAT twists the standard circle equation so that it's just a jumble of x's and y's. Completing the square is the only way back to Get Back to Basics:

$$x^2 + y^2 + 6x - 8y = 0$$

$$(x^2 + 6x) + (y^2 - 8y) = 0$$

$$(x^2 + 6x + 9) + (y^2 - 8y + 16) = 0 + 9 + 16$$

$$(x + 3)^2 + (y - 4)^2 = 25$$

The center is (–3, 4), and the radius is 5. For more practice completing the square, see Quadratic

---

Linear Models lesson

The Basics

If it looks like a line and moves like a line, then it probably *is* a line.

Example 1

Ignore the story for a second. Look at the equation. It's very clearly a line:

$$y = mx + b$$
$$L = 2.1m + 0.6$$

In the Linear Properties packet, we focused on slopes and y-intercepts. The same is true here. But when we have a story, the parts of the line take on certain roles. The slope is usually a rate of some kind, like miles per hour or the price for each sandwich. The y-intercept is a starting point because most Models don't involve negative numbers, which restricts the graph to the first quadrant. (Look ahead to Example 3 to see a visual.)

In Example 1, the question asks for "the estimated increase, in centimeters, of the insect's length each month". That sounds like a rate—centimeters per month. They're asking for the slope of the line.

Don't get fooled by the *m* in the equation. The slope is the number attached to the variable. **So the correct answer is Choice C.**

Example 2

The story is long. Is this a Math question or a Reading question? Ignore it for now and focus on the end. This isn't all that different from the last example. Compare the equation to the standard line:

$$y = mx + b$$

$$n = 1,562 - 225d$$

Be careful. There's a slight twist here. The model does not line up exactly with the standard equation. Rearrange it to Get Back to Basics:

$$n = -225d + 1,562$$

The question asks for the meaning of 1,562. If this were a regular line, 1,562 would be the y-intercept. Since it's a model, it's probably something similar to a starting point.

Choices C and D are clearly rates, so both of those are wrong. **Choice B is the correct answer because it's literally the starting amount of wall space that Mark has to paint.**

Linear Models — The Basics

Even though there's a story, you should still think in terms of slopes and y-intercepts.

The slope is usually a rate (how much something increases or decreases) or a cost per unit.

The y-intercept is usually a starting point or flat fee.

If the equation is slightly off, Get Back to Basics by using standard y=mx+b form.

The Twists

Example 3

This is clearly a line, and the choices are clearly in y=mx+b form. Most people start by looking at the y-intercept, which is 9. That eliminates Choices A and C.

Now look at the slope. It looks like we rise one box and run two boxes, so the slope is $\frac{1}{2}$ and the answer must be Choice D.

WRONG! The most common way the SAT twists graph questions is by messing with the scale on the axes. You're so used to just counting the boxes that you don't even bother to look at the scale. Such a common mistake, but also such an easy one to fix. Get in the habit of double checking the units every time. I think you'll quickly start to see for yourself how often the SAT tries to trick you by changing the units.

You can find the slope by counting the boxes AND knowing how much each box is worth. One box on the y-axis (the rise) is equal to 3 units, and one box on the x-axis (the run) is equal to $\frac{1}{2}$. The slope is really a rise of 3 and a run of 1, which is why **Choice B is the correct answer with the correct slope of 3.** To play it safe, Plug Points Into Equations. Test a point that the line passes through.

Linear Models — The Twists

Check your units! The SAT loves to mess with the scale on the axes, so you have to actively check to see what each box represents when you're looking for the slope.

In general, there are a lot of ways that the SAT can twist Linear Models questions. The stories will be weird, but the equations will look like lines.

Answers: Linear Models

#1 — Answer = A
This is a line. Rearrange it to y=mx+b form: $c = 1f + 3$. The question is clearly asking for a slope, and the slope of this line would be 1.

#2 — Answer = D
Turn the text into an equation: $L = AG$. The question gives you the age (A) and the chart gives you the growth constant (G). Substitute them into the equation: $L = (3)(4.4)$. Multiply to get 13.2.

#3 — Answer = C
Plug Points Into Equations. You have an equation from the first question: $L = AG$. The scatterplot is clearly a line, so pick a point that looks like it would be on the line. Both (8, 20) and (10, 25) look like they roughly lie on the line of best fit (not shown). If you test the first one, you're essentially finding the slope of the line, which is the growth constant:

$20 = (8)(G)$. You'd find that G is 2.5, which is approximately the growth constant for the Toothless guppy.

#4 — Answer = C
You can solve this question without using the fact that the two fish are currently 8 centimeters long. This is a rare case where the SAT gives you information you don't need. Instead, use the equation to calculate the length each fish would grow during 18 months. But first, you have to untwist the question by converting 18 months into 1.5 years. For the yellowback stickler, your equation would be: $L = (1.5)(3.7)$. For the blue snapper, your equation would be: $L = (1.5)(3.4)$. You should get that the yellowback grows 5.55 centimeters, and the blue snapper grows 5.1 centimeters. Subtract them to find the difference is 0.45 centimeters.

#5 — Answer = C
The twist is that they tell you that the model only works between 5 and 40 years. But that doesn't affect the estimated increase. That's still the slope of the line. The equation is already in y=mx+b form, and 9 corresponds with the slope.

#6 — Answer = D
Create a y=mx+b style equation. The starting amount (b) is 255,000, and the rate (m) is 120. Since the total weight can't exceed 340,000, you'll need to set up an inequality where the mx+b part is less than or equal to 340,000. Putting all of this information into y=mx+b gives you: $340{,}000 \geq 255{,}000 + 120n$. The slope and y-intercept are reversed, but it's still a line.

#7 — Answer = B
There's a really mean twist in this question! You might be tempted to put 100 in for w, but that is not correct. Devin wants to increase the total weight by 100, so you need to find the starting value first, then increase it by 100. Luckily, this model is already in y=mx+b form, so the starting amount is 80. Adding 100 means that you need to find the value of t when w = 180. Solving for t, you should get 12.5, which is approximately 13.

#8 — Answer = C

This is basically a Rearrange Formulas question. Subtract 80 from both sides, then divide both sides by 8: $t = \dfrac{w - 80}{8}$. You can't simplify this any further because the terms on the top cannot both be divided by 8.

#9 — Answer = B

Plug Points Into Equations. They give you the equation of the line of best fit. They want the y-value when $x = 3$. Use your calculator, and you'll get 38.54.

#10 — Answer = A

Plug Points Into Equations. The twist is that the x-values are NOT 2010 and 2015. The question specifies that t is years since 2010, so the first point is really (0, 46), and the second point is really (5, 52). Only Choice A includes both of those points.

#11 — Answer = A

The twist here is that there are two "x" variables. But this equation still matches up with y=mx+b. Choice A is correct because it describes the 2 as a rate, which makes sense since it's the slope. Choice B is incorrect because 35 would be the y-intercept. Choices C and D are incorrect because nothing in this equation suggests that there is a maximum or minimum.

Quantity & Value lesson

The Basics

These models are essentially Point of Intersection questions with a story. You'll need to create two equations. They're called Quantity & Value because the two equations almost always represent the total quantity/number of items and the total value/cost of those items.

Example 1

The bolded headings are meant to keep you organized. You should follow a similar process when you encounter Quantity & Value questions on the SAT. Start by very clearly stating your variables (the SAT loves to twist these questions by matching the variable with the wrong value (see #2 in the Exercise).

Let d = dimes
Let q = quarters

The Quantity equation will give you the total number of coins:

$$d + q = 15$$

The Value equation will be a little more complex because you need to multiply each variable by the value of that item. In this case, dimes are worth $0.10 each and quarters are worth $0.25 each:

$$0.10d + 0.25q = 2.70$$

To find the point of intersection, either stack the equations and eliminate a variable or manipulate an equation so that you can substitute. Since the Quantity equation is usually very simple, it's probably easier to manipulate it and substitute:

$$\begin{array}{r} d + q = 15 \\ \underline{-d \qquad\quad -d} \\ q = 15 - d \end{array}$$

$$0.10d + 0.25q = 2.70$$

$$0.10d + 0.25(15 - d) = 2.70$$

Distribute:

$$0.10d + 3.75 - 0.25d = 2.70$$

Combine like terms:

$$3.75 - 0.15d = 2.70$$

Subtract:

$$\begin{array}{r} 3.75 - 0.15d = \quad 2.70 \\ \underline{-3.75 \qquad\qquad -3.75} \\ -0.15d = -1.05 \end{array}$$

Divide:

$$\dfrac{-0.15d}{-0.15} = \dfrac{-1.05}{-0.15}$$

$$d = 7$$

The correct answer is Choice B. But one thing to point out is that the number of quarters is 8:

$$7 + q = 15$$

And of course, that's an answer too. The SAT will almost always give you answer choices that represent both of the variables. Get in the habit of rereading the question before you bubble so that you don't accidentally choose the wrong variable.

Quantity & Value — The Basics

Quantity & Value questions are really just Point of Intersection questions with a story. And you'll need to come up with the equations.

Take the time to write out what each variable represents.

Start with an equation that represents the Quantity of items.

Then make an equation that represents the Value of the items. This one will usually have coefficients in front of the variables.

Solve using the stack method or by substituting.

Double check to make sure that you've solved for the correct variable.

The Twists

Example 2

This is a Quantity & Value question that has been twisted into something that seems completely different. But we know it's Quantity & Value because we have two items that have different values (6- and 10-person tables). Stay organized:

Let x = 6-person tables
Let y = 10-person tables

How many tables are there? (Quantity):

$$x + y = 18$$

How many people will be seated at these tables? (Value):

$$6x + 10y = 152$$

Manipulate the Quantity equation so it's in terms of one variable:

$$y = 18 - x$$

Substitute into the Value equation:

$$6x + 10(18 - x) = 152$$

Solve:

$$6x + 180 - 10x = 152$$

$$180 - 4x = 152$$

$$-4x = -28$$

$$x = 7$$

Did we solve for the correct variable?

Let x = 6-person tables

$x = 7$

"how many of the tables are 10-person tables?"

No! Plug back in to find y:

$$7 + y = 18$$

$$y = 11$$

The correct answer is 11.

Example 3

This question has a little bit more going on, but at least we don't need to solve any of the equations. There are two main twists. First, we have inequalities to worry about. Second, we have these other two weird inequalities in addition to the normal Quantity & Value equations.

Start with the Quantity & Value parts. The question says that Mona "needs to order at least 12 pizzas", which sounds like the Quantity of pizzas needs to be greater than or equal to 12. We can eliminate Choices A and B because they have the wrong inequality sign in our Quantity equation. It should be:

$$x + y \geq 12$$

The Value equation should be:

$$14x + 16y \leq 180$$

Both of the remaining choices have this, so it doesn't affect our answer. Still, it's important to know why it needs to look like this. The question says that "her budget for the party is no more than $180", which means the Value of the pizzas needs to be less than or equal to $180.

The remaining inequalities are strange, but just think about what they would be saying. The question tells us that "x is the number of regular pizzas". Turn the two remaining choices into words:

C) $x \geq 1$
The number of regular pizzas is greater than or equal to 1.

D) $x \leq 1$
The number of regular pizzas is less than or equal to 1.

Choice D makes no sense. Why are we limited to just one regular pizza? For that matter, the last inequality would say that we can only have 1

pepperoni pizza, which is just 2 pizzas total. Yet the question already said she needs at least 12 pizzas.

Choice C is the correct answer. The question actually says that Mona needs "at least one pizza of each type" which is why both of the extra inequalities need to be included in the set. She can't order only pepperoni pizzas. She needs at least one regular pizza.

Quantity & Value — The Twists

Quantity & Value models can take many forms, and have weird stories. But the process to solve is very consistent. Look for clues, like two different items that have different values.

Pay attention to inequalities. Sometimes they're testing your knowledge of the symbols (< vs >) more than your knowledge of the equations.

Answers: Quantity & Value

#1 — Answer = 8

Your Quantity equation should be: $h + s = 11$. Your Value equation should be: $5h + 3s = 39$. Since the question wants the number of screwdrivers (s), you should use the "stack" method to eliminate the h-terms. You'll find there are 8 screwdrivers.

#2 — Answer = C

Notice that the second equation in each choice (Quantity) is exactly the same. Focus on the Value equation. The question says that x represents the number of boxes, which weigh 50 pounds each. So Choices A and B are wrong because the variables are matched with the wrong values. Choice C is correct because the total weight must be less than or equal to the plane's capacity, which is 10,000 pounds.

#3 — Answer = 13

Your Quantity equation should be: $r + b = 19$. Your Value equation should be: $2r + 5b = 77$. Since the question wants the number of black cards, you should use the "stack" method to eliminate the r-terms. You should get that there are 13 black cards.

#4 — Answer = D

Choices A and C can be eliminated because they have the wrong Quantity equation. The quantity of memberships is $S + P = 130$. Choice D is correct because it has the correct Value equation, multiplying the variables by the costs given in the question.

#5 — Answer = 2

Set your variables. You can make x the number of 12 petal flowers and y the number of 14 petal flowers. Your Quantity equation should be: $x + y = 16$. Your Value equation should be: $12x + 14y = 196$. Since the question wants the number of 14-petal flowers, you should solve for y. Use the "stack" method, and you'll get that $y = 2$.

Geometry Models lesson

The Basics

Arithmetize. If they're talking about dimensions, give the shape actual dimensions. Draw pictures to help you visualize.

Example 1

This question is begging to be Arithmetized. Pick a value for the width:

Let $w = 10$

So the length is 5 feet shorter than twice the width? Twice the width is 20. Five feet shorter means:

$l = 15$

The perimeter is the sum of all the sides. That's two lengths and two widths:

$$p = 2l + 2w$$

$$p = 2(15) + 2(10)$$

$$p = 30 + 20$$

$$p = 50$$

Now just check the choices to see which one equals 50:

A) $5 - 2(10) = -15$ X

B) $4(10) - 10 = 30$ X

C) $6(10) - 10 = 50$ ✓

D) $2(10)^2 - 5(10) = 150$ X

Choice C is the correct answer. Just so you are aware, Choice D gives the value of the area. Another one of the SAT's tricks.

Example 2

This is another great Arithmetize question. When working with percentages, 10s and 100s are the best numbers to pick because the math will be much easier. Here's the rectangle:

It's a 10 by 10 rectangle with an area of 100. "But isn't that a square?" Yes. But a square is just a rectangle with equal sides.

The question says the length is increased by 20% and the area is decreased by 16%. Since we picked 10s and 100s, we can do this math in our heads:

Just make an area equation to find the value of the missing side:

$$A = lw$$

$$84 = 12w$$

$$7 = w$$

Going from 10 to 7 would be a 30% decrease, **so Choice C is the answer.**

Geometry Models — The Basics

Know the basic area and perimeter formulas for a rectangle:

area = (length)(width)

perimeter = 2(length) + 2(width)

Very rarely, you also need to know the area formulas for parallelograms and trapezoids:

area of a parallelogram = (base)(height)

$$\text{area of a trapezoid } = \left(\frac{b_1 + b_2}{2}\right) h$$

Arithmetize so that you can more easily visualize the geometry. When working with percentages, pick 10s and 100s so the math is easier.

The Twists

Example 3

This question should remind you of something. Lines!

$$y = mx + b$$
$$A = 5p + 100$$

It sounds like they're asking about a rate, so you might be thinking that 5 is the answer because it's the slope. But be careful. They've twisted this question. The slope gives the increase in the area for each additional foot of the perimeter, but the question wants the increase in the perimeter for each additional square foot of the area. See the difference?

The simple solution is to rearrange the line so that it gives the perimeter in terms of the area:

$$A = 5p + 100$$

$$A - 100 = 5p$$

$$\frac{1}{5}A - 20 = p$$

Now it's easier to see that the answer is $\frac{1}{5}$, but you could have Arithmetized from the start:

Let $p = 10$

$$A = 5(10) + 100$$

$$A = 150$$

Now increase the area by 1 additional square foot, like the question says:

$$A = 151$$

$$151 = 5p + 100$$

$$51 = 5p$$

$$10.2 = p$$

Our value of p increased by 0.2, which is equal to $\frac{1}{5}$. **Choice B is the correct answer.**

Geometry Models — The Twists

Sometimes a Geometry Model isn't really about Geometry at all. Think about other question types, and solve accordingly.

Arithmetize to make things easier!

Answers: Geometry Models

#1 — Answer = 25

Arithmetize. You'll have to be clever. If you make $BC = 100$, $AD = 200$, and the height = 1, then you'll have easier numbers to work with. The area of a trapezoid is given by $\left(\frac{b_1 + b_2}{2}\right) h$. Plugging in your values gives the original area as 150. If you reduce BC and AD by 25%, they become 75 and 150, respectively. The new area is 112.5. Find the percent decrease by: $\dfrac{150 - 112.5}{150} \times 100$. You'll get 25 percent.

#2 — Answer = B

You can find the original volume of water in the tank, or you can skip directly to the 1,800 cubic centimeters that are added. This volume of water will have a length of 30 and a width of 20 when it is poured into the tank. That's enough that you could find the height of just those 1,800 cubic centimeters: $1,800 = (30)(20)(h)$. Divide to find that the added height is 3 centimeters. That's in addition to the 10 centimeters that were already in the tank (because it was originally filled halfway), so the total height is now 13 centimeters.

#3 — Answer = 18

As instructed, set the two congruent sides equal to each other: $2x - 11 = x - 3$. Solve for x to find that $x = 8$. Use 8 to find the perimeter. The two congruent sides are 5, and the base is 8, which adds up to 18.

#4 — Answer = 9

Create an equation for the width: $w = l - 8$. Use this equation in the area formula, which is length times width: $153 = (l)(l - 8)$. You'll create a quadratic equation: $0 = l^2 - 8l - 153$. You can factor this into: $0 = (l - 17)(l + 9)$. Since you can only have a positive value, the length is 17, which makes the width 9. You could also have used Guess & Check from the start since the SAT tends to give easy-to-use numbers. Just keep multiplying numbers that are 8 apart until you get 153.

Exponential Models lesson

The Basics

The SAT almost always tests exponential equations in the form of a model, or story. It's important to understand how Exponential Models differ from Linear Models. Notice that linear growth is constant. The line always has the same slope. But exponential growth is curved. As you increase x, you keep going up by larger and larger amounts.

Example 1

Some questions are only testing the definition. Let's go through the choices:

A) This is linear growth because the amount of the increase doesn't change. If Grover makes $100,000 in his first year (initial salary), then he'll get a $1,000 raise each year (1% of initial salary). That's a constant increase of $1,000 per year. Usually we associate percentages with exponential growth, but this time it was a twist to throw you off. And that's why you always read all of the answers!

B) This is more complicated, but it's basically the same as Choice A. This time, Grover would get a raise of $2,000 (2% of initial salary) plus the extra $500. That's a larger increase, but it's still the same amount each year. The constant rate is $2,500 per year, which is linear growth.

C) The key words in this choice are "1.2% of his previous year's salary". This tells us that his salary will increase by more and more as his salary grows each year. For example, he'd get a raise of $1,200 after the first year (1.2% of initial salary), but he'd get a raise of $1,214.40 after the second year (1.2% of his new salary of $101,200). After the third year, his raise would be $1,228.97 (1.2% of his second year salary of $102,414.40). **Since the growth itself is growing, this is an example of exponential growth.** Let's check D just to be sure.

D) This is very obviously linear growth. Grover's salary will increase by the same amount each year, so it's a constant rate.

Choice C is the correct answer.

Exponential Models — The Basics

Exponential growth usually involves percentages.

But make sure the percentage leads to larger and larger growth each year. If the rate of increase is constant, then that's linear growth.

If a model is decreasing exponentially, then it's called exponential decay.

The Twists

Example 2

There are many versions of the Exponential equation in the world, but I prefer to use the **OPEN** equation so that we're consistent with how we learned Percentages. But since the change takes place over time, we'll use a variable exponent on top of the percentage. Otherwise, it's the same equation!

It might be helpful to remember that anything raised to the 0 is 1. That's why the original amount is outside the exponent:

$$(\text{Original})(1+P)^0 = \text{New}$$

$$(\text{Original})(1) = \text{New}$$

$$\text{Original} = \text{New} \quad \text{(when zero time has passed)}$$

In this question, you can tell from the choices that the equation itself doesn't really matter. The only thing to decide is how you represent 2% growth. We'll always think of percentages as decimals when we're dealing with Exponential Models:

$$2\% = 0.02$$

But we don't want to find 2% of the bacteria. We want to add 2% more bacteria. This is why the exponential OPEN formula has a 1 in the parentheses. We add or subtract our percentage, depending on whether we want growth or decay. In this case, we definitely want growth:

$$1 + 0.02 = 1.02$$

Choice B is correct because it shows the correct percentage. Since this is the most common twist, it's very important that you get in the habit of double checking that you've got the right percentage in the parentheses.

Example 3

In this example, we need to construct the Exponential Model from scratch. The original is clearly stated:

$$(O)(1 \pm P)^t = N$$

$$(800)(1 - 0.12)^3 = N$$

$$(800)(0.88)^3 = N$$

Notice that our percentage doesn't actually look like 12% of anything. That's because we're really saying that we want 88% of our value each hour. There's no difference between taking 88% of something and decreasing something by 12%.

Solve for N. Don't forget PEMDAS dictates that we need to deal with the exponent first, and then we multiply:

$$(800)(0.681472) = N$$

$$545.1776 = N$$

To the nearest whole number, the correct answer would be 545.

Use the OPEN formula to build exponential equations the same way you use y=mx+b to build lines. It's the same formula as percent change, but with a variable as an exponent on the percentage.

$$(O)(1 \pm P)^t = N$$

Pay very close attention to the percentages. Percentages should be expressed as decimals. If growth, add the percentage to 1. If decay, subtract the percentage from 1.

If the twist affects the other parts of the equation, you can probably Arithmetize to better understand what's going on.

Answers: Exponential Models

#1 — Answer = 116

Set up an exponential model using the exponential OPEN formula: $100(1 + 0.03)^5 = N$. Use your calculator, and you'll find that the value is approximately 115.92, which rounds to 116.

#2 — Answer = 12

Set up an exponential model using the OPEN formula, but take note that this time we know N and need to solve for O: $(O)(1 + 0.80)^6 = 408$. Solve for O and you'll get that there were 12 wolves in 2005.

#3 — Answer = A

Arithmetize. If $x = 1$, then the grocery store would have 156 customers after 1 year. Since the choices model the number of customers in terms of months, you should find the equation that gives you 156 customers when $m = 12$ because 12 months is the same as 1 year. Only Choice A gives you 156.

#4 — Answer = D

This is a mean question! Even though you're in the Exponential Models exercise, this question says that the cost of the contract increases at a constant rate, which is d dollars per year. A constant rate means linear growth, not exponential. So Choices A and B

are wrong. Since the rate is given by d, Choice D is the answer because the rate needs to be the slope of the line.

#5 — Answer = C

Arithmetize. Even though the question is talking in terms of percents, 5% is NOT the percentage that goes in parentheses. If there were 100 gallons of water in the pool to start, then only 5 gallons would remain after 6 hours. In other words, the 5% tells you the new amount, not the percentage. Your equation should be: $(100)(1 - P)^6 = 5$. Divide by 100 to get $(1 - P)^6 = 0.05$. To get rid of the exponent, raise both sides to the $\frac{1}{6}$ power. You should get: $1 - P = 0.607$. Solving for P gets you $P = 0.393$, which is approximately 39%. If you have trouble getting rid of the exponent, then just Guess & Check with the answer choices by substituting them in for P.

#6 — Answer = B

First, create an exponential model to find the original amount of trees in the forest. Since the rate is given in terms of decades, the exponent will be 7 to represent the 70 years between 1940 and 2010. Your model should be: $(O)(1 - 0.04)^7 = 3,075$. You should get approximately $O = 4,092$. To find the number of trees in 1960, the exponent should be 2 for the 2 decades since 1940: $4,092(0.96)^2 = 3,771$. Do the same thing for 1980, where the exponent will be 4: $4,092(0.96)^4 = 3,476$. The difference is 295, which is closest to Choice B. It's a little off because you rounded along the way. This question has a lot of steps, but they're easy once you have the model.

Rearrange Formulas lesson

The Basics

This is just Algebra! The story rarely matters. The answer choices will help you understand what you're supposed to do.

Example 1

This question doesn't give you an initial equation, but you should memorize the formula for speed:

$$\text{speed} = \frac{\text{distance}}{\text{time}}$$

$$s = \frac{d}{t}$$

Now you can rearrange the formula as asked. Multiply both sides by t.

$$\left(\frac{t}{1}\right) s = \frac{d}{\cancel{t}} \left(\frac{\cancel{t}}{1}\right)$$

$$st = d$$

Choice A is the correct answer.

Example 2

Here's a good example of a question where the story doesn't matter. The choices clearly want you to rearrange this formula to solve for v^2:

$$E_k = \frac{1}{2}mv^2$$

$$(2)\ E_k = \frac{1}{\cancel{2}}mv^2\ (\cancel{2})$$

$$2E_k = mv^2$$

$$\frac{2E_k}{m} = \frac{\cancel{m}v^2}{\cancel{m}}$$

$$\frac{2E_k}{m} = v^2$$

The correct answer is Choice C.

Rearrange Formulas — The Basics

Read the story, but don't worry if it's confusing. It probably doesn't matter. The answer choices often tell you what the question wants.

Show your work, and stay organized. The most common algebra mistakes are just as common here.

The Twists

Example 3

A common twist is to ask you to compare different values in the formula. You could do these algebraically, but the SAT knows the most common mistakes and will make those mistakes into answer choices. You're better off picking values and Arithmetizing.

In this question, the width is constant, so you can make it equal to 1 to keep things simple. Keep the areas simple too. The subscripts help you keep track of each Plot, since each one will have a length and a width:

$$\text{Let } w_A = w_B = 1$$
$$\text{Let } A_A = 3$$
$$\text{Let } A_B = 1$$

The question says that the area of Plot A is 3 times the area of Plot B, so we picked 3 and 1. Just make sure you assign the values to the right plots.

Now use area formula to compare the lengths:

$$A = lw$$

$$3 = (l_A)(1)$$
$$3 = l_A$$

$$1 = (l_B)(1)$$
$$1 = l_B$$

So the length of Plot A is 3, and the length of Plot B is 1. **Since 1 is $\frac{1}{3}$ of 3, the correct answer is B.**

Example 4

Things get complicated when there are squared terms in the formulas. It's very easy to make mistakes, so numbers help a lot. The cylinder formula is given in the Reference Chart: $V = \pi r^2 h$. Start by making two volume formulas for Containers A and B:

$$V_A = \pi (r_A)^2 (h_A)$$

$$V_B = \pi(r_B)^2(h_B)$$

The question says they have the same volume, so we can set the two equations equal to each other:

$$\pi(r_A)^2(h_A) = \pi(r_B)^2(h_B)$$

Get rid of those π's. They cancel out, and they're just in the way:

$$(r_A)^2(h_A) = (r_B)^2(h_B)$$

The question says the radius of A is 4 times the radius of B. Arithmetize with easy numbers:

$$(4)^2(h_A) = (1)^2(h_B)$$

They want the height of A to the height of B, which could be expressed as a fraction like this:

$$\frac{h_A}{h_B}$$

Let's rearrange our equation so it looks like that:

$$(4)^2(h_A) = (1)^2(h_B)$$

$$16h_A = h_B$$

$$\frac{16\cancel{h_A}}{\cancel{h_A}} = \frac{h_B}{h_A}$$

$$\frac{16}{1} = \frac{h_B}{h_A}$$

$$\frac{1}{16} = \frac{h_A}{h_B}$$

So the ratio is 1:16, which is the same as Choice D.

Answers: Rearrange Formulas

#1 — Answer = C

Divide both sides by $5dm$ to get w by itself. You'll get $w = \dfrac{p}{5dm}$.

#2 — Answer = B

Arithmetize. Normally you'd have to use the Reference Chart to find the formula, but it was given here for convenience. You should make the original dimensions of the pyramid a length of 3 (to cancel out the fraction), a width of 1, and a height of 1. This makes the original volume equal to 1. As instructed, multiply the height by 6, which makes it 6. The length and width stay the same, so the new volume is also 6, which is 6 times greater than 1.

#3 — Answer = B

Multiply both sides by v to start: $Lv = (c + s)^2$. Take the square root of both sides to get $\sqrt{Lv} = c + s$. That's all you need to do.

#4 — Answer = C

Arithmetize. Pick convenient numbers. Make $c = 0.5$ and $s = 0.5$ so that the top term becomes 1^2, which is just 1. The original velocity should also be $v = 1$ so that the original length is simply $L = 1$. Double the velocity so that $v = 2$. Now the overall length is $L = \dfrac{1}{2}$, which is a decrease of 50% from the original.

WTF Models lesson

There's no real lesson for these. It's best to let you try your best without much direction. All of the answers are given as one long Exercise. There aren't really that many patterns on these questions. Some will be similar to the Value half of the Quantity & Value models. Others will be like Ratios, so thinking in terms of units will help you stay organized.

Overall, Arithmetizing can help you on the questions where they just want you to generate an equation. When they want you to solve, you might be able to Guess & Check, but that's hard when there are no answer choices.

Most Multi-Part Models will include a variety of the other types of models that we've seen. Remember that you should treat multi-part questions as separate questions. You will almost never need the answer from one of the parts to answer the others. They're independent of each other, and just happen to rely on the same chart, graph, or equation.

Oh, and if you're wondering why they're called WTF Models, just wait until you try some of the hard ones. You'll probably get that "WTF?" feeling and understand.

WTF Models — Summary

Show your work. Stay organized. Read carefully.

Arithmetize to better understand what's going on.

If you're completely lost, take your best guess and move on. But pay attention to where you are in the test. If it's an early question, it's probably easy, so trust your gut. If it's later on in the section, it's probably hard, so it's okay to guess and move on.

Answers: WTF Models

#1 — Answer = B
This is essentially the Value equation. Match the volume to the correct variable: $16w + 20s$. You can't combine these terms.

#2 — Answer = C
The twist here is that you need to convert the percentages into decimals. That eliminates Choices A

and B. Choice C is the answer because it matches the discounts with the correct variables.

#3 — Answer = D
Arithmetize. If Luis rented the truck for 7 days, it would cost him $(7)(\$50) = \$350$. Since 7 days is equivalent to 1 week, you can plug $w = 1$ into all of the choices to see which one also gives you 350. Only Choice D works.

#4 — Answer = A
Arithmetize. You should assume that there were 100 hares originally, in January of 2010. A 10% increase would mean there were 110 hares in December of 2010. A 6% decrease would mean there were 103.4 hares at the end of 2011. Be careful here. The question says that h is the number of hares at the end of 2011, so your numbers make $h = 103.4$. Plug that into the answer choices to see which one gives you 100, which is the number of hares at the beginning of 2010. Only Choice A works.

#5 — Answer = 120
Create two equations: $J + L = 300$ and $L = J + 60$. Substitute the second equation in for L in the first equation: $J + J + 60 = 300$. Solve for J to get that $J = 120$.

#6 — Answer = 5
Create two equations, but be careful with the subtraction that represents the "less than". Your equations should be: $B = S - 3$ and $5B + 3S = 49$. Substitute the first equation in for B in the second: $5(S - 3) + 3S = 49$. Solve for S to get that $S = 8$. But since the question wants the value of a blerg, you need to plug back into the first equation: $B = 8 - 3$. So a blerg is worth 5 points.

#7 — Answer = 46
Create two equations. The first is easy: $x + y + n = 138$. The second should be: $n = \frac{1}{2}(x + y)$. Since the second equation is messy, you should multiply by 2 to eliminate the fraction: $2n = x + y$. Notice that $x + y$ is also in the first equation. You can substitute without ever finding the

values of x and y: $2n + n = 138$. Solve for n and you'll get that $n = 46$.

#8 — Answer = 25

There are many ways to solve this question. The easiest is to focus on the green apples since you know both the percentage and the actual number. The question says that Ivy will pick a total of 11 green apples (6 in the morning and 5 in the afternoon). Those 11 green apples represent 20% of all the apples since it also says that 80% of the apples should be red. You can set up a proportion to find the total number of apples: $\dfrac{20\,\%}{100\,\%} = \dfrac{11 \text{ green}}{x \text{ total apples}}$. Cross-multiply and divide to find that Ivy picks a total of 55 apples. Subtract the 11 green apples and the 19 red apples that she has already picked to find that Ivy needs to pick an additional 25 red apples.

#9 — Answer = B

Since the right side of the inequality is the same for all of the answer choices, you should focus on the left side. The question says that the team will need to win x additional games, so you can eliminate Choices A and D because they're subtracting x. The question also says that the team won 55% of its first 120 games, so Choice B is the answer. There's no need to take 55% of x.

#10 — Answer = D

Subtract H. Subtract B. Divide the whole thing by n. The most common mistake is subtracting H and B at the same time and forgetting to distribute the negative to the B.

#11 — Answer = 39

Set up an inequality such that Venue A > Venue D, as stated in the question. Using the formula and the values from the chart, your inequality should be: $(3000 + 800) + 75n > (3500 + 875) + 60n$. Simplify and solve for n to get that $n > 38.3$. You need to have a whole number of guests, so you MUST go up to the next highest whole number, which is 39. Even though you would normally round down to 38, you can't in this case because then n would not be large enough.

#12 — Answer = 122

First, take 30% off the cost of the band at Venue B by multiplying: $650 \times 0.70 = 455$. Then put the values into the equation: $(5,500 + 455) + 85n = 16,325$. Solve for n, and you should get that $n = 122$.

#13 — Answer = D

Unfortunately, there's no quick way to solve this. You need to set the equation equal to $10,000 and solve for n for each venue. You should get that Venue $A = 82$, $B = 45$, $C = 60$, and $D = 93$, so Venue D allows the most guests for that budget.

#14 — Answer = C

This is essentially a Linear Model. Put the equation into y=mx+b form: $y = Fx + (H + B)$. The y-intercept is the term in parentheses, which is not attached to the x-term. The y-intercept is the hosting fee and the band added together, which is Choice C.

#15 — Answer = B

First, eliminate Choices A and C. The cost needs to be less than or equal to $10,000, so the inequality sign in these choices is backwards. The real question is whether the a belongs in parentheses. Since 75 is the cost per plate, you need to multiply both g and a by 75 to determine the final cost for the people who attend. In other words, you need to subtract $75 for each guest who does not attend. Choice D is wrong because it simply subtracts the number of guests who do not attend without taking into account that each of them would save Lauren $75.

Part Over Whole lesson

The Basics

Part Over Whole questions are remarkably similar to each other. The process is almost always exactly the same. You'll create ratios that relate a value for part of the circle to the value for the whole circle. Let's take a simple example—a quarter of a circle:

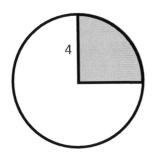

A quarter of a circle forms a 90° angle. If the radius of the circle is 4, then the shaded area is 4π. The arc length for the shaded region is 2π. And the angle could also be expressed as $\frac{\pi}{2}$ radians.

But we often don't have enough information to know all of these things at once. Or at least not immediately. But we can use the fact that all of these parts are the same fraction of the whole:

$$\frac{\text{part}}{\text{whole}} = \frac{90^o}{360^o} = \frac{4\pi}{16\pi} = \frac{2\pi}{8\pi} = \frac{\frac{\pi}{2}}{2\pi} = \frac{1}{4}$$

No matter what, the part is one fourth of the whole circle.

Example 1

Start with the pieces that we know. They give us part of an angle, so we should compare the angle of the shaded part to the whole number of degrees in a circle:

$$\frac{\text{part}}{\text{whole}} = \frac{67.5^o}{360^o}$$

Our ratio will be consistent when we talk about the area because it's still the same fraction of the circle. We don't know the area of the part, so that's our x. But we do know the whole area, so that's the denominator of the fraction:

$$\frac{\text{part}}{\text{whole}} = \frac{67.5^o}{360^o} = \frac{x}{64\pi}$$

Cross-multiply, but keep π as a symbol. You almost never have to use 3.14 to multiply it out.

$$360x = 4320\pi$$

Divide to find x:

$$\frac{360x}{360} = \frac{4320\pi}{360}$$

$$x = 12\pi$$

So the area of the shaded region is 12π. **Choice B is the correct answer.**

Part Over Whole — The Basics

A fraction of a circle will be consistent. It will have the same fraction of the degrees, radians, area, and circumference. You can use ratios to relate these different values.

Put the part over the whole. There are always 360° in a whole circle, so you'll often use the number of degrees as one of the ratios.

Do not multiply out π unless you absolutely have to. π either cancels out or stays as a symbol in the answer.

The Twists

Example 2

The twist here is that there are more steps, but the core of the question is still Part Over Whole because part of a circle is bolded. Start by setting up the ratio. They want the length of the bold arc, so one of our ratios will look like:

$$\frac{\text{bold arc}}{\text{whole circumference}}$$

The bold arc will be x, and we can find the whole circumference because they told us that the radius is 10. Use the Reference Chart if you forget the circumference formula:

$$C = 2\pi r$$

$$C = 2\pi(10)$$

$$C = 20\pi$$

So half our ratio is:

$$\frac{x}{20\pi}$$

We need to set that equal to something. Since there are degree measures in the picture, we probably will end up using degrees and the angle that opens up to the bold arc (the bigger angle JOK, which is right where the letter O is):

$$\frac{x}{20\pi} = \frac{\text{bold angle}}{360^o}$$

Looks like we need to find that bold angle. What do we know? That angle L is 36°. That's not enough to figure out the other angles. Is there anything in the question that we haven't used? Yes. The question tells us that JL and KL are tangent to the circle. The word "tangent" should pop out of the question. It's really important. A line that is tangent to a circle forms a right angle with the radius of the circle:

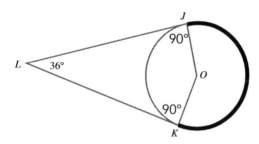

This helps a lot. JOKL is a quadrilateral (four-sided figure), and all quadrilaterals have 360°. We can figure out the smaller angle near center O:

$$360 - 90 - 90 - 36 = 144$$

If we put that angle on our figure, it's clear we can now figure out the larger bold angle where the letter O is:

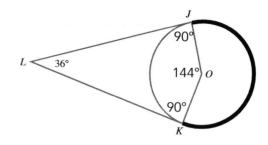

$$360 - 144 = 216$$

Put that into our Part Over Whole proportion:

$$\frac{x}{20\pi} = \frac{216^o}{360^o}$$

Cross-multiply and divide:

$$360x = 4{,}320\pi$$

$$x = 12\pi$$

The correct answer is Choice B. One thing to point out is that Choice A is a trick answer. That's the length of the unbolded part of the circle. Just a reminder to be careful!

Part Over Whole — The Twists

There might be other steps, but everything will come back to Part Over Whole ratios. Start there so you know what to look for.

Use the Reference Chart for circumference and area formulas. It also reminds you that there are 360° and 2π radians in a whole circle.

Answers: Part Over Whole

#1 — Answer = 135
You're given part of the circumference, so use the radius to find the whole circumference, which is 8π.
Set up your Part Over Whole ratios: $\frac{3\pi}{8\pi} = \frac{x}{360}$.
Cross-multiply and divide to find that the angle is 135 degrees.

#2 — Answer = 7/16

You can still use a Part Over While ratio, but you don't need to set it equal to anything. You have part of the circle in terms of radians, so put that over the whole number of radians in a circle: $\dfrac{\frac{7\pi}{8}}{2\pi}$. You can simplify the fraction by multiplying the numerator by the reciprocal of the denominator: $\dfrac{7\pi}{8} \cdot \dfrac{1}{2\pi}$. This reduces to $\dfrac{7}{16}$.

#3 — Answer = 40

There's no need to figure out the angles of a pentagon. Since it's a regular pentagon, it divides the circle into 5 equal pieces. Arc BD is 2 of the 5 pieces. Set up the Part Over Whole ratios with this fraction and the whole circumference: $\dfrac{2}{5} = \dfrac{x}{100}$. Cross-multiply and divide to find that arc BD is 40.

#4 — Answer = 3

You have both the area and angle of the part, so you can find the whole area: $\dfrac{40}{360} = \dfrac{\pi}{x}$. Cross-multiply and divide to find that the whole area is 9π. The question asks for the radius, so use the area formula and solve for the radius: $9\pi = \pi r^2$. The radius is 3.

#5 — Answer = 46, 47, 48, 49, or 50

They give you the radius, so you calculate the whole area, which is 25π. They give you a range of values for the area of the part, so the easiest thing to do is pick something in the middle, like 10.5. At least it gives you a starting point to set up your Part Over Whole ratios: $\dfrac{10.5}{25\pi} = \dfrac{x}{360}$. Cross-multiply and divide to find that $x = 48.128$. You actually need to use the π button on your calculator this time. But since the degree measure has to be an integer, you should round the decimal to 48 degrees even. If you had chosen a different value for the part of the area, you would have gotten other possible values for the degree measure. All of the values above are acceptable because they give a partial area that falls between 10 and 11.

Angle Rules lesson

The Basics

Use the Reference Chart when you can. The most important constant is that supplementary angles add up to 180°. That means angles that lie on the same line will always be equal to 180°.

Example 1

This question is all about constants. Fill in the angles as you find them. Start with the supplementary angles:

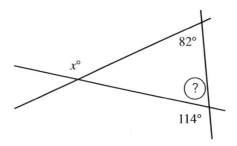

$$180 - 114 = 66$$

If you know 2 angles of a triangle, you can find the third:

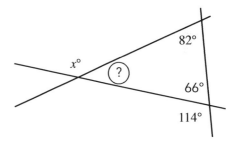

$$180 - 82 - 66 = 32$$

Now use supplementary angles to find x:

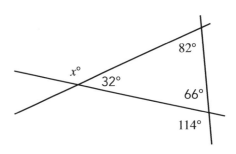

$$180 - 32 = 148$$

The correct answer is 148.

Angle Rules — The Basics

Angles that lie on the same straight line add up to 180°. They are called supplementary angles.

If you're stuck, look for opportunities to use angle constants.

Figures are drawn to scale unless the question specifically says it's not. The angles you get should roughly match the picture. Use that to check your work as you go.

The Twists

Example 2

There are a few other facts that can help you untwist the hard questions. In general, it's a good policy to check the question for unused information. It's very rare that the SAT gives you information that you don't end up using.

In this example, we are told that there are parallel lines. You might remember that two sets of parallel lines make a parallelogram, which has certain rules about congruent angles.

If not, that's okay! Try to make a picture that's similar to the parallel lines picture on the top of The Twists column.

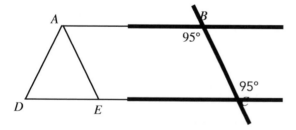

If the top left angle is 95°, then the bottom right angle (which we just created) also has to be 95°. We can use the other set of parallel lines too:

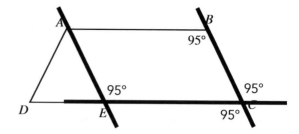

Use supplementary angles to start putting the triangle together:

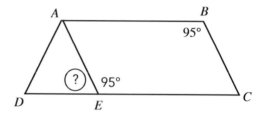

$$180 - 95 = 85$$

There's one more piece of information that we haven't used yet. The congruent sides AD and AE tell us that ADE is an isosceles triangle, which means that the angles opposite those sides are also congruent:

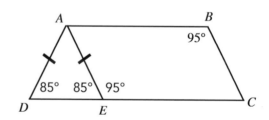

The correct answer is 85.

Angle Rules — The Twists

When two parallel lines are crossed by another line (a transversal), they form congruent angles (alternate interior angles) on opposite sides of the line.

Isosceles triangles have a pair of congruent angles opposite a pair of congruent sides.

Lessons and Answers

Answers: Angle Rules

#1 — Answer = C

If you extend the lines, you'll see the same image that is on the front of the packet. Angle b would also be the unmarked angle to the left of angle a, which means that a and b are supplementary (add to 180°). If $a + b = 180$, then $a = 180 - b$.

#2 — Answer = D

The angles in a triangle must add to 180°, so create an equation: $5x + 7x + 48 = 180$. Solve for x, which is 11 degrees. But be careful! The question doesn't want the value of x. It wants the measure of angle B, which is 7x, or 77°.

#3 — Answer = 52

In this case, you need to know that the total number of degrees in a quadrilateral is 360. First, find the unmarked angle inside the shape, which is $360 - 156 = 204$. Now you can add all the angles together: $204 + x + x + x = 360$. Solve for x, which is 52.

#4 — Answer = C

You need to know that the angles that are opposite each other are congruent, so $a = d$, $b = e$, and $c = f$. Since $b = e$, the equation in the question tells us that $c = d$ too. Substitute b in for e to see why: $b + c = d + b$. Since $a = d$ and $c = f$, then $a = c = d = f$. Choice C says this.

Similar Triangles lesson

The Basics

If you see two triangles and nothing else, you should instantly think of Similar Triangles. Set up ratios, and make sure you compare the correct sides.

You should be able to set up ratios for this question, even if you have no idea why the triangles are similar. Just compare the sides of one triangle to the corresponding sides of the other triangle:

$$\frac{10}{12} = \frac{15}{AE}$$

Here's why this works. The question says that AB is parallel to CD, which means that these angles are the same (think back to the picture from the Angle Rules packet):

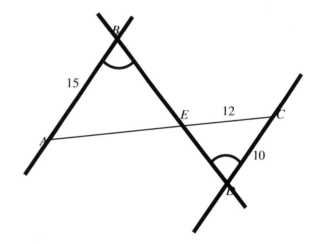

We also know that the angles near point E are congruent because they're vertical angles:

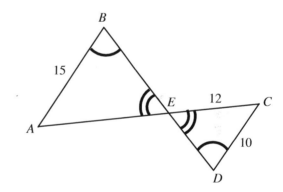

This is all we need to prove that two triangles are similar. The remaining angles must also be congruent because there are always 180° in a triangle.

When you create your ratio, corresponding sides will be opposite the congruent angles. In other words, we know that AB and CD correspond because they're both opposite the congruent angles near point E. Sides AE and EC are both opposite the congruent angles at B and D.

$$\frac{10}{12} = \frac{15}{AE}$$

Cross-multiply and divide:

$$10(AE) = 180$$

$$AE = 18$$

But be careful! Choice A is wrong. Sometimes the SAT twists the question slightly by asking for a different side. In this case, they want the entire length of AC. Since we know AE and EC, we can find AC:

$$18 + 12 = 30$$

The correct answer is Choice D.

Similar Triangles — The Basics

If you see two triangles, there's a good chance it's a Similar Triangles question.

Make sure you compare corresponding sides in your ratio.

Reread the question, just in case the SAT is asking for something different.

The Twists

Example 2

This question involves two triangles, even though they're inside of each other. We know they're similar because they both share angle C, and the parallel lines make the other angles congruent:

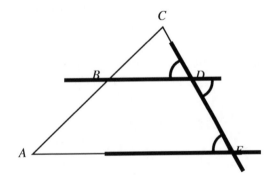

Another twist here is that we're not given all of the side lengths. We're told that the ratio of BD to AE is 2 to 5. Since we're working with ratios anyway, this is actually okay. But if it helps you visualize it more easily, you could just say that BD is 2 and AE is 5. The figure isn't drawn to scale, so it doesn't matter that those lengths don't match the picture.

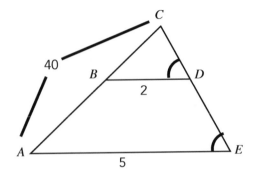

Create the ratio:

$$\frac{2}{BC} = \frac{5}{40}$$

Notice that AC is opposite angle E in the big triangle, and BC is opposite the congruent angle D in the little triangle. That's how we know they correspond.

Cross-multiply and divide:

$$5(BC) = 80$$

$$BC = 16$$

Choice B is wrong. The question is asking for the length of AB, which we can find by subtracting:

$$40 - 16 = 24$$

The correct answer is Choice C. Sometimes it's easier to ignore what they're asking for at first, so you can concentrate on making a ratio. Since AB isn't the side of a triangle, we can't use Similar Triangles ratios to find its length directly.

Answers: Similar Triangles

#1 — Answer = C

You can use ratios to find the length of BC: $\frac{5}{13} = \frac{20}{BC}$. Cross-multiply and divide to find that $BC = 52$. Use Pythagorean Theorem to find the length of AC: $20^2 + AC^2 = 52^2$. You'll find that $AC = 48$.

#2 — Answer = C

The twist here is that there are actually 3 triangles: ABD, BCD, and ABC. The ratio in the question is about the big triangle ABC, so you need to use sides from a triangle that is congruent to ABC. Both of the small triangles have a 52° angle, just like the big triangle, so that's not much help. But only triangle ABD shares an additional angle with the big triangle. They both include angle A. When two triangles have two of the same angles, then they are similar. Your answer should only use sides that are in triangle ABD. In the big triangle, AB is opposite the 52° angle at C, so your ratio should have AD in the numerator because it is also opposite a 52° angle. That's actually all you need to get the answer because Choice C is the only one that has AD in the numerator. Still, BC is opposite angle A in the big triangle, so BD should be the denominator of the ratio because it is opposite angle A in the small triangle.

#3 — Answer = B

Fill in the unknown angles. Angle A is 37° and angle F is 53°. This helps you match the sides in your ratio. AC is opposite the 53° angle, so the correct answer

should have DE in the numerator because it is also opposite the 53° angle. Since AB is opposite the right angle, the denominator should be EF because it is also opposite the right angle.

#4 — Answer = 110

This question is twisted to give you the length of a side that you don't need. They're hoping that you get confused and don't know which side to use in the ratio. Since EC is next to angle C, you need to pick AE because it's next to the congruent angle A. Your ratio should be: $\frac{330}{540} = \frac{EC}{180}$. Cross-multiply and divide to find that $EC = 110$.

Cylinders lesson

The Basics

They give you the formula in the Reference Chart.

Example 1

Just put the information into the formula:

$$V = \pi r^2 h$$

$$144\pi = \pi r^2(9)$$

$$\frac{144\pi}{9\pi} = \frac{\pi r^2(9)}{9\pi}$$

$$16 = r^2$$

$$4 = r$$

Be careful! The question asks for the diameter, not the radius. It's underlined! **The correct answer is 8 because the diameter is double the radius.**

The Twists

Example 2

A common twist is to ask about two cylinders. Sometimes the volume is the same, like when they're pouring liquid from one container to another. Other times, they want you to compare two different cylinders. Regardless, you're still basing everything off the standard cylinder formula.

Let's start this question by looking at the first cylinder:

$$256 = \pi r^2 h$$

Not much to do. Let's move on to the second cylinder. For this one, put the radius and height in terms of the first cylinder's radius and height:

$$V = \pi \left(\frac{r}{2}\right)^2 (3h)$$

Make sure you square the entire r-term. Half the radius means we have to square half the radius. This matters a lot!

Simplify:

$$V = \pi \left(\frac{r^2}{4}\right)(3h)$$

$$V = \frac{3\pi r^2 h}{4}$$

Now what? Look back at the first equation that we mostly ignored. It actually tells us some very important information:

$$256 = \pi r^2 h$$

$$V = \frac{3(\pi r^2 h)}{4}$$

The term $\pi r^2 h$ is in both of our equations. Since we based the second equation off the values in the first, we can just substitute in 256:

$$V = \frac{3(256)}{4}$$

$$V = 192$$

The correct answer is 192.

Cylinders — The Twists

The SAT can twist cylinder questions in lots of ways, but you're usually not straying too far from the standard cylinder formula.

Make sure that you're careful when you are working with the cylinder's radius. Since the term is squared, changes will also need to be squared. Use parentheses, and you should be fine.

Answers: Cylinders

#1 — Answer = 151, 152, 153, 154, 155, 156, or 157
You should start with either the minimum or maximum value of the radius. If you assume the radius is 2.45 inches, then the volume formula will be: $V = \pi(2.45)^2(8)$. Use your calculator, multiplying with the π button to find that the volume is approximately 150.9. You need to round up to an integer, which is 151. If you had started with 2.50 as the radius, you would have gotten the volume as 157.1, which should be rounded down to 157 so that it falls within the range. Any integer in between is also acceptable.

#2 — Answer = 160
Instead of finding the volume of the whole cylinder with and without the rock, just find the volume of the 2 inch height change. Another twist is that they give you the area of the base, which is a circle. This means that you can replace the entire πr^2 portion of the cylinder formula: $V = (80)(2)$.

#3 — Answer = 10
If the radius is equal to the height, then the volume formula becomes: $125\pi = \pi r^2(r)$. The π's cancel, so the equation simplifies to: $125 = r^3$. The cube root of 125 is 5, but the question does not want the radius. Double the radius to find that the diameter is 10.

#4 — Answer = 109

Start by finding the volume of the cylinder portion: $V = \pi(2)^2(6)$. This simplifies to 24π. Next find the volume of the sphere. Since each end is half a sphere, you have one whole sphere. The formula is given in the Reference Chart: $V = \dfrac{4}{3}\pi(2)^3$. This simplifies to $\dfrac{32\pi}{3}$. Add the two values and use the π button on your calculator to find the actual numerical value, which is approximately 108.9. Round to the nearest cubic millimeter, which is 109.

Trigonometry lesson

The Basics

This is where the SAT has a big advantage over the ACT. You do not need to memorize crazy trigonometry formulas. In fact, the most common trigonometry questions require only knowledge of soh-cah-toa.

Example 1

Use soh-cah-toa to go through all the choices.

A) $\sin B = \dfrac{\text{opposite}}{\text{hypotenuse}} = \dfrac{b}{c}$

B) $\cos B = \dfrac{\text{adjacent}}{\text{hypotenuse}} = \dfrac{a}{c}$

C) $\tan B = \dfrac{\text{opposite}}{\text{adjacent}} = \dfrac{b}{a}$

D) $\tan A = \dfrac{\text{opposite}}{\text{adjacent}} = \dfrac{a}{b}$

Choice B gives us exactly what the question wants, which makes it the answer.

Trigonometry — The Basics

Know the trigonometric ratios. Use soh-cah-toa to help you remember them.

The hypotenuse is the side across from the right angle. It is always the longest side.

The Twists

Example 2

A lot of people have trouble with trigonometry because they never really learned what sine, cosine, and tangent mean. They're ratios. They don't give the value of the sides of a triangle. They give a comparison. Just like with other Ratios questions, Part Over Whole questions, and Similar Triangles, the fractions that we make will be consistent.

In this question, we're given the value of sin B, so we should work backwards and think about what that means in terms of the sides:

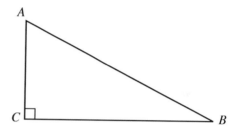

$$\sin B = \frac{3}{5} = \frac{\text{opposite}}{\text{hypotenuse}} = \frac{AC}{AB}$$

The question also gives us the value of AC, so let's put that in our ratio:

$$\frac{3}{5} = \frac{12}{AB}$$

Do what we always do with Ratios. Cross-multiply and divide:

$$3(AB) = 60$$

$$AB = 20$$

Put the side lengths on the picture:

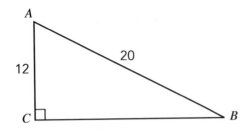

They want BC, and we can get it by using Pythagorean Theorem, which is given in the Reference Chart:

$$a^2 + b^2 = c^2$$

$$12^2 + (BC)^2 = 20^2$$

$$144 + (BC)^2 = 400$$

$$(BC)^2 = 256$$

$$BC = 16$$

The correct answer is 16.

Trigonometry — The Twists

Soh-cah-toa describes different ratios between the sides of a triangle. When questions are twisted, you'll probably need to set up a proportion to compare the trigonometric ratio to the actual side lengths.

You'll almost never need to use the sine, cosine, or tangent buttons on your calculator.

If you have two sides of a right triangle, you can use Pythagorean Theorem to find the third.

Formulas

Example 3

If you can't use soh-cah-toa, then you probably need to use one of these two formulas. You have to memorize them because they're not in the Reference Chart, but they don't come up that often, so they're a low priority.

Understanding why they are true makes them easier to remember:

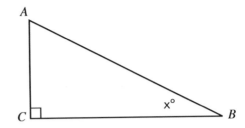

Let's start with $\sin x$. In this case:

$$\sin x = \frac{AC}{AB}$$

How does $\cos(90 - x)$ fit into this? Remember that there are 180° in a triangle. We already know that 90° are accounted for by the right angle. Angles A and B make up the other 90°. In other words:

$$A + B = 90$$

$$A + x = 90$$

$$A = 90 - x$$

Put that on the picture:

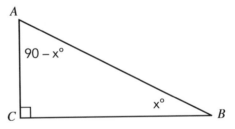

Now find the ratio for $\cos(90 - x)$:

$$\cos(90 - x) = \frac{AC}{AB}$$

It's the same as $\sin x$! That's because the opposite side for angle B is the adjacent side for angle A. The second version of the rule is true for the same reason.

Answers: Trigonometry

#1 — Answer = 5/13

Remember that trigonometry is all about similar triangles. The values are ratios, so the sine of angle A is the same as the sine of angle D. The sine of angle D is the opposite over the hypotenuse, which is $\frac{5}{13}$.

#2 — Answer = 4/3

The twist is that the cosine is given as a decimal. You always see trigonometry as fractions, so convert this to a fraction: $0.8 = \frac{4}{5}$. Now you can use these numbers as values for the side lengths. Since cosine is adjacent over hypotenuse, you can make side a equal to 4 and side c equal to 5. This is a 3-4-5 special right triangle, so side b is equal to 3. This is a common triangle on the SAT, so you should be comfortable filling in the third side without having to go through Pythagorean Theorem. Now find the tangent of A, which is the opposite side over the adjacent side: $\frac{4}{3}$.

#3 — Answer = 3/5

Use the formula on the front of the packet: $\cos a = \sin (90 - a)$.

#4 — Answer = A

Using ratios requires the least amount of memorization because the whole numbers of degrees and radians in a circle are given in the Reference Chart: $\frac{900}{360} = \frac{x}{2\pi}$. Cross-multiply and divide to find that $x = 5\pi$.

#5 — Answer = 0

Draw point D somewhere along line AB, and draw CD, which should divide the 90° angle into two separate angles. You can label angle ACD as x, which means that angle DCB is $90 - x$. You can replace the angle names in the equation with your labels: $\sin (x) - \cos (90 - x)$. Since $\sin (x) = \cos (90 - x)$, your equation is really: $\sin (x) - \sin (x)$. This is equal to 0. Remember that if an SAT Trigonometry question seems really hard, it's probably going to use this rule in some way.

Advanced Geometry lesson

The Basics

There are a lot of geometry rules, but each individual geometry question will use only 3 or 4 of the rules max. The Reference Chart can guide you to the right rule. Try to think in terms of the basic shapes: rectangles, triangles, and circles.

Example 1

This picture clearly involves right triangles. Normally, if we have two sides of a right triangle, we can use Pythagorean Theorem to get the third.

In this case, we only have one side. When that happens, we need to use the special right triangle proportions. These are given in the Reference Chart! Essentially, certain angle measures allow us to know all of the sides of a right triangle, even when we only have one side.

In this question, the 30° and 60° angles should pop. Why are they telling us this? It probably matters. Sure enough, the Reference Chart tells us that 30-60-90 right triangles are special.

Let's match up the proportions on the Reference Chart to the 30-60-90 right triangle on the right side of our picture:

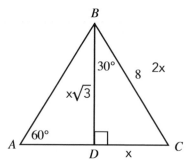

Create an equation using the one side that we know and the corresponding proportion:

$$2x = 8$$

That helps us get the value of DC:

$$x = 4$$

And the value of BD:

$$x\sqrt{3} = 4\sqrt{3}$$

That's what the question wants, so Choice C is the correct answer.

Advanced Geometry — The Basics

If you have two sides of a right triangle, use Pythagorean Theorem to find the third side.

If you have one side of a right triangle, look for 30°, 60°, and 45° angles so that you can use the special right triangle formulas in the Reference Chart.

The Twists

Example 2

Shaded region problems are common on the SAT. If there's a circle involved, it might be a Part Over Whole question. If not, use shapes that you know to build the region, or subtract to get the region as a remainder.

In this question, we know that the area of the big square is 4 because each side is 2.

After that, you might be stuck. But remember that geometry questions rarely give you information that you don't use. The angle in the top right is split into 2x and x. What do we know about this angle? Since it's the corner of a square, it must equal 90°, so:

$$x + 2x = 90$$

$$3x = 90$$

$$x = 30$$

Put those angles on the picture, and you'll see that we've got 30° and 60° angles, not just in that corner, but in all of the triangles. Those should pop. We're working with 30-60-90 right triangles. Use the Reference Chart to remind yourself of the formula. Here's one of the triangles removed from the main picture so that we can more easily see what's going on. I'm also using y so we don't confuse the sides with the x's in the angles:

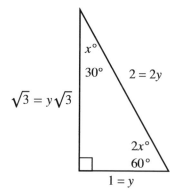

We can find the shaded area by starting with the big square and "chopping off" all of the triangles:

shaded area = big square − 4(triangles)

The area of one triangle is:

$$A = \frac{1}{2}bh$$

$$A = \frac{1}{2}(1)(\sqrt{3})$$

$$A = \frac{\sqrt{3}}{2}$$

So our shaded area equation becomes:

$$\text{shaded area} = 4 - 4\left(\frac{\sqrt{3}}{2}\right)$$

$$\text{shaded area} = 4 - 2\sqrt{3}$$

That's it. Choice D is the correct answer.

Advanced Geometry — The Twists

Be clever.

Solve shaded region problems by focusing on familiar shapes—rectangles, triangles, and circles.

You can build shaded regions by adding together other shapes.

You can also find shaded regions by subtracting away shapes until the shaded area is all that remains.

Three-dimensional shapes can be solved either by using the volume formulas in the Reference Chart, or by finding two-dimensional shapes hidden within the picture.

Answers: Advanced Geometry

#1 — Answer = 1/3

This sounds like a Part Over Whole question, and it basically is. Draw in another radius from point O to point N. You've created an isosceles triangle. Since ON and OM are both radii of the circle, they are congruent, which also means that the angles opposite those sides are congruent. That makes angle N equal to 30°. You can subtract the two 30° angles to find that angle O is 120°. Set up a Part Over Whole ratio: $\frac{120}{360}$. This reduces to $\frac{1}{3}$.

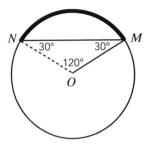

#2 — Answer = C

You can solve this by making two triangles. First, label the point directly below point P (the back bottom left corner) as point R. You can find the length of line QR, which is the diagonal of the base. You've made a right triangle with legs of length 2. Using Pythagorean Theorem or 45-45-90 triangles, you should find that QR is equal to $2\sqrt{2}$. Now you have a second triangle that cuts through the middle of the cube. It has one leg PR, another leg QR, and the hypotenuse is PQ, which is what the question wants you to find. The length of PR is 2, and the length of QR is $2\sqrt{2}$. You can use Pythagorean Theorem to find PQ: $(2)^2 + (2\sqrt{2})^2 = PQ^2$. You'll find that PQ is equal to $\sqrt{12}$, which simplifies to $2\sqrt{3}$. Many three-dimensional shape questions can be solved by making two-dimensional triangles.

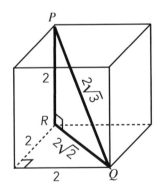

3 — Answer = D

Arithmetize. Let $a = 2$. A hexagon can be divided into 6 equilateral triangles, in this case with sides of length 2. Each of those equilateral triangle can be divided into 2 special 30-60-90 right triangles. In this case, the hypotenuse is 2, which corresponds to the 2x side according to the Reference Chart. Because we picked $a = 2$, the value of x is 1, which makes the side opposite the 30° angle equal to 1 and the side opposite the 60° angle equal to $\sqrt{3}$. You can use these two sides to find the area of the equilateral triangle. The base is 2, and the height is $\sqrt{3}$:

$A = \dfrac{1}{2}(2)(\sqrt{3})$. The area of one equilateral triangle is $\sqrt{3}$. Multiply this by 6 to find the area of the entire hexagon (since there are 6 of these equilateral triangles in the hexagon). The area of the entire hexagon is $6\sqrt{3}$. Choice D gives you this same value when you replace the a with 2.

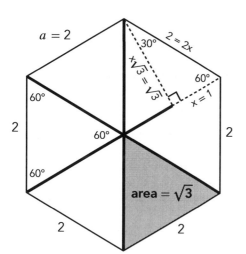

#4 — Answer = B

Very very rarely, the SAT tests the Unit Circle. You need to know which trigonometry functions are positive and negative in each quadrant. Use "All Students Take Calculus" to remember. The first letter of each word tells you the positive function in the quadrants as you cycle through:

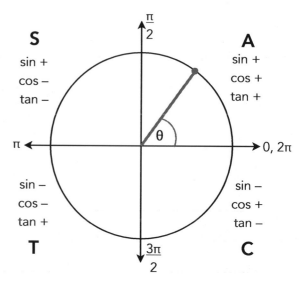

This question tells you that angle x is in the first quadrant, which means that a is positive to start. But $-a$ will need to be the cosine of an angle in either the 2nd or 3rd quadrants because those are the quadrants where cosine is negative. Choices C and D can be eliminated because they actually give the exact same angle. Since 2π is a full circle, C and D are just going around the circle once and ending up where you started. Choice A would be in the 4th quadrant (bottom right), which can't be correct because cosine is positive in that quadrant. That leaves Choice B, which is in the second quadrant, where cosine is negative. If this confuses you, don't worry. It is not commonly tested on the SAT. It only matters if you're shooting for a 750 or better.

Made in the USA
Middletown, DE
17 October 2020